A–Z of Business Tax Deductions

A–Z of Business Tax Deductions

Second edition

Annette Morley BSc Agric (Hons), MBIAC, CTA

Nicola Moore BA (Econ) Hons, FCA, CTA

Bloomsbury Professional

LONDON • DUBLIN • EDINBURGH • NEW YORK • NEW DELHI • SYDNEY

Bloomsbury Professional
Bloomsbury Publishing Plc
41–43 Boltro Road, Haywards Heath, RH16 1BJ, UK

BLOOMSBURY and the Diana logo are trademarks of Bloomsbury Publishing Plc

British Library Cataloguing-in-Publication Data

A catalogue record for this book is available from the British Library.

ISBN: 978 1 52650 731 0

Typeset by Evolution Design and Digital (Kent)
Printed and bound by CPI Group (UK) Ltd, Croydon, CR0 4YY

To find out more about our authors and books visit www.bloomsburyprofessional.com. Here you will find extracts, author information, details of forthcoming events and the option to sign up for our newsletters.

Preface

Welcome to the second edition of *A–Z of Business Tax Deductions*.

Scope

As with the first edition, this publication focuses on unincorporated businesses operated by sole traders, partnerships and limited liability partnerships. Whilst there are some references to comparable treatment for companies where it seems particularly useful, the special regimes for corporate deductions have not been included. Similarly, the rules for capital allowances have been touched upon where appropriate, but they are comprehensively covered in other Bloomsbury Professional publications and are not repeated here.

This second edition continues the aim of providing clarity in areas where there is doubt as to the deductibility for tax purposes of particular expenses incurred by a business. Determining whether a specific cost is allowable or not is a task regularly faced by those working in the tax and accountancy professions. Researching through general reference material and HMRC manuals to find the solution is time-consuming and can be frustrating. This publication has been written as a practical tool to remove that hassle.

Sometimes, an absolute "yes" or "no" to the question of deductibility can be found. More frequently, the classic "it all depends" is the first response. In those instances, the principles behind the legislation have been examined. The aim is that the adviser, by understanding those principles, can determine the correct result for his or her specific problem of the moment.

It is hoped that the A–Z format offers a checklist of topics as well as speedy location of guidance on a particular subject. To provide a wide source of reference, each chapter sets out the main legislation, leading cases and HMRC manuals which guide toward the solution. Of course, these references are appropriate at the date of writing, thus are subject to change over time. Not only does legislation alter, so does the status of recent cases. Judgments can be appealed and although the authors have updated cases for appeals since the first edition of this publication, the possibility of further appeals should be checked prior to relying absolutely on the cases cited.

Amongst the many revisions to be found within this second edition, particularly notable topics are:

- a completely new chapter on trading and property allowances;

- the major changes to property businesses, including the loan interest restriction, the way the cash basis works for properties, and the renewals basis for capital items;
- the amendments to the cash basis legislation for trading businesses.

Acknowledgements

The authors remain grateful to Mark McLaughlin for his inspirational idea and for his interest and comment that lies behind the creation of this title.

The authors express their thanks to David Wright for his belief in the publication and for overseeing this further edition. We appreciate the value provided by Marianne Lee and her careful editing, and to her colleague Jane Bradford for her support.

Especially, we remain grateful to you, the readers – those who purchased our first edition and those who have invested in this updated publication. You will see from the "Scope" section above what we set out to achieve. Only you can judge if we have succeeded. We will always value your constructive comments and suggestions for our future editions.

Annette Morley and Nicola Moore
June 2018

Contents

Table of cases

[*All references are to paragraph number or Appendix*]

C

D

K

L

M

Table of statutes

[*All references are to paragraph number*]

Table of statutory instruments

[*All references are to paragraph number*]

List of examples

List of abbreviations

AIA	annual investment allowance
BIM	HMRC Business Income Manual
BLM	HMRC Business Leasing Manual
CA	HMRC Capital Allowances Manual
CAA 2001	Capital Allowances Act 2001
CH	HMRC Compliance Handbook
CRG	HMRC Complaints and Remedy Manual
CTA 2009	Corporation Tax Act 2009
CTA 2010	Corporation Tax Act 2010
CTM	HMRC Company Taxation Manual
DT	HMRC Double Taxation Relief Manual
EBT	employee benefit trust
EIM	HMRC Employment Income Manual
ESM	HMRC Employment Status Manual
DPB	designated professional body
FCA	Financial Conduct Authority
FIFO	first in first out
FRS	Financial Reporting Standard
	HMRC Flat Rate Scheme Manual
FTT	First Tier Tribunal
GAAP	generally accepted accounting practice
HMRC	Her Majesty's Revenue and Customs
ICTA 1988	Income and Corporation Taxes Act 1988
INTM	HMRC International Manual
ITA 2007	Income Tax Act 2007
ITEPA 2003	Income Tax (Earnings and Pensions) Act 2003
ITTOIA 2005	Income Tax (Trading and Other Income) Act 2005
LIFO	last in first out
LLP	limited liability partnership
MTDfB	Making Tax Digital for Businesses
NIM	HMRC National Insurance Manual
OpRA	optional remuneration arrangements
OTS	Office of Tax Simplification
PIM	HMRC Property Income Manual
PM	HMRC Partnership Manual
R&D	research and development
RI	Revenue Interpretation
RTI	real time information
SAIM	Savings and Investment Manual
SIPP	self-invested personal plan
SP	HMRC Statement of Practice
TCGA 1992	Taxation of Chargeable Gains Act 1992
TIOPA 2010	Taxation (International and Other Provisions) Act 2010
TMA 1970	Taxes Management Act 1970
TMEs	trust management expenses
TSEM	HMRC Trusts, Settlements and Estates Manual
UT	Upper Tribunal

Part A
General principles

Chapter 1

Generally accepted accounting practice

1.1 COMMENT

The starting point for calculating the taxable profits of a trade, profession or property business is based on the accounts prepared in accordance with generally accepted accounting practice ("GAAP").

This publication covers the statutory adjustments that modify the accounting profit or loss in order to arrive at the result for tax purposes; i.e. adjustments which are "… required or authorised by law" (see **Part B**). Where tax law and accountancy principles conflict, tax law takes precedence.

The interaction of accounting and tax law included in this chapter is not intended to provide a detailed analysis of accounting standards but rather to explore the interface between tax and accounting principles. References to relevant accounting standards are included in the applicable sections in **Part B**.

Accounting standards and GAAP are not applicable for traders and property businesses that use the cash basis (**Chapters 2** and **5**).

1.2 STATUTORY BACKGROUND

The requirement to use GAAP is given statutory effect at *ITTOIA 2005, s 25* which says:

> "(1) The profits of a trade must be calculated in accordance with generally accepted accounting practice, subject to any adjustment required or authorised by law in calculating profits for income tax purposes.
>
> (2) This does not—
>
> (a) require a person to comply with the requirements of the Companies Act 2006 or subordinate legislation made under that Act except as to the basis of calculation, or
>
> (b) impose any requirements as to audit or disclosure.

(3) This section is subject to section 25A (cash basis for small businesses) …"

Profits or losses for tax purposes are therefore computed by a two-stage process:

(1) the calculation of the accounting result by reference to GAAP; and

(2) statutory adjustments to arrive at the tax result.

The requirement to comply with GAAP was first introduced into the Taxes Acts in *FA 1998, s 42*, thus creating a statutory linkage between accounting standards and tax law adjustments necessary to arrive at profits for tax purposes.

A change of approach in the drafting of tax legislation for companies during the early 1990s used a new statutory language, referring to accounting terminology ("debits" and "credits") as a framework for computing the tax result (e.g. *FA 1996* Loan Relationships and *FA 2002* Corporate Intangibles rules – now *CTA 2009, Parts 5, 6* and *8*).

The change in legislative emphasis for corporates did not result in the convergence of tax and accounting principles but marked the beginning of different regimes for companies to compute taxable profits and losses for corporation tax.

The rewrite of tax legislation for unincorporated business now found at *ITTOIA 2005* was limited mainly to codifying previous legislation. The tax rewrite project did not attempt to alter tax statute into line with terminology used in accounting standards.

The statutory linkage used to "translate" tax statute from the ordinary principles of commercial accounting into GAAP is found at *ITTOIA 2005, s 27* ("Receipts and expenses"):

"(1) In the Income Tax Acts, in the context of the calculation of the profits of a trade, references to receipts and expenses are to any items brought into account as credits or debits in calculating the profits.

(2) There is no implication that an amount has been actually received or paid.

(3) This section is subject to any express provision to the contrary."

There are further examples of importing accounting terminology into tax legislation, for example the capital allowances regime for long-funding leases (*CAA 2001, Chapter 6A*), but there has been no general shift to import accounting principles as a framework to replace tax legislation as the basis for the computing taxable profits.

A general reluctance to simplify the tax system by alignment with accounting principles is reflected in the questions outlined in the Office of

Tax Simplification's call for evidence (30 November 2017) for a review of accounting deprecation as a replacement for the capital allowances regime. This highlighted a number of issues when relying solely on accounting principles to determine the measure of taxable profits – including the effect of a potential loss of tax to the Exchequer. The final publication of the OTS review of simplifying tax relief for fixed assets concludes that while there are undoubted long term benefits in using accounts deprecation this is not sufficient to make radical changes which would involve complex transitional rules.

Accounting principles continue to be "trumped" by reaffirming pre *FA 1998* tax case law decisions, most recently by the introduction of a statutory rule to ensure recognition of money's worth for barter or similar transactions (*ITTOIA 2005, s 28A, FA 2016, s 71*). The accounting standard FRS 102 (see 1.3 below) defines the measurement of revenue at the "fair value of the consideration received or receivable" (paragraph 23.3) but does not necessarily permit the recognition of income on exchanges of goods and services of a similar nature or value (barter-type transactions, see FRS 102 paragraph 23.6). Notwithstanding the overriding requirement of the accounting standards to recognise the economic substance of transactions it was considered necessary to introduce *ITTOIA 2005, s 28A* to restore tax case law to ensure the recognition of income by reference to money's worth. There is no corresponding statutory amendment dealing with the recognition of an expense for a barter or exchange transaction.

The rewrite project which included drafting *ITTOIA 2005* did not significantly alter the general landscape for taxing unincorporated businesses, and no progress has since been made towards convergence of the methodologies used to compute taxable profits and losses and the results in accounts prepared in accordance with GAAP.

1.2.1 Capital expenditure

The distinction between capital and revenue expenditure is a matter of tax law and not necessarily determined by the accounting treatment (see **Chapter 3**). It is a fundamental principle for tax purposes that no relief is available for capital items, and therefore accounting profits are adjusted to disallow depreciation and capital items expensed to the profit and loss account (*ITTOIA 2005, s 33*).

Capitalised or deferred revenue costs may be deductible at a future date when charged in the accounts, depending on the nature of the expenditure.

The capital allowances regime provides relief for expenditure on assets that fall within the definition of functional plant (*CAA 2001, s 23*) and an ad hoc collection of other assets (e.g. software and knowhow). "Chargeable assets", including land and buildings, or intangibles are mainly dealt with under the capital gains tax rules on a realised basis. During the period of ownership the accounting treatment of an asset has no direct influence on the tax treatment in computing a capital gain or loss, e.g. a revaluation profit on an investment property credited to the income statement will not be taxable until realisation on an eventual sale.

1.2.2 GAAP – exceptions

The introduction of a statutory rule for GAAP in *FA 1998* was accompanied by the withdrawal of the "cash" or "conventional" basis of accounting, which had previously allowed businesses to compute profits on an earnings basis with some adjustments for stocks, debtors and accruals.

From tax year 2013/14 traders may elect to use the cash basis to compute taxable profits. GAAP has no application for the cash basis, as income and expenses are generally taxable and deductible when received and paid. The cash basis resulted in the repeal of the opening years cash basis for barristers and advocates: *ITTOIA 2005, s 160* (see **Chapter 2**).

The cash basis was extended to unincorporated property businesses with effect from 6 April 2017. This is now the default method of arriving at taxable profits and losses for property businesses with annual receipts of £150,000 or less. For tax years prior to 2017/18 property businesses were required to use GAAP to prepare accounts – although by concession HMRC accepted the cash basis if gross annual receipts were less than £15,000 (PIM1101).

1.2.3 Defining GAAP

The framework for preparing the accounts of an unincorporated business is not specifically defined in tax legislation or the accounting standards. There is no accounting requirement for financial information to show a "true and fair" view, as unincorporated businesses are not generally required to audit accounts. An exception to this is the accounts of limited liability partnerships that, under company law, are treated as companies.

ITTOIA 2005, s 25 imposes an obligation to apply GAAP when preparing the accounting information in compliance with accounting standards, but this does not mean that unincorporated businesses must adopt the standard format of accounts required by the *Companies Act 2006* (*ITTOIA 2005, s 25(2)*).

However, full accounts of unincorporated entities that purport to comply with FRS 102 must follow the statutory P&L and balance sheet formats (unless overridden by another statutory framework under which the entity is required to report, see FRS 102, paras 4.1, 5.1). The precise form of accounts will depend on the nature and size of the business.

A profit and loss account will be necessary to derive a pre-tax result that is based on GAAP. A balance sheet may not be required for very small or uncomplicated businesses, but this will be necessary in nearly all other cases in order to operate an accruals basis of accounting.

GAAP is defined at *ITA 2007, s 997*, by reference to "UK generally accepted accounting principles" (BIM31015). This means using accounting standards as applied to UK companies "that are intended to give a true and fair view". Accounts drawn up to comply with International Accounting Standards (and in compliance with *Regulation (EC) No 1606/2002* of the European Parliament) are also accepted as GAAP (*s 997(3)*).

Therefore, unless the cash basis applies, all unincorporated businesses of whatever size must comply with accounting standards and the bar is set at the same level as it is for companies. Businesses that do not comply with GAAP must amend their accounts before making the statutory adjustments required by the Taxes Acts.

1.2.4 Limited liability partnerships

Separate accounting and audit regulations apply to limited liability partnerships (LLPs). An LLP is a body corporate under company law but, for tax purposes, is treated as "transparent" so that profits are attributed to its members in a similar way to a partnership. The format of LLP accounts is subject to *CA 2006* and specific statutory regulations (*Limited Liability Partnerships Regulations 2001, SI 2001/1090*, and *SI 2008/1911*). LLPs that fall within the definition of a medium or large entity will be subject to an audit (in a similar way to companies). Smaller LLPs are permitted to use the micro-entities regime under FRS 105 and HMRC confirm that this simpler accounting framework is acceptable for individual members when filing under self-assessment (see **1.3**).

1.2.5 Accounting records

When submitting a self-assessment return, no attached accounts are required for an unincorporated business except for partnerships with a turnover of more than £15 million (HS229 Information from your accounts).

Small businesses may use the "three line account method" to restrict disclosure to income, allowable expenses and net profit or loss in the self-assessment return where turnover is below the VAT threshold (£85,000 for tax year 2018/19).

Reduced disclosure does not remove the taxpayer's obligation to keep proper underlying records and comply with GAAP. Failure to keep proper records may suggest that accounts have not been prepared in accordance with GAAP. HMRC have statutory powers to prescribe the type of records to be kept by a taxpayer (*FA 2008, Sch 36*). Basic guidance on the type of records that HMRC expect to be maintained is found at Helpsheet 222.

It is proposed that electronic record keeping will be mandatory and given statutory authority through the Making Tax Digital for Businesses (MTDfB) initiative.

The digitalisation of the UK tax system is expected to apply to businesses from April 2019 for VAT reporting and for income tax purposes from April 2020. MTDfB will require businesses to keep and preserve digital records. The aim of MTDfB is to improve compliance and reduce the "tax gap" by filing quarterly returns.

MTDfB is not expected to alter the requirement for businesses to apply GAAP. Taxpayers (other than those using the cash basis) will continue to apply the appropriate accounting policy to finalise annual accounts as a basis for preparing self-assessment returns.

1.3 ACCOUNTING STANDARDS

What accounting standards must be considered by unincorporated businesses in order to comply with GAAP?

Companies Act 2006, s 464 refers to accounting standards as statements of standard accounting practice as prescribed by "such body or bodies as may be prescribed by regulations". The accumulation of best accounting practice and the formulation of accounting standards has been delegated to professional accounting bodies and is not dealt with by direct legislation. The formulation and administration is through the Financial Reporting Council ("FRC", previously the Accounting Standards Board).

For accounting periods commencing on or after 1 January 2015, the accumulated standards, including Statements of Standard Accounting Practice (SSAPs), Statements of Recommended Practice (SORPs), Urgent Issues Task Force notices (UITFs) and other guidance such as Financial Reporting Standards (FRSs), have been replaced. The following standards now apply:

- FRS 100 – Application of Financial Reporting Requirements: Outlining the framework for accounting and reporting.
- FRS 101 – Reduced Disclosure Framework: An alternative to FRS102 and a hybrid accounting standard that combines the measurement principles

of International Accounting Standards "IFRS" with presentation and disclosure aligned to UK GAAP. This standard is used by UK subsidiaries of listed groups.

- FRS 102 – The Financial Reporting Standard applicable in the UK and Republic of Ireland.
- FRS 103 and FRS 104 – Accounting for Insurance Contracts.
- FRS 105 – The Financial Reporting Standard applicable to the Micro-entities Regime.

FRS 102 (as amended by the Triennial Review 2017) is the principal accounting standard used by large and medium sized entities for accounting periods commencing on or after 1 January 2015, from which date this replaced all of the previous standards. Small companies may opt to use a modified standard "FRS 102–1A" which permits a reduced level of disclosure in certain areas.

Amendments to FRS 102 issued in December 2017 primarily affect accounting disclosures for companies and must be adopted for accounting periods beginning on or after 1 January 2019.

As an alternative to using FRS 102-1A, micro entities may choose to use simplified accounting under FRS 105, "Financial Reporting Standard applicable to the Micro-entities Regime" (updated March 2018). This applies for accounting periods commencing on or after 1 January 2016. HMRC have confirmed that FRS 105 is available to unincorporated traders and property businesses.

The limits for micro or small entities with effect from 1 January 2016 are:

	Turnover	Balance sheet total	Employees
Micro-entity	£632,000	£316,000	10
Small entity	£10.2 million	£3.26 million	250

An entity must satisfy two out of three of the criteria for two successive years to fall within the appropriate category.

The accounting changes to comply with new accounting rules under FRS 102 or FRS 105 in most cases are unlikely to affect unincorporated business because statutory tax adjustments for the most part are eliminated when computing taxable profits or losses, e.g. adjustments to depreciation, revaluation of investment properties or intangible assets. Areas where differences may affect the tax result include fair value accounting for financial instruments or forward contracts, or receipt of grant income, where the choice of accounting for these items affect the timing of income and expenses for tax purposes.

1.3.1 Accounting – key concepts

The accounting standards moderate the recognition and measurement of assets, liabilities, income and expenditure and the presentation and disclosure in the accounts (where this is required). Section 2 of FRS 102, "Concepts and Persuasive Principles", summarises the key characteristics in preparing financial statements that are derived from previous standards. The accounting concepts that create tension between the tax and accounting treatment are considered further.

1.3.2 Materiality

Paragraph 2.6 of FRS 102 defines accounting materiality in the following terms:

> "Information is material … if its omission or misstatement, individually or collectively, could influence the economic decisions of users taken on the basis of the financial statements. Materiality depends on the size and nature of the omission or misstatement judged in the surrounding circumstances."

The Taxes Acts do not embrace the concept of materiality, and the accounting treatment of non-material items may need further investigation in order to compute taxable profits or losses.

When considering materiality, a distinction should be made between statutory tax adjustments and the basis of estimates used to prepare the accounts. For example, a disallowance for entertainment should be accurately identified to specific amounts shown in the accounting records rather than extrapolated from other data or by using estimates.

By contrast, an accounting estimate for a provision may be allowable if the amount is computed in accordance with best accounting practice in the accounting period in which it is provided where the underlying expense is revenue in nature, is not disallowed under a specific rule and is accurately calculated (*Owen (HM Inspector of Taxes) v Southern Railway of Peru Ltd*; see **B39**).

In meeting notes issued in September 1997 (*Tax 18/97*) between the ICAEW and the Inland Revenue, it was stated that the use of accounts for tax purposes was restricted by the accounting concept of materiality. This view preceded the change of legislation in *FA 1998* to use accounts prepared in accordance with GAAP. However current guidance at BIM31047 indicates that HMRC's view on this matter has not significantly altered.

HMRC may accept accounting figures rounded to the nearest £1,000 for businesses with a turnover of £5m or more, but qualify this treatment as concessionary (Statement of Practice 15/93), and its use is subject to a number of conditions including demonstrating a compliance cost saving.

1.3.3 Prudence

The requirement to apply prudence when preparing financial statements has long been a cornerstone of accounting standards. Paragraph 2.9 of FRS 102 embraces this principle:

> "Prudence is the inclusion of a degree of caution in the exercise of the judgements needed in making the estimates required under conditions of uncertainty, such that assets or income are not overstated and liabilities or expenses are not understated. However, the exercise of prudence does not allow the deliberate understatement of assets or income, or the deliberate overstatement of liabilities or expenses. In short, prudence does not permit bias."

Tax case law has established that neither a profit nor a loss should be anticipated, and the accounting requirement to apply prudence creates a tension between accounting and tax principles in determining the accounting "profits before tax".

Development of accounting principles for income recognition (FRS 102, Section 23 "Revenue") and the basis on which provisions may be recognised in the accounts (FRS 102, Section 21 "Provisions and Contingencies") have resulted in some degree of convergence of accounting principles and tax law, developed over many years by the courts. For example, "big bath" provisions were acceptable under accounting standards before the introduction of FRS 12 (issued in September 1998) but were disallowed for tax purposes as this conflicted with the tax principle of anticipating losses. Accounting standards no longer permit this type of provision.

1.3.4 Substance over form

In order to present the user of accounts with an accurate summary of the financial position, transactions must reflect the commercial or economic substance rather than the legal form (FRS 102, para 2.8).

Finance lease transactions are an example of substance over form. The legal ownership of an asset remains with the lessor but the accounting shows the substance of the transaction in a similar way to an asset purchased outright, i.e. as a fixed asset and corresponding liability to make payments under the lease.

By contrast, the tax treatment of leases has until recently followed the legal form, with capital allowances claimed by the lessor and rental payments deducted by the lessee. This treatment still applies for most types of short-term leases.

The difference between the accounting and tax treatment of leased assets has resulted in complex and lengthy tax legislation to counteract tax planning strategies developed by lessors (mainly in an attempt to accelerate capital allowances claims). The introduction of long-funding lease rules (*FA 2006*, now *CAA 2001, ss 70A–70YI*) has led to tax legislation imitating accounting by transferring the entitlement to capital allowances claims to the lessee for certain categories of leases, which is based on the economic substance of the transaction being a loan. The tax legislation imports accounting language to define a long-funding lease (see **B29**).

1.3.5 Selection of an accounting policy

FRS 102, Section 10, "Accounting Policies, Estimates and Errors" requires businesses to adopt the most appropriate accounting policy to prepare their accounts and this should be applied consistently. When specific accounting guidance is prescribed for a particular type of transaction, this must be used (except where the effect of doing so would be immaterial). In all other circumstances, paragraph 10.4 of FRS 102 requires that accounting policies are formulated on the following principles:

> "… management shall use its judgement in developing and applying an accounting policy that results in information that is:
>
> (a) relevant to the economic decision-making needs of users; and
>
> (b) reliable, in that the financial statements:
>
> (i) represent faithfully the financial position, financial performance and cash flows of the entity;
>
> (ii) reflect the economic substance of transactions, other events and conditions, and not merely the legal form;
>
> (iii) are neutral, i.e. free from bias;
>
> (iv) are prudent; and
>
> (v) are complete in all material respects."

The policy adopted must conform to recognition criteria and measurement concepts for assets, liabilities, income and expenses and the pervasive principles of Section 2 of FRS 102.

A change in accounting policy may only be made if this is required by an FRS, or when there is clear evidence that the new policy will provide more relevant information on transactions. Only in exceptional circumstances will a departure from an accounting standard be required to conform to a true and fair view.

The tax effect arising from changes to accounting policies is covered in **B1**.

True and fair

ITA 2007, s 997 provides a limited definition of the meaning of UK GAAP as:

> "... generally accepted accounting practice in relation to accounts ... that are intended to give a true and fair view."

The reference to an intention in tax statute to comply with "true and fair" indicates that GAAP may not necessarily reach that view. Accounting standards do not spell out the meaning of "true and fair". However, the FRC and HMRC acknowledge that in most cases the application of correct accounting policies in accordance with accounting standards will result in achieving a true and fair view in the financial statements:

> "Because the standards are formulated with the objective of ensuring that information resulting from their application faithfully represents the underlying commercial activity the FRC envisages that only in exceptional circumstances will departure from the requirement of a standard be necessary in order to ensure a true and fair view. The true and fair view has the ultimate legal override." (BIM31020)

The calculation of profits in accordance with GAAP is a question of fact and not one of law and, ultimately, a dispute between the taxpayer and HMRC is resolved on the basis of expert accounting evidence.

1.4 ACCOUNTING PERIODS

An apportionment is necessary to establish the accounting profits that relate to the relevant tax basis period for a trader:

- when the accounts cover a period of more than 12 months;
- when the opening year rules apply for traders on the commencement of a sole trader or a commencement or cessation of a notional trade when individuals join or leave a partnership or LLP; or
- on a change of accounting reference date.

Time apportionment of profits is used (*ITTOIA 2005, s 203*) unless the taxpayer can justify a more accurate or reasonable method for the allocation. An apportionment is not necessary if accounting records are available to support a more accurate measure of profits, particularly if the accounting records comprise a relatively small number of large transactions (*Marshall Hus & Partners Ltd v Bolton*).

Property businesses that do not use the cash basis are required to disclose the accounting result for periods that coincide with the tax year (5 April or 31 March). Apportionments are made where the accounting reference date does not correspond with the tax year, and (as for traders) this will usually be on a time-apportioned basis (*ITTOIA 2005, s 275*) – but the taxpayer may elect to use a different basis for apportionment where it is reasonable to do so.

1.5 INTERACTION OF ACCOUNTING STANDARDS AND TAX CASE LAW

The accounts of a business provide a measure of profits or losses, but the accounting treatment is not necessarily conclusive for determining profits for tax purposes, where the tax statute takes precedence. The courts have considered the concept of "ordinary principles of commercial accounting", and this is based on case law that has evolved over more than a hundred years.

When the statutory link to GAAP was introduced, it was stated in draft guidance that this was not intended to replace previous case law (Tax Law Rewrite Project ED1). Therefore, the change in statute brought about by *FA 1998, s 42* was not intended to fundamentally alter the interaction between accounting and tax principles, but it marked a change in emphasis on the reliance placed on the accounting and this change coincided with a number of key tax cases around that time. Therefore, *ITTOIA 2005, s 25* retains a two-stage process for establishing accounting profits: 1) use of generally accepted accounting principles in preparing the accounts, and 2) applying the ordinary principles of commercial accounting as established by the courts. The development and convergence of a unified code of accounting standards has enabled the courts to place more reliance on the accounting treatment, particularly when considering the timing of deductions and income recognition.

As previously noted, the introduction of the concept of "true and fair" into tax law required that businesses must use recognised accounting standards "... in so far as they are relevant and material to the computation of profits" (Explanatory Notes to *Finance (No 2) Bill 1998*). In essence this is not significantly different from the previous requirements laid down by the courts to use "ordinary principles of commercial accountancy" when computing the result for tax purposes.

The courts' approach to accounting evidence was summarised by Lord Denning in *Heather v P-E Consulting Group Limited (1972) 48 TC 293* (at page 321):

> "The Courts have always been assisted greatly by the evidence of accountants. Their practice should be given due weight; but the Courts have never regarded themselves as being bound by it. It would be wrong to do so … They are not to be deflected from their true course by the evidence of accountants, however eminent."

The weight of accounting evidence to determine the distinction between capital or revenue expenditure is covered at **Chapter 3**.

If there is more than one acceptable accounting treatment, the courts have considered the most appropriate. The case of *BSC Footwear Ltd v Ridgway [1971]* considered a valuation of stock that was based on the replacement cost reduced by the gross profit margin. The taxpayer considered this to be the best method, as it applied to end-of-line fashion stocks that were expected to be sold at below cost. While it was an accepted accounting basis at that time (this is no longer a valid accounting treatment under Section 13 of FRS 102), it was held that the accounting policy contravened the principle that losses must not be anticipated. On the basis of expert accounting evidence from both sides, the court held that a lower of cost or net realisable value method should be used (see **B55**).

The courts have also considered whether the selection of an accounting policy is appropriate in the context of the corporate loan relationship rules. In the recent First Tier Tribunal decision *Ball UK Holdings Ltd [2017] FTT 0457*, HMRC successfully challenged expert accounting evidence on the choice of functional currency used to prepare the accounts. Therefore the exchange loss on transition to dollars as the functional currency was not allowed. The decision is subject to appeal at the Upper Tribunal.

The application of accounting standards to unincorporated businesses was considered in *Threlfall v Jones* and *Gallagher v Jones [1993]*, where it was held that tax deductions for lump sum lease payments must be spread in accordance with GAAP (BIM31095).

The timing of deductions for accruals for the future cost of a major overhaul of aircraft was considered in *Johnston v Britannia Airways Ltd (1994) 67 TC 99*. The taxpayer company had accrued for repairs using an accepted accounting method at that time and this was one of three possible acceptable accounting treatments. The courts accepted the limits on their right to amend the accounting treatment (Knox J at page 123):

> "The Court is slow to accept that accounts prepared in accordance with accepted principles of commercial accountancy are not adequate for tax purposes as a true statement of the taxpayer's profits for the relevant period. In particular, it is slow to find that there is a judge-made rule of law which prevents accounts prepared in accordance with the ordinary principles of commercial accountancy from complying with the requirements of the tax legislation …"

The Inland Revenue commented on *Threlfall v Jones* and *Johnston v Britannia Airways Ltd* in Tax Bulletin 32 (December 1997), as follows:

> "... the courts were unwilling to identify and apply any principle to over-ride generally accepted accounting treatment concerned with the timing of an item of income or expenditure. These cases illustrate the courts' reluctance nowadays to hold that general accepted accounting treatment should be over-ridden for tax in this way."

This view was based on the codification and maturity of accounting practice through the development of accounting standards and associated guidance introduced and maintained by the professional accounting bodies. It is accepted by the courts that the appropriate accounting treatment may alter over time in accordance with the development of best accounting practice.

Changes to the accounting standard under FRS 12, "Provisions, Contingent Liabilities and Contingent Assets", introduced in 1998, brought about a change in the criteria for recognising provisions and the basis for making best estimates of liabilities. This was followed by the case of *Herbert Smith (a firm) v Honour [1999]*, where the taxpayer claimed a deduction for a provision made for an onerous lease. The amount provided was based on the difference between the future rents payable less estimated rent receivable for sub-letting, which complied with GAAP and was found to be deductible in the year the provision was made (BIM31100).

This decision was followed by a statement from the Inland Revenue (Tax Bulletin 44, December 1999) on the "Interaction of Tax Law and Accountancy Practice":

> "**Allowability of provisions for tax purposes**
>
> Our view can be summarised as follows. A provision made in accounts will be allowable for tax purposes if (and only if):
>
> - it is in respect of allowable revenue expenditure (and not, for example, in respect of capital expenditure);
> - it is required by UK generally accepted accounting practice ("GAAP");
> - it does not conflict with any specific tax rule governing the time at which expenditure is allowed;
> - it is estimated with sufficient accuracy.
>
> Where the first three bullets are satisfied but the fourth is not then only a sufficiently accurate estimate is allowable for tax purposes."

It was unfortunate that the statement made in Tax Bulletin 32 (December 1997) was not followed up by HMRC's approach in *HMRC v William Grant & Sons*

Distillers Ltd and *Small v Mars UK Ltd [2007]*. These cases considered the timing of the disallowance for depreciation when these costs were absorbed into the valuation of closing stock. HMRC argued that the depreciation should be disallowed in the period in which the initial charge was made to profit and loss, i.e. when the stock was manufactured. The taxpayers had followed the relevant accounting standard (*SSAP 9*) to adjust for the disallowance in the period in which the stock was sold and the cost was charged to the profit and loss account, and the courts accepted this approach which followed the timing prescribed in the accounts.

Tax law has been changed (*FA 2008*) to accommodate the principle that an appropriation of stock must be treated as a deemed sale at market value (*Sharkey (HM Inspector of Taxes) v Wernher*). This principle was at odds with the accounting treatment, as no recognition of profit was required by accounting standards. Therefore, the application of the *Sharkey* decision was thrown into doubt following the statutory linkage of GAAP as the starting point in computing taxable profits. The *Sharkey* principle has now been legislated at *ITTOIA 2005, ss 172A–172F* (see **B55**).

1.6 FINALLY

Over recent years there have been a number of attempts to embrace accounting language and concepts when drafting tax statute however, the "holy grail" of aligning the principles of accounting to the basis used for computing taxable profits or losses remains elusive.

1.7 REFERENCES

Legislation

TMA 1970, s 12B

CAA 2001, s 23, Chapter 6A

ITTOIA 2005, ss 25, 28A, 33, 172A–172F, 203, 275

ITA 2007, s 997

FA 2008, Sch 37

CTA 2009, ss 46, 53, 156–161

CTA 2010, s 1127

A–Z of Business Tax Deductions

Companies Act 2006

Small Companies and Groups (Accounts and Directors' Report) Regulations 2008 (SI 2008/409)

Companies, Partnerships and Groups (Accounts and Reports) Regulations 2015 (SI 2015/980)

Large and Medium-sized Companies and Groups (Accounts and Reports) Regulations 2008 (SI 2008/410)

Limited Liability Partnerships (Accounts and Audit) (Application of Companies Act 2006) Regulations 2008 (SI 2008/1911)

Leading cases

Owen (HM Inspector of Taxes) v Southern Railway of Peru Ltd (1956) 36 TC 602

BSC Footwear Ltd v Ridgway (1971) 47 TC 495

Odeon Associated Theatres Ltd v Jones (1971) 48 TC 257

Heather v P-E Consulting Group Limited (1972) 48 TC 293

Marshall Hus & Partners Ltd v Bolton Ch D (1980) 55 TC 539

Threlfall v Jones; Gallagher v Jones (1993) 66 TC 77

Johnston v Britannia Airways Ltd (1994) 67 TC 99

Herbert Smith (a firm) v Honour (1999) 72 TC 130

HMRC v William Grant & Sons Distillers Ltd; Small v Mars UK Ltd [2007] UKHL 15

Ball UK Holdings Ltd [2017 FTT 0457]

HMRC manuals

BIM30000–31115, BIM35201, BIM35205, BIM35210, BIM35215, BIM42051, BIM42215, BIM81065

CH10000

PIM1101, PIM1102

See also

B1, B29, B39, B54

HMRC Helpsheets:

HS222 How to calculate your taxable profits www.gov.uk/self-employed-records/what-records-to-keep

HS229 Information from your Accounts www.gov.uk/government/publications/information-from-your-accounts-hs229-self-assessment-helpsheet/hs229-information-from-your-accounts-2017

James Lole, *Accounting Principles for Tax Purposes* (Bloomsbury Professional, 5th edition)

Andrew Gotch, "The Scope and Implications of Section 42 Finance Act 1998" CIOT Fellowship Thesis, September 2004

OTS – Tax relief for tangible fixed assets using accounts depreciation – 30 November 2017

"Accounting standards: the UK tax implications of new UK GAAP" (21 July 2017): www.gov.uk/government/publications/accounting-standards-the-uk-tax-implications-of-new-uk-gaap

www.gov.uk/government/consultations/ots-depreciation-and-capital-allowances-review-call-for-evidence

What is the best choice for micro-entities: FRS 105 or FRS 102 Section 1A? ICAEW 18 May 2016

Office of Tax Simplification: Accounting depreciation or capital allowances? – June 2018

Chapter 2

Cash basis for unincorporated businesses

2.1 BACKGROUND

The cash basis system of accounting was first mentioned in legislation in the March 2012 Budget. Draft legislation appeared in December 2012. Its final form was presented in the Finance Bill in March 2013 and it was subsequently enacted with effect from 6 April 2013. At that stage it only applied to trades and professions and could not be used by property businesses. *Finance (No 2) Bill 2017, Schedule 2, Part 2* changed that position for 2017/18 and onwards, with a very similar cash basis being made available to small unincorporated property businesses. Originally the cash basis system was heralded as "simplified accounting", following from the principles enshrined in the Office of Tax Simplification (OTS) report, which is where the idea and recommendation started. It is fair to say that the slogan name "simplified" drifted away after the detail of the final form was understood.

Finance (No 2) Bill 2017 also heralded amendments to the rules for trading and professional businesses on the cash basis. These apply to scheme turnover entry conditions and to capital expenditure and receipts. See the detail in the relevant sections below.

Alongside the idea of "simplified accounting" came the idea of "simplified expenses". The latter has also been re-titled, being known now as "fixed rate deductions", although HMRC have retained some reference to the "simplification" form. It is important to understand that, although these concepts emerged together, there is no statutory link between them. Each can be used separately from the other. In the original sketching of the cash basis system, this was not the case insofar as motor expenses were concerned. It was envisaged that all cash basis users would be compelled to use simplified expenses for expenditure on cars and motor cycles.

Fixed rate deductions are examined in **B16**.

Features specific to the property cash basis are explained in **Chapter 5** Property rental businesses.

2.2 THE TARGETS

Self-employed individuals and partnerships carrying on small trading businesses are the ones originally identified by HMRC to use the cash basis. It was always to be an alternative to the preparation of accruals accounts for those who meet the criteria. It is optional; no-one is forced to use the system for tax purposes. However, there are deliberate links with the administration of the Universal Credit (UC) system of benefits, which continues to be brought in gradually by the Department of Work and Pensions and has been progressing since October 2013. Those individuals who claim under the UC could find a benefit from using the cash basis, because their accounts will have been produced within a system which has certain fundamental similarities, although they are far from being identical.

When conceived by the OTS, it was the micro-business that was the target. Turnover limitations for users in the order of £30,000 were mooted. During its enactment, this was extended considerably and the link to UC became more obvious. The detailed conditions are examined below, but note that until 2017/18 users were restricted to those whose annual turnover did not exceed the VAT threshold or, for those within UC, twice the VAT threshold. For 2017/18 and onwards the "relevant maximum" has been unscrambled from the VAT threshold.

It is not possible for companies to use the cash basis; neither can LLPs nor a partnership which has a corporate member.

2.3 THE PRINCIPLES

Using the cash basis means that small businesses can elect to be taxed on the basis of the cash that passes through their financial records, rather than needing to calculate their financial accounts based on generally accepted accounting practice. The latter – GAAP – is also often known as the "accruals basis", and both terms are used here.

The aim is that, over the life of the business, the total receipts and the total payments will all be taken into account once and once only. Transitional rules exist to smooth the accounting differences when businesses do switch between the two systems, as there are some circumstances in which businesses might move from the accruals basis to the cash basis, or they might leave the cash basis for the accruals basis. However, switching frequently between the two systems is not permitted if the criteria for change are not met. That is to prevent use of the cash basis from being abused.

Despite the aim of accounting for all receipts and payments throughout the life of the business and the transitional rules when switching systems, total profits over time of a business that uses the cash basis might not match precisely those of one that uses the accruals basis. For example, loan interest is limited to an annual maximum of £500 under the cash basis. However, even assuming they would reconcile reasonably well overall, there is a very real likelihood that the total tax liability of an individual using the respective systems would differ. The reasons are mainly the effects of timing. For example, under the cash basis:

- the timing differences of when income and expenses are accounted for can result in differing tax rates applying to higher (or lower) profits;
- the date to which businesses make up their accounts has more flexibility, again potentially resulting in tax rate differences; and
- losses can only be set against future profits of the trade, as there is no sideways loss relief. Accordingly, when loss relief is finally given, the extent to which it can be utilised, as well as the rate of tax it saves, could be different.

2.4 ELIGIBILITY – KEY CRITERIA

An election to use the cash basis must be made under *ITTOIA 2005, s 25A*. However, it is *ITTOIA 2005, s 31A* that sets out the conditions which must be met to be able to use the basis.

Section 31A states that:

> "(1) A person may make an election under *section 25A* for a tax year if conditions A to C are met.
>
> (2) Condition A is that the aggregate of the cash basis receipts of each trade, profession or vocation carried on by the person during that tax year does not exceed any relevant maximum applicable for that tax year (see *section 31B*).
>
> (3) Condition B is that, in a case where the person is either an individual who controls a firm or a firm controlled by an individual–
>
> (a) the aggregate of the cash basis receipts of each trade, profession or vocation carried on by the individual or the firm during that tax year does not exceed any relevant maximum applicable for that tax year, and
>
> (b) the firm or the individual (as the case may be) has also made an election under *section 25A* for that tax year.
>
> (4) Condition C is that the person is not an excluded person in relation to the tax year (see *section 31C*).
>
> (5) For the purposes of this section, the 'cash basis receipts' of a trade, profession or vocation, in relation to a tax year, are any receipts that–

(a) are received during the basis period for the tax year, and

(b) would be brought into account in calculating the profits of the trade, profession or vocation for that tax year on the cash basis."

2.5 SECTION 31A IN PRACTICE

As stated above, a prime factor limiting the eligibility of a business to use the cash basis is its turnover ("relevant maximum" in the legislation). It is that of the previous year which determines whether the option exists for the next year.

If an individual has more than one business, it is the aggregate turnover for all his businesses that counts. He cannot look at one in isolation. If the aggregate turnover for all the businesses is below the "relevant maximum" and he makes the election, he must apply the cash basis to all businesses – he cannot then exclude any of them.

If the individual is a partner and he is a controlling partner – i.e. he is entitled to more than half of the assets or of the income – he must aggregate the turnover of the partnership with that of any businesses he carries on separately from the partnership to determine whether the maximum has been exceeded. Again, if the turnover has not been breached and one business is elected for the cash basis, all must be. If the individual is not a controlling partner, no aggregation is needed.

If a partnership does have a controlling partner, all of its separate trades must have their turnover aggregated to determine eligibility. If the result of that review is that all such aggregation permits the cash basis election, all the partnership businesses must follow suit if one makes the election.

ITTOIA 2005, s 31B sets out the way that "relevant maximum" under *section 31A* is calculated. This changed for 2017/18 and onwards.

Prior to 2017/18 the VAT registration threshold at the end of the relevant tax year (i.e. the "previous" year) defined the relevant amount. If the accounting period was less than 12 months, the limit was reduced proportionately. However, it was not increased if the accounting period were to be greater. If the individual in question was claiming universal credit, the relevant amount increased to twice the VAT registration turnover.

A business that claimed the cash basis in the previous year could exceed twice the VAT threshold in the current year before it was required to leave the regime.

All the above turnover limitations changed in 2017/18, instead being based on an amount specific to the cash basis. The joining threshold became, and currently has remained as, £150,000 for mainstream businesses, or £300,000 for recipients of UC. The person must leave the cash basis in the tax year following the year in which the combined cash basis receipts of all their trades exceed £300,000. The exception for the requirement to leave the cash basis is where, in the year subsequent to the one in which the turnover limit was exceeded, the person's total business receipts do not exceed the "relevant maximum".

2.6 ELIGIBILITY – EXCLUDED PERSONS

Excluded persons are listed at *ITTOIA 2005, s 31C*. Summarising, they are persons who are:

- companies;
- partnerships which include a company as a member;
- limited liability partnerships;
- Lloyd's underwriters;
- farming businesses which have a herd basis election in place;
- businesses with a current profit averaging election;
- businesses which, within the seven years prior to the basis period, obtained a business premises renovation allowance;
- businesses which carried on a trade of mineral extraction at any time during the basis period; or
- businesses which own an asset on which research and development capital allowances were claimed at any time before the basis period.

2.7 RULES FOR SPECIFIC TRADES AND PROFESSIONS

2.7.1 Barristers and advocates

Special rules permitting a cash rather than accruals basis which may be used for these professions have existed for many years. The format was modified in 2004/05, with the cash basis being restricted to use during the first seven years of the practice (*ITTOIA 2005, s 160*).

The rules for barristers and advocates differ from the "simplified cash basis" to which this chapter applies. The legislation was repealed for new businesses for 2012/13 onwards, when the new cash basis first applied. However, those already using the *section 160* system can continue its use until the end of the seven-year period if they choose.

2.7.2 Ministers of Religion

There are special rules for deductions that are permitted for a Minister of Religion in respect of his dwelling house, where it is rented and where it is in part used for his profession. The allowance extends to a deduction referenced by the rent paid and also to expenses on the maintenance, repair, insurance or management of the premises. The allowable proportion is set out by statute (*ITTOIA 2005, s 159*).

These deductions are not permitted by a Minister who has elected to use the cash basis.

2.7.3 Dealers in securities

Legislation permits profits and losses from securities that, in accordance with GAAP, are calculated by reference to the fair value of the securities and recognised in the person's statement of recognised gains and losses to be brought into account in calculating the profits of the trade (*ITTOIA 2005, s 149*).

The rule is disapplied where necessary to prevent the same amount from being brought into account twice. Other criteria and conditions are also in point.

For any dealer in securities who has elected to use the cash basis, the concessionary legislation at *section 149* is not permitted.

2.7.4 Dealers in land

Rules apply to dealers in land that are specific to the purchase or sale of woodlands, mineral royalties and lease premiums (*ITTOIA 2005, s 158*). They serve to adapt the particular legislation that is applied to those types of trade, where the purpose would not be met by the short-term holding periods of a person trading in them.

Those particular rules are not available to dealers in land who use the cash basis.

2.7.5 Further detail

There are a few more instances where legislation applied to particular trades or dealings is disapplied for the cash basis. They are set out in *ITTOIA 2005, s 148K*.

2.8 SPECIAL RELIEFS UNAVAILABLE

HMRC, at BIM70050, set out that, in calculating the profits of a trade using the cash basis, some claims and reliefs are not available:

- herd basis rules;
- averaging profits of farmers and creative artists;
- compensation for compulsory slaughter of animals (spreading relief);
- relief for unremittable amounts;
- sound recordings (permitting acquisition of original master version to be treated as revenue cost);
- certain telecommunication rights (permitting treatment of an individual's expenditure and receipts to be treated similarly to those of a trade);
- long-funding leases (allowable portion of finance deduction);
- changes in trading stock (see **2.11** below);
- disposal and acquisition of know-how (amount to be brought into account on disposals whilst trade continues); and
- oil activities.

2.9 THE WAY CASH BASIS WORKS

2.9.1 Starting and ending

To use the cash basis, an election must be made in accordance with *ITTOIA 2005, s 25A*. It is made via the tax return submitted by either the self-employed individual or the partnership, whichever is applicable to the business. The usual time limit applies, i.e. the first anniversary of the 31 January following the end of the tax year which is the first one for which the cash basis has been used.

Once in place, the election has effect for the tax year to which it relates and all subsequent years (*ITTOIA 2005, s 31D*). Nevertheless, the appropriate box on the tax return should be ticked each year.

Therefore, the person remains on the cash basis until either they are no longer eligible (under *ITTOIA 2005, s 31A*) or there has been a change in circumstances so that it is more appropriate for profits to be calculated in accordance with GAAP. If this circumstance arises, the business must elect to calculate profits in that way (*ITTOIA 2005, s 31D*). The legislation does not explain what constitutes "changes in circumstances".

HMRC, at BIM70055, give examples of:

- a business that is expanding and wishes to claim more than £500 interest deductions; and
- a business that wishes to claim 'sideways' loss relief.

The person must leave the cash basis system when their turnover, measured in accordance with *ITTOIA 2005, s 31*, has increased such that the relevant amount has been exceeded. The detail, for years prior to 2017/18 and from 2017/18 and onwards are set out above at **2.5**.

The method of leaving the scheme and notifying HMRC of such is to leave the "cash basis" box on the tax return unticked.

If a person revokes the cash basis election for any of the above reasons, it does not prevent that same person making a cash basis election for a subsequent tax year (assuming all eligibility conditions are met).

2.9.2 Calculation overview

There are two steps to calculating profits on the cash basis:

(1) Calculate the total trade receipts received in the basis period for the tax year.

(2) Deduct the total expenses of the trade paid during the basis period of the tax year (subject to any adjustments required or allowed by law).

According to HMRC, the business can treat income as received and expenses as paid at the date of its choosing. The key point is that the treatment is consistent. Thus, an expense may be paid when a card payment is made, or on the date that entry is shown on the bank statement.

The basis period for a tax year is normally the 12 months to the date to which the accounts are made up in that tax year. There is no special rule about which date that should be.

The broad effect is that the business no longer needs to compute certain figures. These include:

- debtors;
- creditors;
- stock;
- capital expenses; and
- capital allowances.

2.10 INCOME AND EXPENSES

Despite the significant differences from preparing accounts under the accruals basis, for the most part, the rules about expenses and receipts are the same for the cash basis system. It is the principle of being on a paid and received basis that leads to the changes that are apparent.

Income constitutes all amounts received in connection with the business, including output VAT and VAT refunds (where the business is VAT registered) and proceeds from the sale or leasing of capital assets where they are non-durable. Broadly, this means including the sales from plant and machinery or similar, but not from cars as they are excepted. See the section on "Capital expenditure" at **2.12** below for more detail and note the changes for 2017/18 and onwards.

There is no requirement to bring into account as a receipt the value of any goods taken from the business for personal use, such as applies to restaurant and hotel businesses under GAAP. Instead, a fair and reasonable adjustment should be made to reflect an uncommercial transaction. An example might be disallowing as an expense the cost of any such goods.

Income rules are mirrored by the definition of expenses that are deductible. Thus, expenses are allowable when paid and include input VAT and VAT payments (where the business is VAT registered) and the full cost of non-durable assets other than excepted ones.

2.11 PARTICULAR ITEMS

2.11.1 Stock

Where a business has used the accruals basis and changes to the cash basis, stock which has been accounted for as closing stock under GAAP is brought in as a deduction from profits in the first year on the cash basis.

If the business is a new one and commences using the cash basis immediately, stock at each year end is simply ignored.

If a trading business ceases whilst using the cash basis, the value of the stock on hand is brought in as a receipt.

A profession or vocation would deal similarly to a trader's stock with its value of work in progress on transferring to the cash basis and on cessation.

No adjustment for stock or work in progress is required on a change in the persons carrying on the business, provided there is at least one person who is the same in the business both before and after the change. This covers the position where, for example, there is a change in the members of a partnership.

See *ITTOIA 2005, ss 97A, 97B.*

2.11.2 VAT

The cash basis does not affect the way a business should account for VAT. For VAT-registered businesses using the cash basis, business receipts and payments may be recorded either excluding or including VAT. If VAT is included, the net VAT payments to HMRC should be recorded as expenses and net repayments from HMRC as receipts.

2.11.3 Trading allowance

This is covered in detail at **B54**. A key point here is that a business that uses the cash basis is eligible for a trading allowance in the same way as a business that calculates its profits under GAAP. Indeed, if the latter method were used and it resulted in profits exceeding the £1,000 allowance, but had they been calculated under the cash basis they would not have done so (and full cash basis eligibility applies), then the relevant income is treated as not exceeding the trading allowance.

2.12 CAPITAL ASSETS

Fresh legislation was introduced for 2017/18 and onwards to deal with capital expenditure and receipts under the cash basis. The principle behind the rules has remained the same, but the new legislation was designed to provide clearer definitions of capital assets and their consequent tax treatment for cash basis users.

Unfortunately, in so doing the legislation has been extended considerably, see *ITTOIA 2005, s 33A*, and can seem more daunting than previously. Time to adjust is provided by transitional rules, in that for (only) 2017/18 if the old criteria for capital deductions are met they can be used instead of the new ones.

Both old and new rules are set out in separate sections below.

2.12.1 Capital expenditure prior to 2017/18

The legislation permits a business using the cash basis to treat expenditure that would qualify for plant and machinery allowances as a capital expense, with the exception of cars.

The effect is that the principle of determining whether an item is capital or revenue is maintained. The difference is that capital assets that meet the criteria of plant and machinery (except cars) are deductible as expenses in the profit and loss account.

This only applies to "non-durable assets". The costs of acquiring the following are not deductible:

- land;
- cars;
- intellectual property;
- shares;
- investments;
- other businesses; and
- non-depreciating assets.

(*ITTOIA 2005, s 33A – History*)

2.12.2 Capital receipts prior to 2017/18

The principle is that proceeds arising from the disposal of any asset, or rights in it, of a type on which the cash basis permits a deduction on acquisition must be included as a cash basis receipt. "Disposal" includes damages, insurance or other compensation received in respect of the asset. As identified above, the legislation is primarily looking at plant and machinery and it does not include cars.

The requirement to bring in proceeds as a receipt extends to assets which were acquired prior to transferring to the cash basis from the accruals basis. This might seem illogical, as the acquisition cost would not have been a deduction under GAAP. However, its validity is because it would have qualified for capital allowances. Broadly, the asset would either have qualified for annual investment allowance 100% deduction, or at least it would have qualified for a writing down allowance and an adjustment on entering the cash basis system (see **2.15** for more detail).

If only a part of the value of the asset would be a qualifying business item, because of private use, only that same proportion of the disposal proceeds should be included as a receipt.

Where an asset ceases to be used for the purposes of the business, the market value of the asset must be included as a receipt.

Where the non-business use of the asset materially increases, the relevant proportion of the asset's market value must be included as a receipt during the relevant accounting period.

HMRC (at BIM70020) explain their interpretation of the legislation on capital receipts (*ITTOIA 2005, s 96A – History*) and provide examples.

The same manual reference also refers to a person carrying on a trade who receives a grant under the Industrial Development scheme. This must be brought in as a cash basis receipt, even though under GAAP the grant would have been matched to the cost of acquisition of a specified asset.

2.12.3 Capital expenditure for 2017/18 onwards

This legislation tries to clarify the definition of capital expenditure by removing the link from assets qualifying for plant and machinery allowances, which has always created difficulties in interpretation. Instead there is an initial presumption that capital expenditure would not be denied as a deduction for tax purposes. That is set out at *ITTOIA 2005, s 32A(1)*. This presumption is then restricted by *ITTOIA 2005, s 33A(1)* and the remainder of *section 33A's* 14 subsections. The first five subsections are listed below and constitute the main thrust of the deduction restrictions. The remaining subsections define the relevant terms used in the first five. These should be read where *sections 33A(1)–(5)* leave any doubt about a particular asset qualifying as a revenue deduction. "Depreciating asset" (*sections 33A(6)–(7)*) and "intangible asset" (*sections 33A(8)–(11)*) are especially recommended.

ITTOIA 2005, s 33A includes the statements that:

> "(1) This section applies in relation to the calculation of the profits of a trade on the cash basis
>
> (2) No deduction is allowed for an item of a capital nature incurred on, or in connection with, the acquisition or disposal of a business or part of a business.
>
> (3) No deduction is allowed for an item of a capital nature incurred on, or in connection with, education or training.
>
> (4) No deduction is allowed for an item of a capital nature incurred on, or in connection with, the provision, alteration or disposal of–
>
> (a) any asset that is not a depreciating asset (see subsections (6) and (7)),
>
> (b) any asset not acquired or created for use on a continuing basis in the trade,
>
> (c) a car (see subsection (14)),

(d) land,

(e) a non-qualifying intangible asset (see subsections (8) to (11)), or

(f) a financial asset (see subsection (12)).

(5) But subsection (4)(d) does not prevent a deduction being made for expenditure that–

(a) is incurred on the provision of a depreciating asset which, in being provided, is installed or otherwise fixed to land so as to become, in law, part of the land, but

(b) is not incurred on, or in connection with, the provision of–

(i) a building,

(ii) a wall, floor, ceiling, door, gate, shutter or window or stairs,

(iii) a waste disposal system,

(iv) a sewerage or drainage system, or

(v) a shaft or other structure in which a lift, hoist, escalator or moving walkway may be installed."

It can be seen that in essence the nature of the capital expenditure which qualifies as an expense under the cash basis has not significantly changed in 2017/18, it is the method of defining the detail which is fundamentally different.

2.12.4 Capital receipts for 2017/18 onwards

This is set out at *ITTOIA 2005, s 96A*. It now includes capital receipts after leaving, as well as the treatment whilst the business is on, the cash basis. The sheer volume of the legislation can seem daunting. However, the principle is that a receipt mirrors the treatment of the asset on its acquisition, so that there is parity for tax deduction purposes.

The legislation states that it applies where the conditions for either Case 1 or Case 2 are met. Effectively, Case 1 refers to the position where the business is on the cash basis when there is a disposal of the asset. Case 2 is where the business has already left it at the time of asset disposal, but its acquisition was dealt with under the cash basis. Conditions A and B must both be met under Case 1. Condition C and, either, condition D or condition E must be met for Case 2 to be applicable. Between them, the conditions detail the various possibilities of the timing of acquisition and of disposal of capital assets, in conjunction with their application to the business operating under cash basis rules, to ensure that parity for tax purposes is met.

The proceeds received which are cash basis receipts are:

- from the sale of the asset or any part of it;
- in respect of a grant of any right in respect of the asset, or an interest in it; and
- for damages or compensation received.

Thus, proceeds from the sale of assets which were eligible for capital allowances previously will be treated as a trading receipt. However, if proceeds exceed cost, the full proceeds are brought into account.

There is no balancing adjustment for items which were previously subjected to claims for capital allowances.

Broadly, the rules prior to 2017/18 are unchanged in respect of the situation where:

- only a part of the value of the asset would be a qualifying business item, because of private use, ie only that same proportion of the disposal proceeds should be included as a receipt;
- an asset ceases to be used for the purposes of the business, ie the market value of the asset must be included as a receipt;
- the non-business use of the asset materially increases, ie the relevant proportion of the asset's market value must be included as a receipt during the relevant accounting period.

HMRC manual at BIM70020, referred to in the pre-2017/18 situation, has been updated and their interpretation of the legislation on capital receipts is currently relevant.

2.12.5 Capital allowances

In calculating the profits of a trade on the cash basis, payments for plant and machinery which would ordinarily qualify for capital allowances are treated as an allowable business expense. No capital allowances are therefore available in respect of the plant and machinery.

There is an exception for payments relating to the provision of a car. Such payments are not allowable as an expense when calculating cash basis profits. Accordingly, capital allowances are available on the purchase of a car, or on a qualifying business proportion of the cost, where the actual basis is used for the running costs. If the fixed rate deductions for vehicles will be used, no capital allowances can be claimed.

2.13 LOSS RELIEF

Losses incurred under the simplified cash basis cannot be used against other income of the current tax year.

Losses cannot be carried back and used against other income of the previous tax year, irrespective of whether the cash basis was used that year.

Losses cannot be offset against chargeable gains.

Losses *can* be carried forward and used against the next available profits of the same trade, in the same way as for businesses using GAAP.

Losses *can* be carried back for three years on the permanent cessation of the trade, under the terminal loss relief legislation, as for businesses using GAAP.

2.14 EXPENSE RESTRICTIONS

There are certain expenses that are not permitted as a deduction within cash basis rules, or which have restrictions attached:

- Employee benefit contributions can only be deducted if they have been paid in the taxable period (*ITTOIA 2005, s 38(2A)*).
- Contributions to agents' expenses under a payroll deduction scheme will only be allowed for expenses which have been incurred (*ITTOIA 2005, s 72(2A)*).
- Expenses of setting up a SAYE or CSOP option scheme are only allowable for expenses actually paid (*ITTOIA 2005, s 94A(4)*).
- Tenant's deduction for rent paid on a lease premium (*ITTOIA 2005, s 56A(1)*).
- Interest paid on a loan is specifically disallowed (but see below).

2.14.1 Deductible interest

Although the cash basis legislation denies a deduction for loan interest (*ITTOIA 2005, s 51A*), actual interest paid up to a maximum of £500 is permitted.

Furthermore, where the deduction would have been denied in any case because the loan had not been incurred wholly and exclusively for a business purpose, the same deduction is permitted, i.e. up to a maximum of £500. Thus, the loan does not have to be one that entirely finances capital used in the business; it can have a mixed use.

The £500 limit relates to the combined cost of interest on all loans and includes incidental costs of obtaining finance.

Despite the above, payments of interest on purchases are not subject to the £500 limit, provided the purchase itself is an allowable expense (i.e. it is not for cash borrowing). Other examples of interest charges which are outside the restriction are:

- trade credit charged by suppliers of goods or services;
- interest charges for hire purchase or leasing of plant or machinery; and
- credit card interest on allowable purchases.

Note that, in the above instances of interest and credit charges being allowable deductions, if the item purchased is used for both business and private purposes, only the proportion of interest related to the business usage is allowable.

2.15 ENTERING THE CASH BASIS

When entering the cash basis from the accruals basis, adjustments are needed to ensure that income and expenditure are neither omitted completely nor duplicated.

Accordingly, income is adjusted in a logical way for opening/closing debtors so as to ensure that all income is taxed only once. Expenses are similarly adjusted for opening/closing creditors. Accruals and pre-payments are necessarily included in the adjustment process.

2.15.1 Capital allowances

An additional *Chapter 17A* has been inserted into *ITTOIA 2005* to deal with capital allowances adjustments when a business moves to the cash basis system from GAAP. Plant and machinery pools are treated differently from cars. The pool treatment is as follows.

The "unrelieved qualifying expenditure" – effectively the written down value (WDV) of the capital allowance pools – is brought in as an expense in the year of transition to the cash basis, unless for any reason it would not have been treated as allowable had it represented new purchases in that year. That mainly refers to cars which might have a value written down and included within a main pool. Therefore, that value needs to be assessed and excluded from the cost in year one of the cash basis, because of the restriction to the cost of cars as a deduction in the cash basis.

There is an adjustment to be made to the above value of the pool where expenditure on the assets that comprise the WDV has not all been paid for. Primarily this means items bought on hire purchase. In those circumstances, *ITTOIA 2005, s 240D* states that the WDV of the items in question must be compared with the amount already paid. If total payments exceed WDV, the difference can be brought in as an expense in the first year of cash basis. Alternatively, if WDV is less than payments already made, the difference must be treated as an additional receipt. Subsequent payments would then be allowable when made.

Where mileage rate allowances have been claimed, any expenditure incurred in respect of the vehicle is not qualifying expenditure and cannot be carried forward as unrelieved qualifying expenditure. The pool value of cars is in any case precluded, but this extra restriction could apply to motor cycles and other vehicles.

2.15.2 Cars

As set out above, expenditure on cars cannot be treated as a deductible expense under the cash basis. Where a business transfers into the system from GAAP and capital allowances have been claimed on a car then, as explained, the WDV cannot be brought in as a cost. This applies whether the car was within the main pool or special pool. Instead, capital allowances can continue during the cash basis regime. It would not then be possible to change to fixed rate deductions for that vehicle; the actual basis for running costs would have to be used.

2.16 LEAVING THE CASH BASIS

The circumstances when a business might leave the cash basis have been set out above (see **2.9.1**).

Accounting adjustments need to be calculated in the same way as for a business entering the cash basis from GAAP (see above).

The difference is that, because of the likelihood of there being a net income adjustment, a spreading mechanism is available. This is to prevent the hardship that might follow if a significant tax liability became payable in one year. It provides that, upon leaving the cash basis, any adjustment income is spread evenly over the following six tax years (*ITTOIA 2005, s 239A*). However, a person can elect to accelerate this charge if wished (*ITTOIA 2005, s 239B*).

2.16.1 Capital allowances

Where a person leaves the cash basis and they have acquired an asset which would have qualified for capital allowances, if it were not for the cash basis, any unrelieved qualifying expenditure can be allocated to a new capital allowance pool in the next period under GAAP.

The situation envisaged is where an asset was acquired under a hire purchase agreement whilst in the cash basis. These provisions mean that any amount unpaid at the time of leaving the cash basis would be allocated to a capital allowance pool in the first chargeable period in which the person uses the accruals basis. If it were not for this provision, the outstanding hire purchase payments would be omitted from any deductions (*CAA 2001, s 66A*).

2.17 CAPITAL GAINS TAX

Interaction between the plant and machinery rules of the cash basis and capital gains tax is provided for in the legislation. The effect is that no chargeable gains or losses will be applied to an asset sold whilst on the cash basis. If an item is subsequently sold that was acquired whilst on the cash basis, it will be treated as if capital allowances had been applied. Thus the capital gains tax legislation operates in the same way as if the relevant assets had been dealt with under GAAP (*TCGA 1992, ss 47A, 47B*).

2.18 REFERENCES

Legislation

TCGA 1992, ss 47A, 47B

CAA 2001, s 66A

ITTOIA 2005, ss 25A, 31A–33A, 51A, 56A, 57B, 148ZA, 95A–97B, 148K, 160, 239A, 239B, 240A–240E, Part 2, Ch 17A

F(No 2)A 2017, Sch 2

Leading cases

None

HMRC manuals

BIM70000–BIM70100

Chapter 3

Capital or revenue expenditure

3.1 COMMENT

A fundamental principle in calculating the taxable profits of an unincorporated business or trade is that no deduction is allowed for capital expenditure. In order to arrive at the result for tax purposes, capital items expensed in the profit and loss account are disallowed.

Relief for capital expenditure may be available under the capital allowances regime which provides a deduction for "tax depreciation". This applies to a restricted class of assets and is mainly limited to functional plant. Capital expenditure on fixed assets that are chargeable assets for capital gains tax purposes (e.g. land and buildings) are taxed on a realised basis, so that relief for the acquisition and related costs is given on disposal.

The distinction between capital and revenue expenditure is mainly determined by the *effect* of the expenditure in the context of the business. The deductibility of costs as revenue expenses is based on a *purpose* test and only considered once it has been established that the expenditure is not capital (see **Chapter 4**).

This chapter covers tax law for unincorporated business who use generally accepted accounting principles. Separate statutory frameworks apply for traders and property landlords using the cash basis and this is covered at **Chapters 2** and **5**. However businesses using the cash basis are nevertheless required to consider whether expenditure is capital or revenue in nature, before applying the specific statutory framework for deductions of capital items.

This publication applies to deductions for unincorporated businesses and does not cover companies. However, the capital and revenue divide also applies for companies as it does for unincorporated businesses. One key area of difference is the treatment of corporate intangibles, which are subject to the corporate intangible fixed assets regime (see *CTA 2009, Part 8*). Broadly, these rules permit deductions for intangible assets and associated expenditure based on accounting treatment but do not affect other classes of assets.

3.2 STATUTORY FRAMEWORK

The statutory rule for capital expenditure is brief and found at *ITTOIA 2005, s 33* which says that:

> "In calculating the profits of a trade, no deduction is allowed for items of a capital nature."

This denies relief for accounting depreciation and book losses on disposals of fixed assets charged in the accounts where this represents a write down in the cost of an asset (credits for depreciation or a profit on disposal are non-taxable).

A trade also includes a property business (*ITTOIA 2005, s 272*).

Capital expenditure is not identified by the type of item but depends on the effect of the expense for the business. The distinction between capital and revenue has been the subject of a large volume of case law. Decisions based on facts which, on first glance, appear similar have resulted in different conclusions. The courts have acknowledged the problems in assessing borderline cases (see *Heather v P-E Consulting Group Ltd (1972) 48 TC 293* at page 321A, *Strick v Regent Oil Co Ltd (1965) 43 TC 1* at page 29, and *Van den Berghs Ltd v Clark (1935) 19 TC 390* at pages 428–429).

Generally, the following types of expenditure are capital in nature:

- the acquisition or enhancement of an asset that is used as part of the fixed capital of the business;
- payments made to obtain a permanent commercial advantage or to improve the profit-making structure of the business;
- the costs of disposing of an onerous asset or obligation that relates to the fixed capital of the business; and
- abortive costs: where the transaction would have been capital if it had proceeded.

This section considers capital expenditure but similar statutory tests have been applied by the courts to consider the nature of receipts. It is important to note that "tax symmetry" will not necessarily apply to the counterparties of a transaction. For example, the sale of a commercial property by a builder is clearly a disposal of stock on "trade account" and generates an income receipt, whereas a purchaser who acquires a property as a fixed asset of the business will not be entitled to a revenue deduction. The cost of the asset will be deductible on an eventual disposal under the capital gains tax rules.

3.3 BASIC PRINCIPLES

The acquisition, improvement or disposal of an asset is classed as capital. The term "asset" is not defined in tax statute but is generally identified as something which secures an enduring benefit.

The case of *Atherton v British Insulated and Helsby Cables Ltd (1925) 10 TC 155* considered a lump sum paid to set up a pension fund for a company's employees, and Viscount Cave (at pages 192–193) described the characteristics of a capital sum as follows:

> "... when an expenditure is made ... with a view to bringing into existence an asset or an advantage for the enduring benefit of a trade ... there is very good reason (in the absence of special circumstances leading to an opposite conclusion) for treating such an expenditure as properly attributable not to revenue but to capital."

From this basic principle, the courts have distinguished capital and revenue expenditure by considering the following:

- *Fixed or circulating capital*: A permanent change in an asset, including the way in which a business is conducted, which results in an enduring benefit is treated as capital (*Anglo-Persian Oil Company Ltd v Dale*, *Watneys London Ltd v Pike* and *Watney Combe Reid & Co Ltd v Pike*, *Walker v The Joint Credit Card Co Ltd*).
- *Accounting evidence*: The frequency of expenditure and its treatment in the accounts is not necessarily an indicator of whether payments are capital or revenue (*Vallambrosa Rubber Company Ltd v Farmer, Bullrun Inc (SpC)*). The effect on the business and legal form must be considered; for example, periodic payments for acquiring machinery under a hire purchase agreement do not alter the nature of the underlying transaction, and the expenditure is capital in nature where it is made to acquire a fixed asset.
- *Entirety principle*: The replacement of an entire asset is capital expenditure, whereas repairs and maintenance are restricted to the replacement parts of an asset. The distinction is not always clear. The borderline between capital and revenue hinges on identifying the "entirety" (*Bullcroft Main Collieries Ltd v O'Grady*, *Samuel Jones & Co (Devonvale) Ltd v CIR*).
- *Preservation of an asset*: Payments made to preserve an existing asset, where there is no alteration or enhancement, is a revenue expense (*Southern v Borax Consolidated*, *Cooke v Quick Shoe Repair Service*).
- *Onerous contracts*: The *Atherton* principle applies equally to getting rid of an onerous contract or obligation – but the payment of a lump sum to end a trade contract is not necessarily capital and depends on its effect on the business overall (*Anglo-Persian Oil Company Ltd v Dale*, *Vodafone*

Cellular Ltd & Others v Shaw, Van den Berghs Ltd v Clark [1935]). The termination or alteration of a contract to avoid future expenditure will be capital if this alters the rights or entitlement to an asset or the fixed profit-making structure of the business (*Mallett v Staveley Coal and Iron Company Ltd, Tucker (HM Inspector of Taxes) v Granada Motorway Services Ltd*).

3.4 ENDURING BENEFIT

The question of whether a payment creates an asset or secures an enhancement or improvement has been frequently reviewed by the courts since *Atherton*. The effect of the expenditure has guided the courts. However, there is no clear definition of the term "enduring". HMRC (at BIM35901) say:

> "There is no simple yardstick of the length of time for which an asset or advantage must endure before it may be regarded as capital. There are other important considerations such as: how the asset or advantage functions in the context of that particular trade; how it benefits the business, and whether it is obtained by a lump sum or by periodical payments."

3.4.1 Identifying an enduring benefit

In the case of *Tucker (HM Inspector of Taxes) v Granada Motorway Services Ltd [1979]*, expenditure on the alteration of a lease was held to be capital as it secured an enduring benefit. The taxpayer argued that:

- the effect of the payment was to reduce future rentals;
- there was no recognition of an asset in the balance sheet; and
- the lease could not be assigned.

None of these factors were sufficient to classify the expenditure as revenue. In cases where an asset has a defined legal form, such as a lease, the decisions of the courts based on similar sets of facts are generally consistent.

The courts have been less consistent when considering the effect of expenditure on enduring assets that are intangible. *Heather v P-E Consulting Group Ltd [1972]* considered payments to fund a trust to allow staff to acquire shares in their employer company to take control away from shareholders that had a disruptive influence on the company's trade.

The facts of *P-E Consulting* were similar to those of *Atherton*, which was distinguished on the grounds that the pension contribution in *Atherton* was made as initial funding to make the fund solvent. By contrast, in *P-E Consulting* it was found that, on the weight of all the evidence, no enduring asset had been created in making contributions to the employee trust.

Case law has distinguished between the treatment of a commercial trade contract – which impacts on the overall earning capacity of a business – and other types of physical asset, such as leases, that are inherently part of the fixed capital of the business.

A payment made to commute an onerous trade contract was found to be deductible as revenue in *Vodafone Cellular Ltd & Others v Shaw [1997]* when the taxpayer made a substantial one-off payment to end a licence. The technology covered by the agreement had become out of date. It was found that the agreement was an "ordinary commercial contract made in the course of trade". The contract did not serve as fixed capital of the business, so that the release payment did not secure an enduring benefit and was accepted as a revenue deduction.

The principle established in *CIR v Carron Company [1968]*, that for a payment to be treated as capital it must be identified with an asset, was upheld by Millett LJ in *Vodafone* (at page 433I):

> "… the principle that a payment made in order to commute or discharge a liability to make recurring revenue payments is itself a revenue payment is subject to an important qualification. If the liability to make recurring revenue payments is reduced or brought to an end by the modification or disposal of an identifiable capital asset, then any payment made for the modification or disposal is itself a capital payment."

Vodafone established that the effect of a payment should be considered at the time it is made. It should be noted that the nature of the licence agreement played a significant part in the outcome in *Vodafone* and the decision may not necessarily be transferable when considering other types of intangible assets.

In the more recent First Tier Tribunal decision, *Ingenious Games LLP and Others v HMRC [2017] UKFTT 429*, the Tribunal found that the impairments made against film distribution rights were capital in nature. HMRC's argument that the expenditure represented an asset with an enduring benefit was based in part on the accounting treatment which capitalised the initial purchase as a fixed asset of the business. Income derived from the rights was likely to be arising over a minimum of five years however income from the run off rights could extend for a longer period and this pointed towards the payment for the rights being capital in nature. The Tribunal decision provides a comprehensive summary of the tests to be considered when evaluating whether expenditure is capital in nature.

3.5 FIXED OR CIRCULATING CAPITAL

The distinction between fixed and circulating capital is not always clearly defined. In accounting terminology, stock, debtors and consumables are generally circulating capital, whereas goodwill, plant, business premises and intellectual property rights are part of the structure of a business.

In *John Smith & Son v Moore [1921]*, reference was made (at page 282) to the economic principles established by Adam Smith, where fixed capital was referred to as what the "… owner turns to profit by keeping it in his own possession, circulating capital as what he makes profit of parting with it and letting it change masters".

The initial intention of the taxpayer treatment will influence the treatment of expenditure. The case of *Gloucester Railway Carriage and Wagon Co [1925]* considered a company that manufactured railway carriages for sale. The sales were made outright or by hire purchase arrangements and some units were used for short-term hire. The taxpayer argued that the hired assets were capital (so that the proceeds on eventual sale were non-taxable at that time). On the facts, it was found that the main purpose of the trade was to sell carriages and the short-term hire did not result in the stock becoming fixed capital. (Note: this decision may be of assistance to traders, such as property developers or dealers, who are unable to sell stock and temporarily hire assets. There is no presumption of an appropriation from stock to fixed assets, and the *Sharkey* principle will not apply if stock is temporarily hired – see **B55**.)

The accounting treatment of expenditure may provide some evidence on whether a payment creates an enduring benefit but is not necessarily conclusive when considering the dividing line between capital and revenue (*Heather v P-E Consulting Group Ltd*; BIM35035).

Example – Fair value adjustment

ABC LLP acquires stock of £50,000 and goodwill of £75,000 on the purchase of a business. Fair value accounting adjustments are required to bring stock valuation in line with the accounting policy for the purchaser and this is dealt with by the following adjustment in the accounts:

Dr Stock (Balance sheet)	£10,000
Cr Goodwill Intangible assets (Balance sheet)	£10,000
Dr Stock cost of sales (P&L)	£60,000
Cr Stock (Balance sheet)	£60,000

ABC LLP can only claim £50,000 for stock as revenue deduction for tax purposes. The £10,000 fair value adjustment for goodwill is disallowed as capital.

Fees or costs relating to the formation, renewal, merger, dissolution or variation of a partnership or limited liability partnership are capital, as these relate to the fixed structure of the business (but see the Special Commissioners' decisions on demutualisation at **3.7.5** below).

The costs in dealing with disputes between partners are capital in nature (*Connelly & Co v Wilbey (1992) 65 TC 208*), but generally legal expenses for protecting the rights over the assets of a business are revenue expenses. In *Linslade Post Office and General Store v HMRC [2012] UKFTT 457 (TC)*, a claim against partners by another individual for a share of the partnership assets had no substance. The dispute was held to be for the protection of the trade and not the rights to the ownership of the business.

The effect of a payment or receipt in the context of the structure of the business is an important indicator. The *Van den Berghs* case considered the cancellation of agreements that were fundamental to the way the company conducted its business, and the compensation received was treated as capital as it related to the "whole structure of the Appellants' profit-making apparatus". The contracts under dispute were not incidental to the profit-making capacity of the business but regarded as part of the fixed framework.

The deduction of foreign exchange losses on a long-term borrowing for unincorporated businesses is treated as a capital expense as it relates to fixed capital (*Beauchamp v F W Woolworth plc [1989]*; see **B17**).

3.5.1 Acquisition of a business

The purchase or acquisition of share capital and the associated costs (including stamp duty) are capital expenditure. When a bundle of assets are acquired that comprise a business (e.g. goodwill, intellectual property rights, and property), the costs will be capital. This includes the associated legal fees and stamp duty land tax (see **B30**).

Initial expenditure on advising a business on an acquisition or sale may be capital or revenue, depending on the nature of the costs and stage of the transaction. For example, a management review of general strategic issues that affect the existing business may include commissioning a report to gather information on competitors; this expenditure may be classed as revenue as it does not enhance the existing business and has no identifiable enduring benefit. On the other hand, the costs of due diligence to investigate a specific target will be capital expenditure, whether or not the transaction is carried through to its conclusion (*ECC Quarries Ltd v Watkis*).

The settlement of liabilities that have been assumed as part of a purchase of a business is capital expenditure (*Triage Services Ltd [2006] SpC 519*, *Parnalls Solicitors Ltd [2010] UKFTT 261 (TC)*).

3.6 ACCOUNTING PRINCIPLES VERSUS LEGAL FORM

The statutory rule that capital expenses are not deductible (*ITTOIA 2005, s 33*) prohibits relief for capital items, regardless of the accounting treatment. For tax purposes, the capital or revenue nature of an expense is a question of law, so that the legal form of a transaction will generally override the accounting treatment.

Herbert Smith v Honour [1999] found that a provision for ongoing rentals due on an onerous lease was deductible because no asset was disposed of. This contrasts to a payment for the surrender of an onerous lease in the Special Commissioners' decision in *Bullrun Inc v Inspector of Taxes [2000]* that was treated as capital (BIM35625). The surrender payment was made by instalments, although the accounts reflected the whole amount as an expense in the period of surrender and this was agreed as the correct accounting treatment. The taxpayer's argument that the payment was a commercial contract and did not affect the whole structure of the company's profit-making apparatus was rejected. The Special Commissioners rejected the *Van den Berghs* principle as the payment specifically related to the lease which was a fixed asset of the business and the payment was not attributed to goodwill or the business's general capacity to earn profits (*Vodafone Cellular Ltd & Others v Shaw* was distinguished).

3.6.1 Capitalised revenue expenditure

Deferred expenditure that is revenue in nature is deductible when charged to the profit and loss account (Tax Bulletin, June 2001; BIM42215). If revenue expenditure is capitalised in the accounts as part of fixed assets, apportionment of the depreciation charge will be required to split this between disallowable capital and a revenue element that will be deductible.

Staff costs and other expenditure that relate to the development of assets to be used as physical fixed assets of the business are capital in nature, and the write-off through deprecation will not establish a revenue deduction (*McVeigh v Arthur Sanderson & Sons Ltd*). Capital expenditure for the construction of plant and machinery may be eligible for capital allowances, if this relates to functional plant or software (*CAA 2001, ss 4, 5*).

Capitalised interest costs are deductible when charged to the profit and loss account, and the distinction for interest on fixed or working capital borrowings is not relevant to obtaining a deduction (*ITTOIA 2005, s 29*).

For the treatment of in-house software expenditure, see **B48**.

3.7 ENTIRETY

The concept of an enduring benefit has been extended by the courts by the development of the entirety concept, which is based on the distinction between the replacement of an entire asset and the repairs and maintenance of parts of the asset. This was described in *Lurcott v Wakely & Wheeler [1911] 1 KB 905* (at page 924) as follows:

> "Repair is restoration by renewal or replacement of subsidiary parts of a whole. Renewal, as distinguished from repair, is reconstruction of the entirety, meaning by the entirety not necessarily the whole but substantially the whole subject-matter under discussion."

Case law dealing with entirety mainly focuses on physical assets, but the principles also apply to intangibles.

3.7.1 Borderline cases

In *Bullcroft Main Collieries Ltd v O'Grady [1932]*, expenditure on the replacement of a pithead chimney was a standalone structure. The new chimney was in a different location and was an improvement on the pre-existing chimney which had become unsafe. It was decided that the expenditure was for an entirely new asset and therefore capital.

This contrasted to the decision reached in *Samuel Jones & Co (Devonvale) Ltd v CIR (1951) 32 TC 513* where a chimney situated in the centre of a factory was demolished and a new one built in the same location. The expenditure was treated as a repair because there was no appreciable improvement and the chimney was part of a larger entirety, being the whole factory.

Identifying an entirety is based on the physical, commercial and functional role of the asset in the business. In *Brown v Burnley Football and Athletic Co Ltd* the replacement of a sports stadium at a football ground was found to be capital, as it was a self-contained structure. The properties surrounding the pitch were not a single unit but had been added to over the years and had separate distinct functions.

The cases of *Auckland Gas Co Ltd v CIR [2000]* and *Transco Plc v R A Dyall [2002]* considered the replacement of gas pipelines but reached different decisions on whether expenditure to maintain gas pipe infrastructure was capital or revenue. The nature of the work undertaken in both cases involved replacing existing cast iron and steel pipes with polyethylene pipes by inserting new pipes into the old structure. The renewal of the pipes by Auckland Gas allowed for the system to take a higher gas pressure and increased overall capacity. It also allowed natural gas to be supplied (not previously used in the old network). This was held to be capital expenditure.

The programme of renewal by Transco was a "like for like" replacement, with no enhancement of functionality (despite the difference in materials used). The pipework was replaced gradually at a rate of 1% p.a. of the entire of the system. The costs were held to be revenue.

A replacement or repair using modern materials does not necessarily enhance the original asset. In *Conn v Robins Bros Ltd Ch D [1966]* the structural repairs to a 400-year-old building were accepted as revenue. Certain enhancement expenditure was distinguished in the accounts (e.g. installing underfloor heating) and was not claimed as a revenue deduction.

The distinction between an improvement and repair and the effect of using different materials was tested in the First-tier Tribunal decision of *G Pratt and Sons v HMRC [2011] UKFTT 416 (TC)*. Resurfacing a farm drive was claimed as a repair by the taxpayer. HMRC argued that the drive was enhancement expenditure, as different materials were used to that of the original. The existing tarmac drive had continued to be used by suppliers for deliveries on a daily basis before the work was carried out. There was no alteration to the pathway of the drive or the functionality of the asset, and so the taxpayer successfully claimed a revenue deduction.

3.7.2 Notional repairs

When expenses are incurred for more than one purpose, an identifiable part may be apportioned and deducted as revenue expenditure if the amount is wholly and exclusively for the purposes of the trade (*ITTOIA 2005, s 34(2)*). However, the construction of a new replacement asset or the improvement of a new asset, in lieu of repairs, is not sufficient to characterise the expenditure as revenue; in other words, the capital cost will not be treated as notional repairs (*William P Lawrie v CIR [1952]*). The tax principles for deductions of repairs and renewals expenditure are covered in **B44**.

3.7.3 Effect of expenditure

The effect of the payment for the business, rather than how monies are applied by the recipient, determines whether payments are capital or revenue. In *Bolam v Regent Oil Co Ltd [1956]*, contributions made by a petrol supplier to independent filling stations to cover the costs of decoration, re-siting petrol pumps and maintenance in return for an exclusive supply arrangement was treated as a revenue deduction. The agreements covered different periods of between one and five years, and the payments were formulated on sales or future sales revenues. It was found that the contributions were in the nature of rebates. The payments of a lump sum in advance did not alter the nature of the payments.

3.7.4 State of asset on acquisition – Law Shipping case

When a business has neglected to keep an asset in good repair, the accumulated maintenance costs do not generally change the nature of the expenditure from revenue to capital. A notable exception is where an asset has been acquired in a condition where it cannot be used or is not fit for purpose. The well-known case of *Law Shipping v IRC (1923) 12 TC 621* established the principle that, if an asset is acquired but cannot be used until essential repairs are carried out, the costs are capital in nature, according to Lord Clyde (at page 626):

> "It is obvious that a ship, on which repairs have been allowed to accumulate, is a less valuable capital asset with which to start business than a ship which has been regularly kept in repair. And it is a fair inference that the sellers would have demanded and obtained a higher price than they actually did, but for the immediate necessity of repairs to which the ship was subject when they put her in the market."

This approach contrasts with the *Odeon* case where the owners had chosen to defer maintenance expenditure but the theatres continued to operate normally for many years (*Odeon Associated Theatres Ltd v Jones*; see **B44**). Therefore, the *Law Shipping* principle applies if the price of the asset has been impaired and this is reflected in the sum paid by the purchaser but does not apply to regular maintenance costs (BIM35450).

3.7.5 Protecting the business

The principle of deductibility for revenue items is based on a purpose test, whereas capital expenditure considers the effect, and this distinction has proved troublesome for the courts, particularly when considering the effect on goodwill. The general rule is that payments made to preserve an existing business without securing an advantage are revenue.

In the case of *Lawson v Johnson Matthey plc [1992]* a parent company made a large capital contribution to its insolvent banking subsidiary in order to save its own business. The payment was part of an agreement to dispose of the subsidiary's shares to the Bank of England for a nominal sum. The Revenue argued that the payment facilitated the disposal of shares and was a capital cost of getting rid of an onerous asset. The House of Lords reversed the decisions of the lower courts and held that the payment was revenue, as the share transaction was incidental to the financial rescue operation. The effect of the financial rescue was to ensure that the parent company would not be open to claims from creditors due to a loss of financial confidence in its subsidiary so that it could continue to trade.

The outcome of *Johnson Matthey* does not sit easily with other decisions where capital payments have been made to discharge onerous assets or obligations.

The effect on the costs of converting building societies to banks was considered in four Special Commissioners decisions: *Halifax plc v Davidson [2000] SpC 239, Woolwich plc v Davidson [2000] SpC 240, Northern plc v Davidson [2000] SpC 241* and *Alliance & Leicester plc v Hamer [2000] SpC 242*). The costs incurred by the societies comprised external legal and other advisory costs, together with in-house staff and administrative expenses. The costs were incurred for obtaining the necessary regulatory approvals (including Bank of England authorisations and Stock Exchange listings). It was agreed that the expenses under dispute were properly written off to the profit and loss account. The taxpayers argued that the conversions were driven by the wish to operate in a more flexible regulatory regime. The Special Commissioners found that no permanent advantage was created by the transfer from building society status to a listed company and, accordingly, the expenses were not capital in nature (cash bonuses paid to members were accepted as capital sums).

In *Morgan v Tate & Lyle*, the costs of an anti-nationalisation campaign were found to be for keeping the existing trade intact, as there was no improvement of the existing asset. Other cases that considered the effect on the profit-making structure of the business covered elsewhere include: *Vallambrosa Rubber Company Ltd v Farmer*, *Cooke v Quick Shoe Repair Service*, *Walker v The Joint Credit Card Co Ltd*, *Parnalls Solicitors Ltd v CIR*, *Anglo-Persian Oil Company Ltd v Dale* and *Vodafone Cellular Ltd & Others v Shaw*.

3.7.6 Intellectual property

Course fees for business proprietors to obtain new expertise or skills to put them into a position to trade are regarded as capital costs, i.e. an intangible asset of the business (*Dass [2006] SpC 570*). Courses that provide general updates may be deductible as revenue expenses.

The purchase of patents is treated as capital when used as fixed assets of the business and may qualify for capital allowances (see **B34**).

Know-how is treated as capital expenditure (*ITTOIA 2005, s 192*) and may qualify for capital allowances.

The costs of developing a copyright such as a book or film rights are specifically deductible as revenue expenses by offset against royalty income. The capital asset is regarded as the creative abilities of the individual as author. However, the purchase of a copyright from the author or another person may be a capital asset when it is used as part of the fixed capital of a business. A lump sum or periodic payments (royalties) to use trademarks or copyrights may be deductible as revenue expenditure if the use of the intangible is for a limited period and the amounts are written off to profit and loss accounts in accordance with GAAP (BIM35701, BIM35725).

3.8 LAND AND ASSOCIATED RIGHTS

The nature of a payment must be considered in the context of the trade.

In the case of *Strick v Regent Oil Co Ltd [1965]*, the taxpayer entered into exclusive agreements to supply filling stations. This was dealt with by a sale and leaseback on the customer's premises. The value of the transactions was linked to the expected future petrol sales of the garage owner. The legal form of the sale and leaseback prevailed to characterise the payments as capital. The taxpayer's trade did not extend to granting property leases (*Bolam v Regent Oil Co Ltd* was distinguished).

The cost of reinstating land to its original state is capital expenditure where this was used as part of the fixed capital of the business (*Mallett v The Staveley Coal and Iron Company [1928]*).

The cost of land for mining is a fixed asset, but raw materials extracted and awaiting further production are stock in trade (*Golden Horseshoe (New) Ltd v Thurgood (1933) 18 TC 280*). The cost of landfill sites and preparation costs to receive waste are capital expenditure (*Rolfe v Wimpey Waste Management Ltd (1989) 62 TC 399*).

3.9 EXCEPTIONS TO GENERAL PRINCIPLES

General principles for establishing the capital and revenue divide do not apply for the following types of expenditure:

- *Interest expenses*: The deductibility of interest is not determined by the nature of the underlying debt (i.e. long or short term), and no distinction is made between the application of debt for fixed assets or working capital (*ITTOIA 2005, s 29*; see **B31**).
- *Incidental costs of obtaining loan finance*: Subject to certain conditions, the costs of securing loan finance for a trade or property business are permitted as a deduction (see **B24**).
- *Integral features*: Where repairs expenditure on an integral feature (*CAA 2001, s 33A*) is 50% or more than the benchmarked cost of entirely replacing the system during any 12-month period, the expenditure is deemed to be capital and will instead qualify for capital allowances (*CAA 2001, s 33B*; see **B44**). Note: this treatment does not apply to repairs generally.
- *Patent design rights and trademarks*: The costs of a grant or registration of patents, design rights and trademarks are specifically deductible as revenue expenses (*ITTOIA 2005, ss 89, 90*; see **B34**).

- *Renewals basis*: Prior to 6 April 2013 a renewals basis was generally available as an alternative to capital allowances. This allowed a deduction in computing profits for the cost of a replacement of capital items less the proceeds of sale (or scrap value) of the item being replaced. Where the replacement was an enhancement, the deduction was restricted to the cost of replacement on a like-for-like basis (see **Chapter 5**, **B44**, **B62**). The renewals basis is no longer available – except for domestic items purchased by a residential property business.

- *Tools*: Statutory relief was previously available on a renewals basis for tools that would otherwise be treated as capital items. This treatment applied for expenditure incurred before 6 April 2016 (see **B53**).

- *Lease premiums*: A premium paid for a property lease of 50 years or less is subject to a deduction for notional rent (with part of the premium allocated as capital). The tax treatment of short lease premiums is covered at **Chapter 5** and **B28**.

- *Interaction with capital gains tax*: Where insurance or compensation is received for an asset that is not entirely lost or destroyed, the funds may be used for repairs. The expenditure will be revenue in nature if there is no material improvement to the original asset. The compensation will be taxable as a capital gain if it is derived from a chargeable asset. A taxpayer may claim to treat the capital receipt as held over against the cost of the original asset and (where necessary) the replacement expenditure. If so, the repair or replacement costs will be capital and will not be eligible as a revenue deduction, and become part of the capital gains base cost (*TCGA 1992, s 23*).

- *Payments made to a retiring partner*: There is a body of case law covering the capital versus revenue divide on payments made to retiring partners. However, this is subject to non-statutory guidance for capital gains tax and partnerships: *Statement of Practice D12, 8. Annuities Provided by Partnerships*. Annual payments made to a retired partner in excess of a defined formula are treated as a capital receipt. The corresponding capitalised value of the excess annuity payments are treated as capital acquisition costs by the remaining partners (*TCGA 1992, s 37*; CG28400).

- *Sea walls*: Capital expenditure on a sea wall is allowable as a deduction over a fixed 21-year period for the owner or tenant of premises (*ITTOIA 2005, s 315*).

- Contributions to a flood or coastal erosion risk management projects (under an application through the Environment Agency) are treated as a deductible expense for a trader. This takes priority over a capital allowances claim subject to no "disqualifying benefit" being received by the payer or a connected person, as a result of making the expenditure. A subsequent refund of the contribution or payment for services in connection with the work is taxable (*ITTOIA 2005, ss 86A, 86B*).

3.10 A CAUTIONARY TALE

The physical, commercial and functional effect of expenditure in the context of the business defines the capital and revenue divide. This presents difficulties in applying general principles, particularly for borderline cases. Lord Denning summarised the dilemma in *Heather v P-E Consulting Group Ltd (1972) 48 TC 293* (at page 321A):

> "The difficulty arises because of the nature of the question. It assumes that all expenditure can be put correctly into one category or the other: but this is simply not possible. Some cases lie on the border between the two: and this border is not a line clearly marked out; it is a blurred and undefined area in which anyone can get lost. Different minds may come to different conclusions with equal propriety. It is like the border between day and night, or between red and orange. Everyone can tell the difference except in marginal cases; and then everyone is in doubt. Each can come down either way."

The conundrum in bringing together accumulated cases to define capital and revenue expenditure is succinctly summarised by Lord Reid in *Strick v Regent Oil Co Ltd (1965) 4 TC 1* (at page 29):

> "It may be possible to reconcile all the decisions, but it is certainly not possible to reconcile all the reasons given for them."

3.11 REFERENCES

Legislation

TCGA 1992, ss 23, 37

ITTOIA 2005, ss 29, 33, 33A, 34(2), 58, 68, 86A, 86B, 271A, 272, 307B, 315

CTA 2009, s 53, Part 8

Leading cases

Vallambrosa Rubber Company Ltd v Farmer (1910) 5 TC 529

Lurcott v Wakely & Wheeler [1911] 1 KB 905

John Smith & Son v Moore (1921) 12 TC 266

Law Shipping v IRC (1923) 12 TC 621

Atherton v British Insulated and Helsby Cables Ltd (1925) 10 TC 155

Gloucester Railway Carriage and Wagon Co Ltd v CIR (1925) 12 TC 720

Mallett v Staveley Coal and Iron Company Ltd (1928) 13 TC 772

Anglo-Persian Oil Company Ltd v Dale (1931) 16 TC 253

Bullcroft Main Collieries Ltd v O'Grady (1932) 17 TC 93

Van den Berghs Ltd v Clark (1935) 19 TC 390

Southern v Borax Consolidated (1940) 23 TC 597

Cooke v Quick Shoe Repair Service (1949) 30 TC 460

Samuel Jones & Co (Devondale) Ltd v IRC (1951) 32 TC 513

William P Lawrie v CIR (1952) 34 TC 20

Morgan v Tate & Lyle Ltd (1954) 35 TC 366

Bolam (HM Inspector of Taxes) v Regent Oil Co Ltd (1956) 37 TC 56

Strick v Regent Oil Co Ltd (1965) 43 TC 1

Conn v Robins Bros Ltd Ch D (1966) 43 TC 266

Commissioners of Inland Revenue v Carron Company (1968) 45 TC 18

McVeigh v Arthur Sanderson & Sons Ltd (1968) 45 TC 273

Odeon Associated Theatres Ltd v Jones (1971) 48 TC 257

Heather v P-E Consulting Group Ltd (1972) 48 TC 293

ECC Quarries Ltd v Watkis (1975) 51 TC 153

Tucker (HM Inspector of Taxes) v Granada Motorway Services Ltd (1979) 53 TC 92

Walker v The Joint Credit Card Co Ltd (1982) 55 TC 617

Watneys London Ltd v Pike; Watney Combe Reid & Co Ltd v Pike (1982) 57 TC 37

Beauchamp v F W Woolworth plc (1989) 62 TC 542

Lawson v Johnson Matthey plc (1992) 65 TC 39

A–Z of Business Tax Deductions

Vodafone Cellular Ltd. & Others v Shaw (1997) 69 TC 376

Halifax plc, Woolwich plc, Northern plc v Davidson and Alliance & Leicester plc v Hamer [2000] SpC 239, 240, 241, 242

Bullrun Inc v Inspector of Taxes [2000] SpC 248

Auckland Gas Co Ltd v CIR (2000) 73 TC 266

Transco Plc v R A Dyall [2002] SpC 310

Triage Services Ltd v Revenue and Customs Commissioners [2006] SpC 519, [2006] STC (SCD) 85

Parnalls Solicitors Ltd v Revenue and Customs Commissioners [2010] SFTD 284

G Pratt and Sons v HMRC [2011] UKFTT 416 (TC)

Acornwood LLP and others v Revenue and Customs Commissioners [2014] SFTD 694 ("Icebreaker Partnerships")

Ingenious Games LLP & Others [2017] TC05893

HMRC manuals

BIM35000–BIM35910, BIM35200+, BIM35300+, BIM35400+, BIM35500+, BIM35700+, BIM35800+, BIM46900, BIM70035

PIM2030, PIM1095

CG15700, CG28400

See also

Chapter 2, **Chapter 4**, **Chapter 5**, **B17**, **B18**, **B24**, **B31**, **B20**, **B38**, **B44**, **B34**, **B48**, **B56**, **B62**

HMRC Capital v Revenue Expenditure Toolkit – 6 April 2016

Revenue Tax Bulletin June 2001

Chapter 4

"Wholly and exclusively"

4.1 COMMENT

At the cornerstone of defining the deductibility of expenses for business purposes, other than for those specifically permitted or denied by statute, lie the two key questions:

- is the expenditure capital or revenue in nature?
- is the expenditure wholly and exclusively for the purposes of the trade?

We have reviewed the "capital or revenue" debate in the previous chapter. Here we focus on "wholly and exclusively".

4.2 STATUTORY BACKGROUND

The statutes that set the legal basis are:

- *ITTOIA 2005, s 34*
- *CTA 2009, s 54*

The phrasing of the above legislation, for unincorporated and incorporated businesses respectively, is identical. It reads (using *ITTOIA 2005, s 34*):

> "(1) In calculating the profits of a trade, no deduction is allowed for–
>
> (a) expenses not incurred wholly and exclusively for the purposes of the trade, or
>
> (b) losses not connected with or arising out of the trade.
>
> (2) If an expense is incurred for more than one purpose, this section does not prohibit a deduction for any identifiable part or identifiable proportion of the expense which is incurred wholly and exclusively for the purposes of the trade."

The distinction from the equivalent employment legislation is important. The latter prohibits deduction of expenses unless "wholly, exclusively and necessarily" incurred in the performance of the employee's duties. The omission of the word "necessarily" from the legislation affecting business profits leads toward a subjective element being introduced. Thus, when establishing the purpose of a trader when he incurred a particular expense, it is more a matter of whether the expense was determined upon for business or for personal reasons. He need not show it was indubitably necessary to have expended on a particular item to carry out his trade.

It can be seen from a reading of the legislation that the definition of what is an expense incurred "wholly and exclusively for the purposes of the trade" is not actually prescribed. Indeed, the law sets out what is not deductible. It has to be deduced that anything falling outside that exclusion will be allowed as a business cost.

This section of the law as it was enacted by *ITTOIA 2005* is different in format from its predecessor (*ICTA 1988, s 74*) but not in intent. The *ICTA 1988* legislation attempted to be more prescriptive in setting out what was available as a deduction. However, the key phrase "wholly and exclusively" was enshrined in *ICTA 1988, s 74(1)(a)*. As a result, a first step when analysing whether expenditure is deductible or not is to consider: "is it *capable* of satisfying the wholly and exclusively test?". The determination of that response should then be a matter of law. If it has passed that test, it is then a matter of fact as to whether the particular item meets the "purposes of the trade" part of the rule.

4.3 IMPORTANCE OF CASE LAW

The lack of definition of deductible expenses in the legislation has led to case law becoming the benchmark. This is underlined by the regularity of new cases appearing in order to test their particular facts.

Accordingly, in this chapter it is necessary to refer to a selection of key cases to demonstrate the principles which can then be applied to particular circumstances. Throughout this publication, leading case law relevant to each specific expense has been indicated. Inevitably, there will be some duplication with the cases highlighted herein. However, that is necessary where they explain a different focus.

4.4 UNDERSTANDING THE STATUTE

Although *ITTOIA 2005, s 34* is brief, the words express individual points that must be understood if the statutory meaning is to be applied properly in practice. These can be identified as follows: is the item of expenditure:

- for the purposes of the trade?
- wholly for the trade purposes?

- exclusively for the trade purposes?
- properly subject to apportionment?

4.5 PURPOSES OF THE TRADE

This is generally the easiest of the factors to meet. Expenditure incurred by a business, whether decided upon by a sole trader, partner or company director, is likely, at the least, to include a business motive in its purpose. Therefore, contentions which arise are generally within the scope of the other factors, often that of "exclusively".

It is particularly important to determine a trade purpose because, as explained above, this is the first step of the analysis and, if expenditure fails here, the law has not been met, and so it would be irrelevant to move to "wholly and exclusively". Moreover, it is accepted that it is for the taxpayer to establish his purpose in incurring the expenditure which, where there is doubt, a Tribunal will determine on the basis of fact.

An example of a taxpayer not establishing trade purposes and consequently failing the "wholly and exclusively" test is that of *Patel [2015] TC 04617.*

This case before the First Tier Tribunal (FTT) followed after some disputed issues had been settled with the aid of the alternative dispute resolution (ADR) process. The appeal dealt with the three remaining issues relating to Mr Patel's tax return. Two of those related to whether items of expenditure formed valid deductions in Mr Patel's trade. The third requested the suspension of penalties already levied by HMRC.

Mr Patel, a self-employed pharmacist, claimed an interest deduction in respect of a loan taken out by him personally to finance the acquisition of guaranteed equity bonds with the purpose of providing him with income in his retirement. He described this as a "self-invested personal plan" or "SIPP" but the FTT – represented by Judge Aleksander, and Derek Speller FCA – disputed this description in their findings.

Mr Patel also claimed that he was entitled to a deduction in his trade for the cost of acquiring the bonds as part of his "SIPP".

The FTT found that the purchase of the bonds was not a contribution to an approved pension scheme for which a statutory relief applied. Furthermore, the expenditure on the bonds was not of a revenue nature, and even if it was, it would not have been incurred wholly and exclusively for the purposes of Mr Patel's trade. Accordingly Mr Patel was not entitled to a deduction for the purchase of the bonds.

As regards the loan interest – the FTT decided that the loans were taken out to finance the purchase of the bonds. Given that the expenditure on the bonds had been found to be capital in nature, and that they were not acquired wholly and exclusively for the purposes of Mr Patel's trade, it followed that the interest incurred on the loans was not deductible, also through not having been incurred wholly and exclusively for the purposes of his trade.

Interestingly, Mr Patel did succeed in his claim for the penalties to be suspended. One of the conditions imposed by the FTT was that he must engage the services of a professional adviser who was a member of the ICAEW, the ACCA or the CIOT.

In *Robinson v Scott Bader Co Ltd*, Waller LJ, in the Court of Appeal, discussed whether the test is subjective or objective and concluded that it depends on the circumstances. He elaborated:

> "The phrase with which the Case is concerned is 'for the purposes of'. In my judgment 'purpose' contains an ingredient of 'intention'. It is very difficult, but perhaps not impossible, to determine this without some element of subjectivity. Indeed, in many cases the test will be wholly subjective."

The Judge went on to say:

> "It would be impossible in such a case to do other than make the decision subjectively. In considering the purposes of a company there may be room for some objectivity, but it will normally be to assist in making the subjective decision."

(See BIM37065 and BIM38250 for a more detailed analysis of this case.)

We are therefore left in something of a limbo on the question of whether it is an objective or a subjective purpose of the taxpayer at the point of incurring the expenditure that is the key aspect. We can probably conclude that, in most cases, it is bound to have been the taxpayer's subjective decision at the time which matters, and it is the object of that decision that determines whether the purpose was for the benefit of the trade or for something else. Of less importance is the effect of the disbursement when it is ultimately made. Impartial (i.e. objective) evidence of the taxpayer's intention at the time is likely to assist, rather than relying on his subsequent recall. Thus, contemporaneous notes and board minutes will always be valuable.

Taking the above into account, there can still be difficulties in interpretation of "business purpose", as the following sections illustrate.

4.5.1 In the capacity of the trader

The taxpayer might have believed that the expenditure was made for the purposes of his trade and that might have been his intention. Yet in law he could be judged to have made it in a different capacity and not as that of the trader in question.

One of the early cases which set this principle, *Strong & Co v Woodfield* in 1906, ruled against an innkeeper who paid damages to a guest hurt when a chimney collapsed. He then claimed the expense as a deduction when calculating his profits. Lord Davey decided that the company was acting as a landlord not an innkeeper when deciding to pay damages, because it had happened not as a result of his innkeeper business, but in his role of occupying the property.

Despite the above, HMRC's current practice would be more inclined to accept that damages of that nature had been paid for the purposes of the trade. They have referred to that particular case (BIM37300, BIM38510). They note that Lord Davey's conclusion was criticised in later judgments and now must be seen to be of doubtful utility.

However, HMRC do not dismiss the principle of the "capacity test", explaining the idea based on a number of other cases as:

> "If the liability in question did not fall on the payer as a trader but, for example, as landlord, householder or citizen, then the taxpayer failed the statutory test and the deduction was denied."

Another "capacity test" case is that of *Smith's Potato Estates*. There, the company's claim for legal fees incurred in an appeal against a tax liability was denied. In a majority verdict, it was decided that such litigation had not been incurred by a trader for the purposes of his trade, but, partly at least, for the purposes of his relationship to the Crown as a taxpayer.

In the case of *Fairrie v Hall*, a sugar broker was a selling agent in London for Galban Lobo SA (a Cuban company). Mr Fairrie disagreed with the buying policy of the Ministry of Food, as he believed it was adversely affecting the interests of Galban Lobo SA and himself. In his exchanges in connection with the deputy director of the Ministry of Food, Mr Fairrie was found in court to have been libellous. Mr Fairrie then claimed his legal costs as a deduction. Macnaghten J, using the capacity test, found that the expenditure was not allowable. He concluded "The loss fell upon the Appellant in this case in the character of a calumniator of a rival sugar broker. It was only remotely connected with his trade as a sugar broker".

In *Vaines v Revenue and Customs Commissioners [2018] EWCA Civ 45*, the previous judgments of the FTT (found for Mr Vaines) and the Upper Tribunal

(UT) (found for HMRC) were considered by the Court of Appeal. The key issue was whether a payment made by Mr Vaines to a German bank, Bayerische Landesbank, to settle a debt liability claim was deductible from his profit share in the law firm SSD LLP, of which he was a member when the payment was made. The Court of Appeal determined against Mr Vaines, primarily on the basis that the liability had been incurred whilst Mr Vaines was a member of a previous law firm, the German HH GbR. As such, it had not been a payment made in his capacity of partner in SSD LLP. Consequently it could not be a deduction from SSD's trading profits.

4.5.2 Earning profits of the trade

Where costs have been incurred which are of a capital nature, e.g. for the enduring benefit of the trade or to put oneself in the position to be able to trade, they are not allowed as a revenue deduction. However, provided the capital definition is not in point, the requirement for expenditure to be for the purposes of the trade can be met without showing that it secured an increase in profit. It is sufficient that the payment in question was made for the purpose of benefiting the business and in the expectation that an advantage to the business would follow.

In *Mitchell v Noble (B W) Ltd*, it was held that a lump sum payment had been made for the purpose of preserving the reputation of the company. It had been paid to secure the resignation of a director. Avoiding the adverse publicity, had there been legal proceedings between the company and the director, was deemed necessary to prevent financial loss. It was not necessary to prove that there would in fact have been a loss to the company; it was sufficient that the company believed this to be the case. Thus the trade purpose was established.

Expenditure to earn future profits was adequate to obtain a ruling in the *Vallambrosa Rubber Co Ltd v Farmer* case, where only a part of the rubber plantation had reached the production stage. The remainder was still in the growing stages. Nevertheless, the maintenance costs of the entire estate were allowed, because of the expectation of earning profits in the future from the entirety. There was no need even to prove afterwards that financial gain had followed. The trade purpose existed at the time the expenditure was made.

In Morley v Lawford & Co a guarantee that was called upon was decided as a deduction, because the purpose of giving the guarantee (for the costs of an exhibition) had been in the expectation of the taxpayer that he would obtain contracts of work as a result. The fact that he did not obtain any work did not change his purpose at the time of making the guarantee.

4.5.3 Applying profits of the trade

In law, following from the phrasing of *ITTOIA 2005, s 34*, there is a distinction between expenses required to earn profits and those which are paid out of the profits. HMRC consider this at BIM37800 onwards. Whilst in many circumstances the difference will be clear, there have been instances when recourse has been made to the courts.

In *Thomson (Archibald) Black & Co Ltd v Batty* the company incurred expenditure in applying to the court to have its capital reduced. The purpose was to distribute its profits more efficiently by paying dividends. The costs incurred in achieving this were held not to be deductible, as although the company was acting in its own interests, the expenditure itself was directed toward the more advantageous application of the profits already earned.

Two cases particularly illustrate the line between the deductible and not, in this context.

In *British Sugar Manufacturers Ltd v Harris* the Special Commissioners and the High Court had decided against the company, but the Court of Appeal determined that a deduction from profits of the expenditure claimed should be allowed. British Sugar, in return for technical and financial expertise, had agreed a percentage share of their net profits to outside companies which were able to provide those skills. Ultimately the deduction was allowed because it represented a payment in exchange for services provided. It was not merely an application of profits already earned. BIM37830 analyses the case in detail.

In contrast, in the *Pondicherry Railway Co* case, a payment based on a percentage of net profits to the French Government was not made in return for any services. It was a legal requirement to make the payment based on the ascertained net profits of the business. Accordingly, it was not deductible.

4.6 WHOLLY FOR TRADE PURPOSES

On first reading, it is difficult to see why it is needed to include both the words "wholly" and "exclusively" in the legislation. Indeed, they are generally referred to as the single phrase "wholly and exclusively".

An explanation as to what is separately intended by the word "wholly" is given in *Bentleys, Stokes & Lowless v Beeson.* In that case, Romer LJ in the Court of Appeal said that, in the phrase "wholly and exclusively", the word "wholly" referred to the quantum of money and the word "exclusively" referred to the purpose. He further noted that the Crown conceded that the word "wholly" referred to the quantum of the money expended.

It is from there that we deduce that, if the amount of the expense is to a material extent for a non-business purpose, the whole is strictly disallowable. Where an amount of expenditure is incurred for more than one reason, it is dual expenditure. If not all the money has been spent for business purposes, the full amount of the expenditure fails the statutory test of "wholly", as there is no provision within that phrase at *ITTOIA 2005, s 34(1)* that allows just a business proportion to be deductible from income. Fortunately, *s 34(2)* assists, as is examined below, but its application only where there is an identifiable part of dual expenditure stems from this interpretation of the word "wholly".

4.7 EXCLUSIVELY FOR TRADE PURPOSES

The legislation disallows any expenditure not incurred wholly and exclusively for the purposes of the trade, profession or vocation. (From hereon, the practice of following *section 34(1)* and frequently rolling the two key words together, wherever appropriate, is continued.)

This means that the rule is only satisfied if the taxpayer's sole purpose for incurring the expense is for the purpose of their trade, profession or vocation. If there is any non-trade purpose, the whole expenditure is not allowable against income.

This vital concept is best examined in parts, as follows.

4.7.1 Incidental benefits

As so often occurs in tax, there are exceptions even to a very strict rule. BIM37400 sets out the position where non-business purposes are incidental to the main business purpose. The circumstances would be very few. It means that an incidental or unsought benefit does not impose a disallowable duality of purpose, but the furtherance of some non-trade objective would do so.

HMRC provides examples of "incidental" as:

- The trader in the course of his or her business may meet interesting people or travel to desirable destinations.
- A self-employed consulting engineer may travel to exotic locations to advise on projects. The travel and the exotic locations may be benefits but, where there was no private purpose, they are incidental to the carrying on of the profession and the cost is allowable.

Examples determined by the courts are:

- *Bentleys, Stokes & Lowless v Beeson.* The case involved a firm of solicitors, where it was customary to arrange a business meeting with a client during lunch. The firm claimed the cost of the lunches as a business deduction. Fees were always chargeable and only one partner of the solicitors would be involved. It had already been agreed that the quantum was not in dispute (see "wholly" above). The issue was whether the taxpayer's exclusive purpose was for their profession. In the Court of Appeal, Romer LJ determined in favour of the taxpayer. Within his reasoning he observed that entertaining inevitably involves an element of hospitality but that did not mean that it would be automatically disallowable (see below). The question to address was not whether the expenditure results in a personal benefit accruing to the trader but whether it was incurred solely for the purposes of the trade.

Note: the *Bentleys* case was heard in 1952, before *ITTOIA 2005, ss 45* and *46* were enacted. The latter specifically disallow all entertaining costs, so that would very likely have altered the outcome of the case. However, the principle set out by the judge remains valid. It could be utilised where other types of non-business purpose not specifically disallowed by statute are, in fact, so minor as to be incidental to a main business purpose.

- In *Bourne and Hollingsworth Ltd v Ogden* the "no incidental benefit" principle was considered. However, the High Court decision found that a significant charitable donation had been claimed as a trading expense. It was determined that the element of munificence or beneficence was sufficient to provide a purpose to the company's decision to make the payment, other than that of enhancing the trade. In previous years, donations had been allowed by the Inspector, but they were small in comparison to the year in question. Accordingly, they could no longer be viewed as "incidental" to the purposes of the trade. Note that specific legislation which applies to individuals making charitable donations and companies making qualifying donations could, currently, apply to this type of expenditure.

4.7.2 Benefits to a third party

It does not prevent an expense from being deductible simply because it also results in a benefit accruing to a third party. The result of making the payment is different from the purpose of making it.

This is clearly exemplified where corporate structures are concerned. One company in a group might incur an expense which can be determined as having been made for the sole purpose of benefiting that company's trade. If it also, as a result, happens to benefit another company in the group, that does not mean that the duality of purpose rule has been invoked and the cost accordingly disallowed.

In *Robinson v Scott Bader Co Ltd* (also referred to above in the context of objective and subjective purposes) a UK parent company continued salary payments for a key employee whilst he was seconded to a French subsidiary. The latter was failing so, without doubt, it benefited from the arrangement.

Nevertheless, the parent company established to the satisfaction of the Commissioners that the purpose of the secondment was solely to benefit its own trade. This depended substantially upon the success of the French subsidiary. Waller LJ said that the inevitable result of sending the employee, at the taxpayers' expense, to France would be to improve the running of the French company, but that was not the purpose of Scott Bader in doing so.

Where, however, the taxpayer can be shown to have intended to provide a benefit to the third party at the time when he decided upon the expenditure, that intention will taint the payment with a duality of purpose and the deduction will not be allowed.

The case of *Garforth v Tankard Carpets* showed where the line had been stretched too far in respect of benefit to a third party. Basically, Tankard Carpets had given security by way of a guarantee in favour of an associate company. The guarantee was called in and the company claimed as a trading loss the expenditure that it had to meet under the guarantee. Walton J highlighted that it was necessary to identify the purpose in the mind of the company's director at the time the guarantee was given. In this instance the judge determined that there were too many links with the associate company for the original purpose of Tankard Carpets to be solely for the benefit of its own trade. It must have been in part for the benefit of its associate. Accordingly, the sole purpose test was failed.

4.7.3 Duality of purpose

The above sections hone the decision-making process when faced with allowing a deduction for business purposes. We know that we need to focus on the taxpayer's object when deciding to incur the expense – although a subconscious motive will also be taken into account. We know it must have been solely for the benefit of the trade – and that does not include the benefit of the taxpayer. We know that, if a purpose other than for business existed at the critical time, it will be fatal to the deductibility of the expense, unless it was truly incidental. Yet we also know that, merely because there is an inevitable and consequential benefit to a third party, the deduction will not automatically be prohibited.

Particular difficulties arise where the expenditure may have some personal element, such as the provision of food or clothing in the case of an individual trader (see BIM37900). Similarly, as commented above, in the case of a company, the equivalent might be to benefit another company in the same group.

The remaining issues on whether or not a duality of purpose existed when an expense was incurred are reviewed through the following case law.

Mallalieu v Drummond

This well-known case remains valuable in setting criteria where the personal motives of an individual taxpayer are concerned. Having succeeded in the High Court and the Court of Appeal, the case ultimately failed in the House of Lords.

The principle determined was that expenditure on ordinary clothing worn by a trader during the course of their trade has a duality of purpose. This remains so, even where particular standards of dress are required by, for example, the rules of a professional body.

The courts had to decide whether a barrister was entitled to a deduction for expenditure on replacement and laundering of professional clothes. She claimed it on the basis that she had to choose a particular style of dress to carry out her profession when appearing in the courts. She did not wear those clothes at any other time.

Lord Brightman's decision was based upon the fact that a second purpose, that of fulfilling her needs as a human being as well as the needs of professional propriety, must have existed in Ms Mallalieu's mind when she purchased and then maintained her wardrobe. He accepted that it was not the main purpose. He accepted that it was probably not even a conscious purpose. Nevertheless, Lord Brightman concluded that the non-allowable purpose was not so obscure in her mind that she merely arrived at it "fortuitously, fortunately, accidentally or incidentally".

Norman v Golder

Mr Norman, a shorthand writer working in the courts, had suffered from a severe illness and had incurred medical expenses as a consequence. Mr Norman stated that his illness was the direct result of working in unfavourable conditions. He also contended that the expenses should be deducted in computing his taxable profits, as being expenditure wholly and exclusively incurred in connection with his professional work. There were other claims made by Mr Norman in addition, but the deduction of medical expenses was the key element.

Lord Greene, in ruling that the expenses could not be deducted, explained that:

> "It is also impossible to argue that doctor's bills represent money wholly and exclusively laid out for the purposes of the trade, profession, employment or vocation of the patient. True it is that if you do not get yourself well and so incur expenses to doctors you cannot carry on your trade or profession, and if you do not carry on your trade or profession you will not earn an income, and if you do not earn an income the Revenue will not get any tax. The same thing applies to the food you eat and the clothes that you wear. But expenses

> of that kind are not wholly and exclusively laid out for the purposes of the trade, profession or vocation. They are laid out in part for the advantage and benefit of the taxpayer as a living human being."

Murgatroyd v Evans-Jackson

This case was also one of medical expenses, although on first viewing might seem to have more merit than that of Mr Norman.

As the result of an accident, Mr Evans-Jackson ruptured a disc in his spine, and he was advised by a neurologist that he should receive electrical treatment. He normally worked as a trade mark agent, partly from an office in London and partly from one in Dublin. To enable himself to continue his trade whilst in hospital, he paid to be treated privately, so he had his own room. He paid to have equipment fitted into his room so he could continue his work from there whenever practicable. Mr Evans-Jackson then claimed 60% of his total hospital costs as being deductible from his income.

Ironically, Plowman J pointed out that the claim to deduct only 60% of the costs pointed to the fatal duality of purpose and that no deduction was due. The judge went on to say that it may have been more plausible to claim the whole of the costs. However, he did continue to assure that such a claim would also have failed.

The reasoning given included the following:

> "The whole object of going into the nursing home in the first place was to receive treatment for the injury that he had sustained. It seems to me that it would offend common sense to say that at any rate one of his motives or purposes in going into the nursing home was not to receive treatment for that injury."

Spofforth & Prince v Golder

Here, a firm of two chartered accountants claimed a deduction for certain legal costs that they had paid to defend successfully one of the partners in court proceedings. The partner had been charged with conspiracy to defraud the Revenue. There were also associated legal costs incurred by the partner who was not involved in the proceedings.

The High Court, affirming the decision of the Commissioners on the main point, held that neither the costs of defending the accused partner nor the costs in respect of the legal advice and assistance to the other partner were admissible deductions. However, a deduction was allowable in respect of any legal costs incurred by the firm up to the issue of the summons.

The reason was that the purposes of the legal costs initially were those of the partnership obtaining advice on its own legal position. However, at the point when the summons was issued, the nature of the costs changed. At that point, there must inevitably have been a personal motive for the partner defending himself against criminal action. Similarly, there was for the partner who was not accused but inevitably became concerned for his own position.

Accordingly, the change created a duality in the purpose of the legal costs and they had to be disallowed in their entirety from that point on.

Executive Network v O'Connor

This case reinforces the view that dealings between a trader and close relatives will almost inevitably include a private purpose and awareness of the beneficial effect on a third party resulting from particular expenditure.

The company (EN) was a specialist recruitment and personnel consultancy firm. Mr Toms was the majority shareholder and a director. His wife ran an equestrian business and its riders included their children. EN made sponsorship payments to the equestrian business over a period of six years. HMRC disallowed each of these.

EN appealed, on the basis that the payments were made for the benefit of EN's trade. This was supported by the fact that it had substantial income from clients who were also involved in equestrian sponsorship. Furthermore, EN also claimed that any benefit to the other parties was incidental. Providing that benefit was not a purpose of EN's expenditure.

The Special Commissioners' decision concluded that the expenditure was not allowable. They took into account, and believed, that the sponsorship payments were laid out for the purpose of EN's trade. Nevertheless, they also said:

> "we cannot displace from our minds the conclusion that 'personal benefit' played a part in the decision to make the sponsorship payments."

Furthermore, they found that the annual decision as to the level of the sponsorship was directed as much at the needs of Mrs Toms' business as at the potential benefits that EN might derive from sponsorship. They also concluded that the financial benefit to the equestrian business was more than incidental.

Healy v R & C Commrs

Mr Healy was an actor whose home was in Cheshire. He entered into a contract to appear in a musical in London, during which time he stayed in rented accommodation in London. Mr Healy claimed a deduction for the accommodation expenses against his acting income. The deduction was denied by HMRC on the basis that under *ITTOIA 2005, s 34(1)(a)* the expenses were not incurred wholly and exclusively for the purposes of the appellant's profession. In a previous hearing the FTT found in favour of the appellant *(Healy [2012] TC 01940)* and HMRC appealed to the Upper Tribunal (UT) on the basis that the FTT had erred in law in failing to consider if the appellant had a dual purpose in incurring the expenditure. The UT agreed with HMRC that the FTT had not applied the wholly and exclusively test properly. Consequently the UT set aside the FTT decision and remitted the case to the FTT for a fresh hearing (*R & C Commrs v Healy [2013] BTC 1,958*).

In the new FTT hearing the FTT remained in agreement that the expenditure on the accommodation was for the purpose of the appellant's trade as a self-employed actor. However they considered a new angle, that when Mr Healy entered into the tenancy agreement he had also considered its suitability for friends and family to stay, as well as for himself. As a result, he decided to rent a three bedroom flat. The FTT considered that for the purposes of *ITTOIA 2005, s 34(1)* this was a separate aim from his business need. Consequently the accommodation had a dual purpose, both enabling him to perform his acting duties and enabling him to host his personal visitors in London. As the latter was not a business purpose, there was a duality and the "wholly and exclusively" purpose was not met.

McQueen v R & C Commrs

Here, a Special Commissioner decided that expenditure on motor rallying carried on by the sole proprietor of a business was wholly and exclusively laid out for the purposes of the trade and so could be deducted in computing the taxpayer's profits.

There were particular facts which prevented the "private purposes" rule which would more usually have applied to a case with this headline. The taxpayer argued that the advertising costs in respect of a rally car were wholly and exclusively laid out or expended for the purposes of the trade. An associated claim for capital allowances in respect of the rally car was allowable. The taxpayer contended that the expenditure on motor rallying was for the purposes of the trade and resulted from a rational and, in retrospect, successful commercial decision. So far as any benefit accrued to the taxpayer personally by way of the motor rallying expenditure, that benefit was purely incidental and could not rightly be said to have been the purpose of the expenditure.

The findings of fact were that the taxpayer was using his skill and enthusiasm for motor rallying as the best means available to him for promoting his business.

He enjoyed it and it had given him satisfaction in just the same way as running an evidently successful business had done. Nevertheless, the securing of the private satisfaction of success on the rally circuit could properly be described as an incidental effect of the payment. Standing back and looking at all the circumstances, the tribunal was satisfied that the particular object that the taxpayer sought to achieve from the disputed expenditure on motor rallying was the promotion of the business.

Travel, subsistence, fines, legal expenses

The above, and other similar subjects, are key topics in interpreting the role of "duality of purpose" in determining deductibility of an expense. They are examined in detail in **Part B** of this publication and it would be unhelpful duplication to refer to the detail further here. Nevertheless, it is recommended that relevant chapters should be reviewed to reinforce the principles involved.

Intrinsic duality of purpose

HMRC's view of the type of expenditure which would be bound to have a duality of purpose, whether decided consciously or otherwise, is expressed at BIM37900. HMRC identify:

- ordinary "civilian" clothing;
- food for sustenance;
- having somewhere to live;
- wishing to enjoy good health;
- wishing to avoid a criminal conviction – especially if there is a custodial sentence; and
- helping one's nearest and dearest.

4.8 SUBJECT TO APPORTIONMENT

The interpretation of *ITTOIA 2005, s 34(2)* (and *CTA 2009, s 54(2)*) is vital for extending the circumstances when a deduction from business profits is allowable against its income where "duality" is concerned (see **4.6** above).

The importance is that, without this section, amounts expended by a business would fail to be a deduction because the particular amount expended had not been wholly for the business. In mitigation, the phrasing of the section (see above) allows that, if a particular part or proportion of the expenditure can be defined as wholly for business, it can be allowed.

This still requires that:

- the part or proportion of the expenditure has been validly assessed as being wholly incurred by the business;
- that same proportion is not tainted by duality of purpose, i.e. there was no other reason or motive for that part of the expenditure to have been incurred other than for the benefit of the trade, and that benefit was of a revenue and not a capital nature.

An example of the latter is the *Murgatroyd v Evans-Jackson* case (see **4.7.3** above). As there was an intrinsic personal purpose to the expenditure on medical care, the apportionment of expenses failed. The duality of purpose took precedence.

The case of *Lochgelly Iron and Coal Co Ltd* provides a good example of straightforward apportionment. The company paid a levy to an association of coal-owners. The association duly spent its levies on a variety of objects. Some of those would have been allowable as a deduction if the company had spent them direct, and some would not. As the different objects were identified separately by the association, the company was able to apportion its payment of the annual levy accordingly. The court held that that was the way to process the expenditure, and it allowed deductions based thereon.

HMRC confirm, at BIM37007, that there should be a distinction between cases where a definite part or proportion of an expense has been laid out or expended wholly and exclusively for the purposes of the trade, profession or vocation, and where an expense has been incurred for a dual purpose.

HMRC then clarify that the appropriate part or proportion should not be disallowed on the grounds that the entire expense is not laid out or expended wholly and exclusively for the purposes of the trade, profession or vocation.

There are several types of expenditure that particularly lend themselves to apportionment. These are where there is a regularity of pattern. Keeping accurate records in an appropriate format for a representative period ought to suffice to underpin the apportionment. Common examples are:

- motoring costs;
- use of home as office;
- telephone costs; and
- mortgage interest.

Suggestions as to the various ways that apportionment might be calculated are examined in the relevant sections in **Part B** of this publication (e.g. **B33**, **B57** and **B59**).

The overriding approach to apportionment is that, where feasible, the method used should be fair, reasonable and based on fact.

4.9 REFERENCES

Legislation

ITTOIA 2005, s 34

CTA 2009, s 54

Leading cases

HMRC (at BIM38600) summarise the cases to which they have referred

Strong & Co of Romsey Ltd v Woodfield (1906) 5 TC 215

Vallambrosa Rubber Co Ltd v Farmer (1910) 5 TC 529

Lochgelly Iron and Coal Co Ltd v IRC (1913) 6 TC 267

Mitchell v Noble (B W) Ltd (1927) 11 TC 372, CA

Morley v Lawford & Co (1928) 14 TC 229

Bourne and Holingsworth Ltd v Ogden (1929) 14 TC 349

Pondicherry Railway Co Ltd v ITC (Madras) (1931) 10 ATC 365, PC

British Sugar Manufacturers Ltd v Harris (1937) 21 TC 527

Norman v Golder (1944) 26 TC 293

Spofforth & Prince v Golder (1945) 26 TC 310

Fairrie v Hall (1947) 28 TC 200

Smith's Potato Estates Ltd v Bolland (1948) 30 TC 257, HL

Thomson (Archibald) Black & Co Ltd v Batty (1950) 31 TC 495

Bentleys Stokes & Lowless v Beeson (1952) 33 TC 491

Murgatroyd v Evans-Jackson (1967) 43 TC 581

A–Z of Business Tax Deductions

Garforth v Tankard Carpets (1980) 53 TC 342

Robinson v Scott Bader Co Ltd [1981] STC 436, (1981) 54 TC 757

Mallalieu v Drummond [1983] BTC 380, STC 124, CA; [1983] STC 665, HL

Executive Network v O'Connor [1995] SpC 56

Healy [2015] TC 04425

McQueen v R & C Commrs [2007] SpC 60

Patel [2015] TC 04617

Vaines v Revenue and Customs Commissioners [2018] EWCA Civ 45

HMRC manuals

Generally BIM 37000–38600; particularly BIM37300, BIM38510, BIM37800–37860, BIM37830, BIM37065, BIM37007, BIM37400, BIM38250, BIM37900

Chapter 5

Property rental businesses

5.1 COMMENT

The tax principles and framework for deductions by unincorporated property businesses are generally the same as those of trades, professions or vocations. However, there are a number of exceptions which are covered in this chapter.

The cash basis that was initially introduced only for trades and professions has been extended to property businesses from 6 April 2017. The intention was to simplify the tax computations of smaller landlords however the property cash basis is complex, in particular when computing relief for finance expenses and navigating the rules for deductible capital expenditure.

Unless the taxpayer elects to use general accepted accounting practice (GAAP), the cash basis is the default basis applicable to property businesses with gross annual rents of less than £150,001, this contrasts to the cash basis for traders where taxpayers who qualify must "elect in" (**Chapter 2**).

The cash basis has no application to certain landlords, including: trustees of a trust, members of a limited liability partnership, companies, or partnerships that include corporate partners.

Sections **5.3–5.9** cover property businesses that use GAAP (i.e. landlords who are not within the property cash basis or have elected out of the regime). Applying generally accepted accounting principles does not necessarily require a property business to comply with the Companies Act 2006 or impose any particular framework for financial disclosure or to undertake an audit (see **Chapter 1**).

Section **5.10** covers landlords using the cash basis.

This publication deals with the tax principles for business deductions and therefore the treatment of receipts of property businesses (particularly premiums) is not covered except where this is required to explain the treatment of corresponding expenditure (section **5.5**, **B28**).

Unincorporated property businesses will be required to keep electronic records under the Making Tax Digital for Business project which is expected to apply for VAT registered businesses from April 2019 and for income tax from April 2020.

For individuals who receive small amounts of property income (for example renting a garage), the property allowance introduced by *F(No 2)A 2017 (ITTOIA 2005, ss 783A–783BQ)* is available from 6 April 2017. The allowance of up to £1,000 p.a. is available to cover letting receipts. No further expenses may be deducted and a taxpayer may elect not to use the allowance. Where property income is offset in full by the allowance a taxpayer is not required to disclose the income in their self-assessment return (see **B54**).

The computation of property income by companies is broadly similar to that of unincorporated businesses. For companies, one notable difference is that interest and related expenditure for loans to finance property businesses are dealt with under the loan relationship legislation. The restrictions that apply limiting relief for interest expenses (see **5.4**) are not relevant to companies (see **B31**). Companies are not permitted to use the cash basis.

5.2 STATUTORY FRAMEWORK

A property business consists of the generation of income from land in the UK or overseas. This includes rents or other receipts for the exploitation of land or rights over land (*ITTOIA 2005, s 266*). "Other receipts" are widely defined to include:

- a licence to occupy land;
- the exercise of any other right over land;
- annual payments from land (e.g. ground rents and certain types of wayleaves); and
- the right to use a caravan or houseboat at only one location.

The following activities are *not* property businesses and are treated as trading activities (*ITTOIA 2005, ss 9–12*; PIM4300):

- income from farming and market gardening;
- mines, quarries, gravel pits, brickfields, ironworks, gasworks, waterworks, canals and docks;
- markets, fairs, tolls, bridges and ferries, railways;
- fishing rights;
- other commercial occupation of land, e.g. licences for sporting rights;
- furnished holiday letting (*ITTOIA 2005, s 322*; PIM4100);

- caravan and mobile home parks with material activities in operating the site (*ITTOIA 2005, ss 20, 875*);
- hotels, guest houses and bed and breakfast;
- letting surplus business accommodation (*ITTOIA 2005, s 21*);
- wayleaves arising from electric telegraph or telephone wires or pipes (*ITTOIA 2005, s 22*; see **B61**); and
- tied premises.

The distinction between a trade and a property business is not always clear cut and will depend on the extent of the additional services provided by the landlord. In some instances, income and expenses will need to be allocated between a property letting business and a trade.

UK and overseas lettings are treated as separate property businesses and taxed accordingly. The deemed trading status for furnished holiday letting apply to properties in the UK and the European Economic Area.

When a room is let to a lodger in the taxpayer's only or main residence, rental income below £7,500 p.a. is exempt under the "rent-a-room" rules.

5.3 CALCULATION OF PROFITS– GAAP BASIS

Unless the cash basis applies (see **5.10**), generally accepted accounting principles must be used as the starting point when calculating taxable profits of a property business, in a similar way to that of a trade. Underlying accounting records must be sufficient to support this position (see **Chapter 1**). Current proposals for Making Tax Digital for Businesses, which is expected to be introduced in April 2020 for income tax purposes, will require each individual of a jointly owned property to maintain a digital record of their income and expenditure.

The rules for adjusting expenses generally apply to property businesses in the same way as for trades (see **Part B**).

For overseas property businesses, the taxation of income attributed to non-UK domiciles is taxable on a remittance basis (*ITTOIA 2005, s 832*).

Rent and other income paid in respect of UK property to non-resident landlords is subject to deduction of income tax at the basic rate (PIM4810; see **B43**).

Small businesses with turnover below the VAT threshold (£85,000 for tax year 2018/19) can make a minimum disclosure of accounting information when completing the self-assessment return.

Property businesses are taxed on profits for periods aligned to the tax year; so if the accounts are drawn up to a date other than 5 April (or 31 March) apportionments must be made (*ITTOIA 2005, s 275*). There is an exception to apportionment for partnerships that have letting income which is ancillary to a trade, in which case the basis period is the accounting reference date of the trade.

The profits of a property business were previously computed by reference to matching income and expenditure with individual properties, and the offset of excess expenditure was determined by the nature of the lease ("Schedule A" rules). All receipts and expenditure of properties are combined as a single property business if the person is acting the same legal capacity, for example:

- Property held by as trustee or personal representative is a separate business from other properties held by an individual.
- Income from UK and overseas property businesses is treated as separate activities.
- The share of income and expenses from joint interests in property is allocated between individuals in the relevant proportions and included with other sources of property income.
- Income received by spouses or civil partners is automatically divided equally, unless the underlying beneficial ownership is formally divided in different proportions and an application is made to split income and expenses on that basis ("Form 17" claim).

5.3.1 Partnerships

The joint ownership of property for letting does not normally constitute a partnership unless landlords also provide additional services. However, a formal partnership or limited liability partnership (LLP) may be used to operate a letting business, and the profits and losses will be allocated and taxed on the partners and members as a property business.

The following points should be considered when computing income of partnerships or LLPs:

- Property income that is ancillary to a trade or profession is treated as a separate property business for a partner and is distinguished from other sources of property income that the individual may receive.
- Property that is temporarily surplus to the requirements of a trading partnership is treated as trade income where the amounts are "relatively small" (*ITTOIA 2005, s 25*).
- Partnerships that include services provided in conjunction with letting may be treated as trading (e.g. fully serviced office accommodation).

5.4 REVENUE EXPENDITURE

The capital versus revenue divide and the "wholly and exclusively" rules apply when computing taxable profits or losses of property business in a similar way to trades, professions and vocations.

The permissive and restrictive rules for expenses that apply to compute the profits of a trade are imported for property businesses at *ITTOIA 2005, s 272* (PIM1103; see **Part B**).

The terms of a lease set out the respective responsibilities of the landlord and tenant. Deductions against property income for expenditure on rent and council tax or business rates, insurance and general repairs are available if the lease prescribes that this is an obligation of the landlord. Expenditure relating to common areas of a property (e.g. hallways, foyers, lifts or stairways) will also be deductible if costs are revenue in nature and where the expenses are not the responsibility of the tenants or are recharged to tenants as a management charge.

Costs may need to be apportioned between capital and revenue on the purchase or sale of a property. For example, consideration paid to acquire a freehold with a tenant in situ may include an additional amount for outstanding rent due to the previous owner. This is deductible as a revenue expense by the new owner against rental income.

Other costs deductible as revenue expenses include:

- *Advertising*: Costs of placing adverts for new tenants on websites or in newspapers. Fixed advertising such as billboards may qualify for capital allowances.
- *Collection of rents*: Agents' fees, staff salaries and other collection costs will be allowable, subject to the amounts being set at a commercial rate.
- *Bad debts*: Irrecoverable rents are deductible where the amounts are proven to be bad debts (see **B3**).
- *Interest*: Generally a deduction for interest expenses for a property business is available in a similar way to that of a trade and may be subject to restriction where only part of the loan is used for funding the property business and part is for personal use. For residential properties, changes introduced by *Finance (No 2) Act 2015* have brought about restrictions for interest relief to an amount equivalent to the basic rate of income tax (for interest on "dwelling-related loans") – see **5.4.1**.
- *Legal fees*: The costs associated with the purchase or sale of a property (including stamp duty land tax) are capital expenditure and are not permitted as deductions when computing property income. This applies equally to an assignment of a short lease as well as the purchase of a long lease or freehold.

- Professional fees and the associated costs of granting a new sub-lease for a period of more than one year are also capital in nature. The costs of renewing an existing lease (without any amendment to the terms) for a period of less than 50 years are allowable. But part of the cost attributed to the capital element of a premium is disallowable (see **B30**).
- *Shared premises*: Apportionment of costs will be necessary when premises are shared by a landlord with the tenant. This may also require splitting loan interest costs.
- *Sea walls*: A landlord or tenant who incurs capital expenditure on a protective sea wall or embankment (where the expenditure does not qualify for capital allowances) may claim a revenue deduction on a time-apportioned basis over a fixed 21-year period (*ITTOIA 2005, s 315*). The provision applies to protection from the sea or a tidal river but does not extend to inland rivers and waterways.

5.4.1 Relief for finance costs – dwelling-related loans

For residential property letting, restrictions apply to limit relief for interest to an amount equivalent to the basic rate of income tax. This restriction applies whether the taxpayer uses GAAP or the cash basis. Other finance costs that represent an economic equivalent to interest and incidental costs of obtaining loan finance are also subject to restriction.

The restriction operates after any disallowance of part of the interest expenses for the following:

- For landlords using GAAP or the cash basis: interest that is not incurred wholly or exclusively for the business (e.g. where a property is used privately or drawings have been made that result in the loan funding being applied for non-business purposes); and
- For landlords using the cash basis: a further "loan to value" restriction may apply (see **5.10.3**).

The income tax relief restriction is being phased in over three tax years as follows:

Tax year	Unrestricted proportion of finance costs deducible against rental income	Restricted proportion – relief at basic rate of income tax
2017/18	75%	25%
2018/19	50%	50%
2019/20	25%	75%
2020/21	0%	100%

For examples on restrictions to interest relief see **B31**.

A dwelling-related loan relates to borrowing for a dwelling house and land occupied or enjoyed as its garden or grounds, from which property income is generated. It covers funds applied for the acquisition or construction of a dwelling house and associated land.

Interest on borrowing for commercial properties, furnished holiday letting, property development or dwellings used as part of a trade are *not* subject to restriction.

A "dwelling-related loan" (*ITTOIA 2005, s 272B)* is defined as borrowing that relates to a dwelling-house and a just and reasonable apportionment is made where only part of a loan relates to a residence. The costs of servicing loans used to acquire, create or adapt a dwelling-house fall within the restriction together with other costs of servicing or setting up the loan. The legislation does not define a dwelling-house. There is a body of tax and other case law that has considered the meaning of a dwelling-house and a residence for the purposes of principal private residence relief *(TCGA 1992, s 222*). The application of the capital gains tax interpretation of a dwelling-house for the purposes of applying the interest restriction is not free from doubt.

The application of the restriction for interest on a dwelling-related loan will not apply to certain types of residential property receipts that are classified as trading income. The following income is (or may be) taxable on trading principles: wayleaves; caravan parks; receipts from surplus business accommodation; rent derived from tied premises (see **5.2**). HMRC guidance (PIM2054) confirms that the restriction of interest relief does not apply to residential mobile home parks.

5.5 DEDUCTIONS FOR PREMIUMS

Statutory rules apply to split the payment of a premium for a lease of 50 years or less between capital and revenue. A premium for a lease with a term in excess of 50 years is a capital payment, and relief is only available under the capital gains rules on disposal or assignment. These rules have no application for landlords or tenants using the cash basis.

The calculation of notional rent deductions for a trader is covered at **B28**.

Example – Lease premiums: calculation of notional rent

A trader pays a premium of £30,000 for a 10-year lease.

The capital and revenue elements are split, and the notional rent deduction for the tenant is computed as follows:

Total premium paid to landlord (L)	30,000
Less: Capital element* 2% × (10 – 1)	(5,400)
Notional rent deduction spread over 10 years	24,600

* The capital cost of the lease is calculated as: Premium X (50 – Y/50)

where Y = term of the lease (in months) less the first 12 months.

A revenue deduction is available to a trader (T) of £24,600 at £2,460 per annum.

The landlord is subject to income tax on £24,600.

The above calculation also applies to sums payable instead of rent and variation or surrender payments if these are provided for under the original terms of the lease (*ITTOIA 2005, ss 277–282*).

When a landlord pays a premium to acquire a short lease that is then sub-let, relief is not available for notional rent under the mechanism illustrated above – which applies to tenants who are using the property for a trade.

Instead, when a non-trader sub-lets a property and becomes an intermediate landlord, a deduction can be claimed by reference to a premium treated as revenue in the hands of the superior landlord (*ITTOIA 2005, s 288*).

Example – Calculation of notional rent: property sub-let

Extending the example above, if the tenant (T) is not trading, no relief is available for notional rent. The relief available to T on the grant of a sub-lease by T to Z is illustrated in the following examples:

(i) No premium on grant. Annual rent £3,000 p.a.

In this case, T will be able to claim a notional rent deduction equivalent to the revenue part of the premium paid to L; i.e. £2,460 p.a. can be deducted against rental income of £3,000 p.a.

(ii) Z pays a premium to T of £15,000 for a five-year sub-lease, with no annual rent.

T can claim an amount equivalent to 5/10ths of the superior landlord's revenue receipt, being the proportion of the life of the sub-lease over the life of the head-lease; £24,600 × 5/10 = £12,300; this can be relieved as follows:

	£
Premium received by T	15,000
Less: Capital element 2% × (5 – 1)	(1,200)
Taxable as income	13,800
Less: Relief for premium paid	(12,300)
Net amount chargeable as income	1,500

Where the relief for the premium on the sub-lease is more than the premium received (the part taxable as income), the excess is spread and deductible over the period of the sub-lease.

5.5.1 Duration of lease

When the lease or other factors mean that the lease is unlikely to continue for its full duration, an earlier date (on which the lease is expected to terminate) is used to determine the lease term (*ITTOIA 2005, s 303*). This will have implications for the allocation of a premium between capital and revenue.

For example, if a long lease (over 50 years) is reclassified as a short lease, the receipt and payment are not capital amounts. Part will be retained as capital, but an element of the premium is treated as income in the hands of the landlord, with a corresponding revenue deduction for the tenant (see examples above).

The rules have been amended for leases granted on or after 6 April 2013 so that no deduction is now available for the tenant if part of the premium is reallocated as income in the hands of the landlord due to the actual lease period being less than the term provided in the lease agreement (*ITTOIA 2005, s 61(5A)*).

5.5.2 Assignments of leases

The rules for notional rent deductions in respect of premiums on the *grant* of a lease do not apply to an *assignment* or transfer of an existing lease. The consideration paid on assignment is capital expenditure, and a disposal of a lease (long or short) is subject to capital gains tax rules. A reduction in base cost applies for a lease with a life of 50 years or less under the rules for wasting assets (*TCGA 1992, Sch 8*).

5.5.3 Repairs and renewals

A revenue deduction is available for repairs or restoration of land where this does not result in a replacement of the whole asset or there is no significant enhancement (see **Chapter 3**). The use of up-to-date materials and techniques for repairs does not necessarily indicate an improvement (*Conn v Robins Bros Ltd*).

HMRC accept that, if work undertaken on a property includes an element of capital improvement and repairs, an apportionment can be made between capital and revenue costs (PIM2020). This approach is not entirely supported by case law principles.

Repairs will be treated as capital expenditure if essential work must be carried out to make the property suitable for letting, including modifications to comply with safety regulations (*Law Shipping* case).

Special rules apply for repairs expenditure on items defined as integral features, including:

- electrical and cold-water systems;
- heating and air conditioning;
- lifts and escalators; and
- external solar shading.

If the expenditure on repairs to the above items would be treated as a revenue deduction, the amounts are classified as capital if, over a 12-month period, the accumulated repair costs exceed 50% of the cost of an entire replacement. If the rental activity is a qualifying activity, capital allowances can be claimed as part of the special rate pool, subject to any prior claim for an Annual Investment Allowance (*CAA 2001, ss 33A, 33B*; see **B44**).

If a landlord receives a grant or contribution, this must be offset against the relevant expenditure. Contributions made by a tenant to the landlord under the terms of a lease to cover repairs and maintenance are taxable in the hands of the landlord as rent and cannot be directly offset against repairs expenditure (*ITTOIA 2005, s 226*).

If the landlord meets the cost of maintenance but the obligation under the lease rests with the tenant, a revenue deduction is unlikely to be available. This will depend on the circumstances; for example, if the landlord pays for the repairs as part of a settlement to secure early termination of the lease and vacant possession of the property, the amount will be a capital in nature (*Mallett v The Staveley Coal and Iron Company Ltd [1928]*; CG71262).

From the tenant's perspective, when a surrender agreement releases a tenant from a liability to make good dilapidations (or other onerous liabilities under the lease), the value of the release is treated as a capital receipt in the hands of the tenant.

5.6 REVERSE PREMIUMS

A reverse premium is a payment made by a landlord to a tenant for an inducement to enter into a lease (and is distinguished from a rent-free period where no payment is made). A reverse premium is treated as a revenue receipt and is taxed as income when recognised under GAAP (*ITTOIA 2005, ss 101, 311*).

For both traders and landlords who are tenants, the receipt of a reverse premium is taxable in full in the year in which the lease is entered into if the parties are connected and the arrangements are not at arm's length (*ITTOIA 2005, ss 102, 311*).

The tax treatment for the landlord who makes the payment of a reverse premium is determined by general principles; in other words, a one-off payment to secure a tenant will be capital expenditure in creating an asset with an enduring benefit and, as such, will be non-deductible (unless the lease is for one year or less). Reverse premiums paid by property developers where property is held as stock is distinguished; a reverse premium will be a revenue expense being a cost of sale.

5.7 CAPITAL ALLOWANCES

Generally, capital allowances are not available for expenditure on or alterations to land, buildings or structures (*CAA 2001, ss 21, 22*), except for expenditure incurred by a landlord that falls within the definition of plant and machinery. The structure of the building may include fixtures or integral features (*CAA 2001, s 33A*), and these will be eligible for capital allowances claims by the landlord except where:

- the lease is for a dwelling house (furnished or unfurnished); or
- the items fall within the definition of "non-background plant" under the long-funding lease rules (see **B29**).

Claims for industrial building allowances, agricultural building allowances and enterprise zone allowances were withdrawn from the tax year 2011/12 (*CAA 2001, Part 3*).

Business premises renovation allowances at 100% are no longer available for expenditure on converting or renovating unused business premises in a disadvantaged area unless the expenditure was incurred before 5 April 2017.

5.7.1 Dwelling houses

The letting of a dwelling house as part of a UK or overseas property business is *not* a qualifying activity (*CAA 2001, s 35*), so that expenditure on plant, equipment or fixtures does not qualify for capital allowances. The exceptions to this rule are:

- equipment used by the landlord to maintain properties;
- plant installed in common areas (e.g. a lift for access to flats);
- properties used for UK or EEA furnished holiday letting (*CAA 2001, ss 249, 250A*);
- expenditure on assured tenancies incurred between 10 March 1982 and 1 April 1992 (*CAA 2001, s 491*); and
- flat conversion allowances for expenditure incurred after 10 May 2001 and before 6 April 2013 (*CAA 2001, s 393A*).

5.7.2 Replacement domestic items relief

For tax years 2016/17 onwards landlords can claim the cost of replacing certain equipment used exclusively by a tenant where these items would not otherwise be deductible due to being capital in nature. The initial purchases of domestic items do not qualify for a deduction. The relief applies to all types of residential letting – furnished, unfurnished, or part furnished. Furnished holiday letting businesses can claim capital allowances and therefore cannot claim the relief. Landlords within rent-a-room are also unable to claim the relief (unless an opt-out election is made).

Typically a domestic item includes furniture appliances and utensils (see **B62**). A deduction is not available for fixtures, i.e. items that when installed become part of the premises, for example expenditure on boilers and heating systems are not treated as a domestic item.

5.7.3 Tax years before 2016/17 – wear and tear allowance

A "wear and tear" allowance preceded the replacement domestic items relief for tax years prior to 2016/17. The allowance was intended to cover tax depreciation on furniture and free-standing equipment (see PIM3215) and computed at 10% of the "relevant rental amount".

The wear and tear allowance did not apply to unfurnished tenancies (see **B53**, **B62**).

5.7.4 Tax years before 2015/16 – landlord's energy saving allowance ("LESA")

For energy saving expenditure incurred *before* 6 April 2015, landlords may claim a LESA allowance of up to £1,500 for:

- cavity wall and loft insulation; and
- other items listed by regulation, including hot water insulation, draught-proofing, solid wall and floor insulation (*ITTOIA 2005, ss 312–314*; *SI 2007/3278*).

The relief included expenditure on dwelling houses but did not apply to furnished holiday lets or rent-a-room properties.

5.8 RENT-A-ROOM

Rent from letting residential accommodation under "rent-a-room" arrangements is exempt from income tax if gross rents are £7,500 or less. This applies to letting accommodation in a taxpayer's main or only residence (e.g. a lodger or bed and breakfast business). The limit for receipts is divided when a property is jointly owned, if the property is the main residence of each of the individual owners and they jointly let the accommodation.

No relief is available for expenses, and capital allowances cannot be claimed (PIM4000; *ITTOIA 2005, Chapter 1, Part 7*). If receipts exceed £7,500, the excess gross rents are taxable, with no relief available for expenditure.

A taxpayer may find it beneficial to elect out of the rent-a-room arrangements if:

- taxable profits are lower when computed using conventional property business rules, compared to the excess gross receipts under rent-a-room; and
- the additional services provided amount to a trade activity rather than property business (e.g. a bed and breakfast or guest house), so that losses may be offset against other sources of income (PIM4020).

The annual property allowance of up to £1,000 cannot be used where a taxpayer has chosen to deduct actual expenses to compute taxable profits instead of using rent-a-room relief (see **B54**).

5.9 LOSSES

The losses of a property business can be used as follows:

- Carried forward for offset against profits of the same property business in a future tax year. For this purpose UK and overseas property businesses are treated separately.
- If losses are derived from capital allowances claims or agricultural expenses, these amounts may be claimed as sideways loss relief against other sources of income (subject to the overall cap on loss utilisation from 2013/14 – *ITA 2007, s 24A*).
- *BUT* no sideways loss relief is available for capital allowances derived from Annual Investment Allowances (*ITA 2007, s 127A*).
- Excess expenditure on a property that is not let on commercial terms is not deductible under general principles. By concession, HMRC allow excess expenses to be matched against future income from the same property (PIM2220).
- With effect from tax year 2011/12, losses of a furnished holiday letting trade cannot be relieved against other sources of income.
- Post-cessation expenditure can be relieved in a similar way to that of post-cessation trade expenses (*ITA 2007, s 125*; see **B37**).

5.10 PROPERTY CASH BASIS

The cash basis is extended to property businesses with effect from 6 April 2017. A summary of the cash basis for traders is covered in **Chapter 2**.

The cash basis treats income and expenses as taxable and deductible at the date of receipt or payment.

While heralded as a tax simplification for landlords, the property cash basis includes complex rules, particularly on restricting interest expenses where debt exceeds the value of the properties (see **B31**) and separate rules for deductions of capital expenditure (see **5.10.2**).

The property allowance cannot be used where the taxpayer obtains relief for expenditure under the property cash basis (see **B54**).

5.10.1 Statutory framework

The cash basis is the default position for unincorporated property businesses that have receipts of £150,000 or less received in a tax year (proportionately reduced where letting has commenced or ceased during the year). The limit of £150,000 per annum is measured by the total receipts of the business, rather than the receipts allocated to each landlord – when a property is jointly owned. Where an individual owns interests in different property businesses the application of the cash basis must be considered separately for each.

In any tax year where cash receipts of the business exceeds £150,000 the cash basis no longer applies, there is no period of grace and the taxpayer must use GAAP. This contrasts to rules for traders where an adjustment from the cash basis to GAAP is required in the tax year following the year during which the turnover for an individual's combined trades exceeds £300,000.

Requirement to use the property cash basis is defined by exclusion and the cash basis will *not* apply to:

- company landlords, including partnerships that include a corporate partner;
- trustees of a trust;
- a limited liability partnership;
- spouses or civil partners with a share in a jointly held property business (with beneficial entitlement to equal shares) where one individual has elected to use GAAP, unless a declaration is made to treat the income as unequal shares (Form 17 process);
- where a claim has previously been made for business premises renovation allowances and a balancing event arises in the tax year;
- where an election has been made to opt out of the cash basis.

A landlord may opt out of the property cash basis for a particular tax year by making an election within the usual time limit for amending a self-assessment return but the election must be made for each tax year in order to continue to use GAAP (unless the taxpayer falls outside of the cash basis due to exceeding the annual maximum or falling within one of the other exclusions above).

The cash basis applies to all types of letting, i.e. commercial and residential. Furnished holiday letting is treated as a deemed trade for income tax but is not within the trader cash basis rules. UK and overseas property businesses continue to be treated as separate sources of property income.

Where an agent manages the business on the landlord's behalf, the timing of receipts and payments are determined by the dates on which the agent receives rents or pays the expenses, and not when the funds are transferred to the landlord.

Cash receipts include money's worth in lieu of rent (*ITTOIA 2005, ss 28A, 272ZA*). HMRC have confirmed that security deposits are not immediately treated as taxable income. A deposit is held on behalf of the tenant until the end of the lease or the amount is applied to offset against dilapidations or unpaid rent. The amount will be taxable at the time the landlord becomes absolutely entitled to the funds (PIM1095).

Where a property business ceases, post-cessation receipts and expenses are taxable or deductible in the tax year in which the amounts are received or paid (see **B37**).

Generally the property cash basis uses the same principles to consider deductibility of expenditure in a similar way to the rules for computing property income under GAAP; i.e. no deduction is available for expenses that are not wholly and exclusively incurred for the purposes of the business or for losses that are unconnected with the business.

The rules governing the computation and split of premiums between income and capital for premiums paid or received on the grant of a lease (see **5.5**) have no application to the property cash basis.

Losses of a property business computed on the cash basis can be carried forward in a similar way to losses computed using GAAP, i.e. with no relief for sideways losses against other sources of taxable income or chargeable gains (see **5.9**).

5.10.2 Capital expenditure and receipts

A specific set of rules apply to disallow certain types of expenditure "of a capital nature". The legislative approach, which is consistent with the cash basis for traders (see **Chapter 2**), is then adapted to include relief for certain types of depreciating assets.

The capital allowances regime does not generally apply to the property cash basis, except that capital allowances may be claimed for cars (*CAA 2001, s 1A*). Transitional adjustments are required for assets qualifying for capital allowances when starting or leaving the cash basis.

The taxpayer must first assess whether a payment is capital and if so, no deduction is available where it falls within one of the following classes of expenditure (*ITTOIA 2005, s 307B*):

- capital costs in connection with the acquisition or disposal of a business;
- capital expenditure on education or training;
- expenditure on the provision, alteration or disposal of land, unless the asset is installed or fixed to land and is a "depreciating asset" (e.g. a fixture);
- capital expenditure on an "ordinary residential property" – whether or not the expenditure relates to a depreciating asset. Apportionment may

be necessary for depreciating capital assets where a property has mixed residential and commercial use. An "ordinary residential property" *excludes* furnished UK or EEA furnished holiday letting, so these types of businesses may claim capital expenses where the cost falls within the definition of a "depreciating asset";

- other categories of assets where expenditure does not qualify include:
  - cars (defined by *CAA 2001, s 268A*);
  - an asset not used on a continuing basis in the business;
  - a financial asset (financial instrument or arrangement capable of producing an economically equivalent return);
  - a "non-qualifying" intangible.

Depreciating assets are defined as assets with a useful life of 20 years or less, or which will decline in value by 90% or more within 20 years of purchase.

Certain types of capital expenditure on fixtures *may* be deductible (except for expenditure relating to an ordinary residential property). However the following classes of expenditure are specifically *excluded* from the definition of a depreciating asset for all types of property:

- a building;
- walls, floors, ceilings, shutters, windows, doors and gates;
- sewerage or drainage systems;
- shafts, lifts, hoists and escalators.

The legislation does not directly refer to capital payments for leases but the general rule that no deduction is available for the provision of land so this excludes a deduction for a lump sum premium and HMRC guidance confirms this view at PIM1095.

A landlord who sub-lets a property from an interest that is a short lease (i.e. with a term of 50 years or less) may wish to opt out of the cash basis in order to obtain relief for part of the premium paid (see **5.5**).

There is no outright restriction on relief for capital expenditure for intangible assets – although the acquisition of an intangible by a property business is unusual and this provision might in practice be limited.

Deductions for intangibles are within the cash basis if the rights fall within the definition of intangibles used in the Financial Standard applicable for Micro-entities: FRS 105, Section 13 "Intangible assets other than goodwill". This includes internally generated intangible assets or intellectual property.

Intellectual property is further defined as:

- patents, trademarks and registered designs, plant breeder rights (UK registered or similar rights registered overseas);
- unregistered information or techniques with industrial, commercial or other economic value; and
- licences in connection with the above rights.

No relief is available for purchased goodwill (*ITTOIA 2005, s 307B(2)*). Furthermore FRS 105, Section 13:

- does not permit the recognition of goodwill;
- does not permit capitalising internally generated intangibles; and
- requires that all expenditure in connection with intangible assets must be written off as incurred.

ITTOIA 2005, s 307B(14) defines a "qualifying" intangible as an asset, or right to an asset, which must cease to exist within 20 years. Relief for intangibles can be claimed under the cash basis when the conditions above are satisfied.

Intangible expenditure is treated as "non-qualifying" if the business grants a sub-licence in respect of the intangible to another person.

Where capital receipts relate to expenditure that was previously deductible then the amount is included on the disposal of the asset or where an amount is refunded, this is taxable at the time of receipt. The taxable amount is proportionately reduced if only part of the original expenditure was not deductible. When a large "one off" capital receipt arises this may result in the business no longer qualifying for the cash basis and consequently total receipts exceed £150,000, in which case GAAP must be used.

If an asset ceases to be used and the cost has previously been claimed then a deemed sale at market value arises. Similarly if a taxpayer becomes non-resident and no longer continues to be taxable under the cash basis the assets of the business are deemed to be sold at market value.

Capital gains tax rules do not apply on a disposal of an asset if it has been used in the business and the cost was previously deductible under the cash basis. Disposals of land and buildings and other chargeable assets for which relief is not available under the cash basis therefore remain subject to capital gains tax rules.

5.10.3 Restrictions for finance costs – loan to value

The property cash basis limits relief for interest and incidental finance expenses by reference to a "loan to value" restriction and this applies to all types of let property (i.e. commercial and residential lettings – *ITTOIA 2005, s 307D*). The restriction for interest relief to the basic rate of income tax for residential letting (other than furnished holiday accommodation) is computed after any restriction to the deduction of interest under the loan to value rule.

The tax relief for interest costs is therefore computed in three stages:

- apportionment of interest between business and non-business elements;
- restriction of interest by reference to statutory rule for "loan to value"; and
- for dwellings, limiting relief to the basic rate of income tax – see **5.4.1**.

The restriction to finance costs applies on relevant loans when the total outstanding amount of the loan principal ("L") immediately before the end of the tax year (or before the business permanently ceases), is more than the value of all relevant properties "V".

V is the sum of the market value of the properties at the time these were first used in the business plus enhancement expenditure. The value of V includes properties that continue to be owned at the end of the tax year plus any properties which have been sold during the year – but does not include the value of any properties disposed of during previous tax years.

Example – Restrictions for finance costs: loan to value

Anushka has let two residential properties for many years and from tax year 2017/18 uses the property cash basis. Details of the properties at 6 April 2017 are as follows:

	Cost	**Value**	**Original mortgage**
	£000	£000	£000
Property A	300	400	275
Property B	250	350	175

Property A was re-mortgaged on 31 May 2017 and the loan was increased to £325,000.

On 31 December 2017 Property B was sold for £350,000 and the mortgage of £175,000 was repaid in full.

The total interest expense before adjustment is £22,000 for tax year 2017/18 and £20,000 for tax year 2018/19. No part of the interest costs relate to non-business property.

The Loan "L" to Value "V" restrictions for 2017/18 and 2018/19 are:

Tax year 2017/18

$$\frac{\text{Business related interest before restriction}}{\text{Total interest}} \times \text{Loan principal at the end of the year} =$$

22,000/22,000 × £325,000 = £325,000 ("L").

L, the relevant loan at 5 April 2018 is £325,000

V is £550,000 being the original cost of property A *plus* property B

As V is > L there is no interest restriction for tax year 2017/18 as the original cost of Property B may still be taken into account at 6 April 2018 (the end of the tax year of sale).

Tax year 2018/19

$$\frac{\text{Business related interest before restriction}}{\text{Total interest}} \times \text{Loan principal} =$$

20,000/20,000 × £325,000 = £325,000 ("L").

L, the relevant loan at 5 April 2019 is £325,000

V is £300,000 being the original cost of property A only

As V is < L a restriction of interest applies by using the following formula: V/L × Business related interest =

£300,000/£325,000 × £20,000 = **£18,462**

Further examples of restrictions to deductible interest are shown at **B31.2.2**.

The loan to value calculation does not apply where GAAP is used and some landlords may wish to opt out of the property cash basis to avoid the restriction on deductible interest.

5.10.4 Starting and leaving the cash basis

Transitional rules will apply for property businesses that have not opted out of the cash basis and where:

- GAAP was used prior to 6 April 2017; or
- the business no longer qualifies for the cash basis.

In order to ensure no "double counting" of income or expenses on entering or leaving the cash basis, an appropriate adjustment is made to exclude amounts previously accounted for on an accruals basis and subsequently received or settled during a later tax year in which the cash is used.

Example – Starting and leaving the cash basis

David has operated a property business for many years. As at 31 March 2017 the balance sheet includes:

	Debtor/(creditor)
Security deposits held on behalf of tenants	(£10,000)
Pre-paid rents received at 31 March 2017	(3,000)
Provision for bad debts for the period to 31 March 2017	(£1,000)
Repairs and maintenance services invoiced but not paid	(£2,000)

The tenants have continued to occupy the properties in 2017/18 and no claims for damages have been made against the deposits.

On entering the cash basis the following transitional adjustments will be made:

- Security deposits: not taxable in 2017/18 as the landlord has no entitlement to income. All or part may be taxable in a future tax year.
- The pre-paid rents have not been taxed under GAAP and will be taxable in 2017/18 under the cash basis as the amounts have been received.
- The provision for bad debt against rent income receivable is ignored when moving to the cash basis unless the rent is settled, at which time the receipt will be taxable.
- The settlement of the repairs and maintenance invoice during 2017/18 will be ignored as relief has been claimed under GAAP on an accruals basis in the year ended 31 March 2017.

The transitional adjustment is limited to £3,000 income for the pre-paid rent.

Similar principles apply when leaving the cash basis to ensure income and expenses are not taxed twice.

Where a property business previously using GAAP has claimed capital allowances, the full amount of any residual tax written down value is deductible on commencement of the cash basis, except where the cost of purchasing the asset is outstanding (e.g. an asset acquired on hire purchase), in which case the deductions may be allowed on payment. This is subject to the excluded assets at **5.10.2**.

On leaving the cash basis a transitional adjustment is spread evenly over the next six tax years (*ITTOIA 2005, ss 334A, 239A*), subject to an election by the taxpayer to accelerate the charge (*ITTOIA 2005, s 239B*).

5.11 REFERENCES

Legislation

TCGA 1992, s 222

CAA 2001, ss 1A, 35, 66A, 70A–70YI, 249, 250A, 393A, 491, Part 3A, Part 4A, 268A

ITTOIA 2005, ss 9–12, 21, 60, 61, 63, 263–266, 271A–271E, 272ZA, 272A–272B, 274A–274C, 276A, 307C, 307D, 307G, 308A–308C (repealed 2016/17 and subsequent years), 311A, 312–314 (repealed 2015/16 and subsequent years), 322–328B, 330, 334A–334E, 783BC, 783BF, 784–802, 832, 869

ITA 2007, ss 24A, 117–127C

Capital Allowances (Leases of Background Plant or Machinery for a Building) Order 2007 (SI 2007/303)

Energy-Saving Items (Income Tax) Regulations 2007 (SI 2007/3278)

Leading cases

Lurcott v Wakely & Wheeler [1911] 1 KB 905

Law Shipping v IRC (1923) 12 TC 621

Mallett v The Staveley Coal and Iron Company Ltd (1928) 13 TC 772

Salisbury House Estate Ltd v Fry (1930) 15 TC 266

William P Lawrie v CIR (1952) 34 TC 20

Conn v Robins Bros Ltd Ch D (1966) 43 TC 266

Odeon Associated Theatres Ltd v Jones (1971) 48 TC 257

HMRC manuals

BIM46255, BIM41060

CG70700C, CG71100, CG71262

PIM1000+, PIM1900, PIM2005, PIM2030, PIM2068, PIM4100, PIM4800, PIM1090–PIM1098

Property Rental Toolkit 2016/17

See also

FRS 105 – The Financial Standard applicable to the Micro-entities Regime (revised March 2018)

Chapter 3, B1, B31, B28, B30, B38, B37, B44, B61, B62

Part B
Business deductions

B1

Adjustments on a change of accounting basis

B1.1 COMMENT

The starting point for computing taxable profits or losses is the accounting result prepared in accordance with generally accepted accounting principles.

On a change to an accounting policy or the correction of an accounting error, the financial statements will be amended and a prior period adjustment may be required. Consequently, the accounting period in which income and expenses are credited or charged will alter.

Where the interpretation of tax law is revised, the *timing* of tax adjustments from a basis used in an earlier accounting period may also alter. This applies specifically to the disallowance of depreciation when the accounting policies for fixed assets or stock and work in progress are revised (*HMRC v William Grant & Sons Distillers Ltd; Small v Mars UK Ltd*).

Where the business applies valid accounting policies and complies with current tax law, both before and after the change in the choice of an accounting policy, then the adjusted expenses or income are dealt with by statute as "adjustment income" (*ITTOIA 2005, ss 226–235*). The rules ensure that income or expenses do not fall out of account or are not taxed or relieved more than once when computing taxable profits or losses over the periods during which accounting policies are amended.

It is important to note that the adjustment income rules do *not* apply in the following circumstances:

- Corrections to accounting errors or accounts – previously prepared on an invalid accounting basis.
- Amendments to tax law – changes to statute, case law or interpretation and practice do not alter the previous basis on which taxable profits are computed (BIM34070).

- A change in accounting policy following the acquisition of a business – the purchaser is not bound by the accounting treatment adopted by the predecessor business.
- Barristers and advocates, where separate statutory rules apply on ceasing to use the opening year cash basis so that adjustment income is spread over 10 years (repealed from tax year 2013/14, grandfathered for those already in the regime).
- A change from a realisation basis to a "mark to mark" (fair value) basis for stock where the spreading election is made (*ITTOIA 2005, s 237*; BIM34115).
- Relevant foreign income charged on a remittance basis.

B1.1.1 Cash basis transitional rules

When a business moves to or from the cash basis, the adjustment income rules ensure that income and expenses are not omitted, or taxed or relieved twice. On leaving the cash basis, adjustment income is automatically spread over six tax years beginning in the first period in which the whole amount would otherwise be charged. The taxpayer may elect out of spreading and instead be taxable on the whole amount in the accounting period of change (*ITTOIA 2005, ss 239A, 329A, 334A*).

Property businesses that come within the cash basis from 6 April 2017 will be required to make transitional adjustments in moving from GAAP. Capital expenditure previously qualifying for capital allowances is dealt with by separate statutory rules (*ITTOIA 2005, ss 334B–334E*). The timing of the adjustment will be taxable or deductible on the last day of the first period of account to which the change applies.

The net adjustment income on reverting back to an accruals basis can also be spread over six tax years when a property business leaves the cash basis (see **Chapters 2** and **5**).

B1.1.2 Accounting policies

For unincorporated businesses using GAAP the accounting result must comply with the relevant accounting standards, as this is used as the starting point for making statutory adjustments to arrive at the taxable profit or loss.

The timing of the adjustment made to taxable profits depends on the nature of the accounting adjustment, which will generally fall into one of the following categories:

- refinement or revision of accounting estimates;

- changes in accounting policies – invalid to valid; or
- changes in accounting policies – valid to valid.

B1.1.3 Changes in accounting estimates

A change in an accounting estimate is not a change of accounting policy (Section 10 of FRS 102).

Revisions to calculations of estimates made in a previous accounting period that previously complied with GAAP will be taxable or deductible in the accounting period in which the adjustment is made. This includes impairments against closing stock and bad debts, or provisions for warranties or other liabilities. The adjustment income rules do not apply in these circumstances, and the accounting and tax adjustment takes place in the accounting period during which the revision is made; i.e. the tax treatment follows the accounts.

Example – Change in accounting estimate

XYZ Partnership provided £300,000 against the cost of extended warranties in the year ended 30 April 2017 for a product with an established rate of component failure. The provision was made in accordance with FRS 102, Section 21. The closure of the extended warranty period and reduction in customers eligible to claim for products sold before April 2017 resulted in a revision to the opening provision on 1 May 2017 to £75,000. The accounting recognition of the credit to profit and loss account of £225,000 is made in the year ended 30 April 2018 (FRS 102, paragraph 10.16) and this amount is taxable in respect of that accounting period (the basis period for tax year 2018/19).

B1.1.4 Changes in accounting policies – invalid to valid basis and accounting errors

Under Section 10 of FRS 102 a prior period adjustment is required if there is an error in the accounts of a previous period and the amount is material.

The presentation in the accounts requires:

- restatement of the comparatives for the prior period(s) in which the error occurred; or
- if the error occurred before the earliest period presented in the accounts, a restatement of the opening balance sheet for that earlier period.

When a business has used an invalid policy or has made an accounting error, the tax computations should be amended in the accounting period in which the error arose.

The requirement to adjust for an accounting error in the appropriate tax year underlines the long-established statutory principle that taxable profits must be computed on the basis of correct accounting principles (*Bombay Commissioner of Income Tax v Ahmedabad New Cotton* Mills *Co Ltd*) and applies notwithstanding that the accounting standards may permit an adjustment in a later period (e.g. on the grounds of materiality).

Example – Accounting error

ABC Partnership made an impairment provision of £75,000 against stock and work in progress at 30 April 2016. The provision was overstated by £50,000 due to an error in the formula used to absorb production overheads. No prior period accounting adjustment was required and the over-provision was adjusted in the profit and loss account for the year to 30 April 2017, where the closing stock provision was calculated at £10,000.

The adjustment for the provision credited to the accounts for the year ended 30 April 2017 was £65,000 (£75,000 – £10,000) and comprised:

- £50,000 adjustment in respect of the error in opening stock; plus
- £15,000 movement for the current year.

The error was not considered fundamental, and no accounting prior year adjustment was made.

For tax purposes the adjustment income rules do not apply, as an invalid basis was used for valuing stock at 30 April 2016.

The amount over-provided is disallowed in the partnership tax computation for the year ended 30 April 2016, and £50,000 of additional taxable profits will arise for that basis period (2016/17). The corresponding adjustment made to reverse the over-provision in the following year's accounts will not be taxable.

B1.1.5 Changes in accounting policies – valid to valid

Section 10 of FRS 102 allows a business to change its accounting policies from an existing valid accounting basis to a new valid basis when:

- this is required by a new Financial Reporting Standard (or other guidelines); or
- the results would be more reliable by adopting the new accounting policy.

The adjustment in the prior period is dealt with through the Statement of Changes in Equity (SOCE), and the opening balance sheet in the period of change is amended to restate opening balances.

On a "valid to valid" change of accounting policy, the accounting debit or credit required to bring all of prior years' results onto the new accounting basis is treated for tax purposes as arising on the *last* day of the first accounting period in which the change is adopted and applies to both net adjustment income or net adjustment expenses. (Note: for companies, the adjustment is deemed to arise on the *first* day of the accounting period in which the change is made.)

For unincorporated businesses, net adjustment income is a standalone category of taxable income but trading losses may be offset against taxable profits in the usual way. The taxable amount is not subject to class 4 National Insurance.

The following are exceptions to the general rule outlined above to determine the timing for taxing adjustment income and adjustment expenses:

- for stock and work in progress or depreciation where a tax adjustment has arisen in a previous accounting period which is followed by a change of accounting policy, adjustment income or expenses on a change from a "valid to valid" basis are taxable or deductible in the accounting period the assets are realised or charged to the profit and loss account (*ITTOIA 2005, ss 235, 333, 334*);
- when expenses have previously been deducted in full, and the effect of the change in accounting policy under the new basis spreads the expense over more than one period of account, the original deduction stands and no deduction is permitted for the expenses for the period after the change (*ITTOIA 2005, s 234*);
- for adjustment income on a change in accounting policy for trading stock from a realisation basis to a "mark to market" (fair value) basis the amount is brought into account when realised (i.e. sold or written off). Alternatively the taxpayer may elect for an income adjustment to be spread over six years beginning with the period of change in accounting policy (*ITTOIA 2005, ss 236, 237*).

Example – "Valid to valid" change of accounting policy: exception for stock and work in progress

ABC partnership changes its accounting policy on valuing stock and work in progress to absorb borrowing costs. Previously interest was written off on an accruals basis (as incurred). The old and new policies comply with FRS 102.

At the year ended 31 December 2016 closing stock and work in progress is increased by £30,000 for interest expenses previously charged to the P&L account and for which tax relief has previously been claimed:

Dr Closing stock 31/12/2016	£30,000
Cr Reserves 31/12/2016	£30,000

The stock is sold in the year ended 31 December 2018.

Under the general rule for adjustment income an increase in taxable profits would be taxed in the year ended 31 December 2017 but this does not apply to accounting adjustments for stock and work in progress. Tax deductions for interest have already been claimed in the periods up to 31 December 2016. When the stock is realised in the year ended 31 December 2018 the interest element included in cost of sales must be disallowed so that the net effect is that interest is deducted once under the old accounting policy. The tax adjustment for stock in the year of sale ensures that the interest deduction is not double counted.

Example – "Valid to valid" change of accounting policy

XYZ Partnership applied a "last in first out" (LIFO) basis for valuing stock in accordance with FRS 3. FRS 102 no longer permits LIFO as an acceptable valuation method, and the business changes its accounting policy for the year ended 31 May 2015 to "first in first out" (FIFO) to comply with the new standard. The effect is to increase opening and closing stock values by approximately 10%:

	Opening stock at 1 June 2014
Original – LIFO	£250,000
Revised – FIFO	£275,000
Prior year adjustment	£25,000

The stock was sold in the year ended 31 may 2015.

The business moves from an old valid to new valid accounting treatment. The credit to prior year reserves of £25,000 will be taxable as a separate trade receipt and treated as arising on the last day of the accounting period of change; i.e. 31 May 2015.

Example – "Valid to valid" change of accounting policy

ABC LLP has set up an opening holiday pay accrual on transition to FRS 102 of £80,000, in respect of the year ended 30 November 2017. No recognition of this liability was required under old GAAP. The provision has been accurately computed. All holiday must be taken by the end of the holiday year at 31 May 2018 otherwise the entitlement is lost. An adjustment is made to reflect the opening liability of £80,000 at 1 December 2016.

The net charge for the year to 30 November 2017 is:

Reversal of opening balance 1 December 2016	(80,000)
Charge at 30 November 2017	90,000
Charge to P&L	10,000

The adjustment expense is the provision brought forward of £80,000 which will be deductible in the accounting period ended 30 November 2017 (tax year 2017/18), so the total provision of £90,000 will be deductible in full in the accounting period of transition.

B1.1.6 Change in statutory interpretation

The timing of a statutory tax adjustment may alter due to a change in the interpretation of tax law. A valid tax basis applies to tax adjustments when the previous treatment was in accordance with the practice and interpretation of tax law prior to the change.

Example – Depreciation: timing of disallowance

ABC Partnership added back in full the depreciation charged in the profit and loss account for the year ended 30 June 2006 of £40,000. At the year-end, £7,000 of the depreciation charge had been carried forward as part of manufactured stock. All the stock was sold in the next accounting period.

Following the *William Grant* and *Mars* decisions, a disallowance for depreciation in stock is made at the time the items are expensed to profit and loss account in the year to 30 June 2007. A disallowance of £7,000 for depreciation in stock is required in the year ended 30 June 2007. As "gross" depreciation of £40,000 was already adjusted for under the old "valid" tax basis, this results in a double disallowance of £7,000 for the depreciation carried forward in stock. A deduction is given under adjustment income rules to offset the effect of the disallowed depreciation in the year to 30 June 2007.

B1.1.7 Summary

Adjustment	*Tax effect*	*Adjustment Income rules?*
Change in accounting estimate: no accounting error in previous periods *Or* Change in accounting treatment: no change in accounting policy	Tax adjustment in the accounting period in which the revision is made	No
Accounting error: prior period accounting adjustment required or error adjusted in current period accounts *Or* Adjustment from an invalid to valid accounting basis: prior period accounting adjustment or error adjusted in current period accounts	Tax adjustment made in prior period to apply GAAP in computation of taxable profit/loss – subject to statutory time limits for discovery assessments	No
Adjustment from a valid to valid accounting basis	Prior period adjustment taxed or deducted on last day of the first accounting period of change	Yes
Adjustment for change of interpretation in tax law – timing of statutory disallowance for depreciation	Previous disallowance or deduction adjusted on last day of accounting period in which change of law took effect	Yes

B1.2 REFERENCES

Statutory references

ITTOIA 2005, ss 226–240, 329–334A, 334B–E, 832

FA 2006, Sch 15

CTA 2009, ss 180–187

Leading cases

Bombay Commissioner of Income Tax v Ahmedabad New Cotton Mills Co Ltd [1929] 8 ATC 575

Pearce v Woodall Duckham Ltd (1978) 51 TC 271

HMRC v William Grant & Sons Distillers Ltd; Small v Mars UK Ltd HL [2007] STC 680

HMRC manuals

BIM34000–BIM34135, BIM51120 onwards, BIM34110, BIM70090

See also

Chapter 1, **Chapter 2**, **Chapter 5**, **B3**, **B54**, **B55**

Sections 10, 21 FRS 102

B2

Advertising and sponsorship

B2.1 COMMENT

Advertising costs are generally deductible where the purpose of the expenditure is to promote the goods and services of the business, with a view to generating sales and profitability.

Advertising typically covers a broad range of media including publications, TV, radio, billboards, public relations, conferences, trade fairs, websites and social media.

Deductibility is determined by the nature of the underlying expenditure, and certain types of advertising will be disallowed under general principles, such as:

- capital expenditure – expenditure that creates an enduring benefit (**Chapter 3**);
- gifts, entertainment and hospitality (see **B13**, **B19**); and
- expenditure with a dual purpose (**Chapter 4**).

The cost of promotional goods or services may be deductible where these are of a type normally sold by the business. Other gifts and entertainment are disallowable except where hospitality or entertainment provided by the trader is part of the ordinary trade and this would reasonably be expected to be part of the service to customers.

Generally, sponsorship is an allowable expense where the purpose of the payment is for publicising products and services or promoting brand awareness. Expenditure will be disallowable where it is incurred for non-business purposes; e.g. the motive is derived from a personal interest or hobby of the proprietor and this is more than incidental to the overall business purpose.

B2.1.1 Capital expenditure

Capital expenditure on advertising may include:

- The initial costs in setting up a website by an unincorporated business.
- Estate agent fees where a property is held as a fixed asset rather than stock. These costs may instead be deductible as incidental costs of disposal when computing the chargeable gain or loss on disposal. Advertising for a new tenant via an agency or other media is allowable as a revenue expense of a property business.
- Permanent signage such as billboards will not be deductible, but may qualify for plant and machinery capital allowances where expenditure is incurred on functional plant used for a qualifying activity.
- The costs of registering certain intellectual property rights such as a copyright (but registration or renewal of trademarks is deductible – see **B34**).

B2.1.2 Placement of goods and services

Samples of goods or services given to the general public are an allowable expense where the items are of a kind that relates directly to the trade (*ITTOIA 2005, s 47*; BIM45071).

The costs of placing goods or services at the disposal of an individual or another business are also allowable. Examples of this include:

- A business making designer clothes or jewellery worn by a celebrity or sports personality.
- Free accommodation provided by a hotel for review by an independent travel critic.

The cost of providing entertainment is only allowable if it is integral to the type of services provided by the trade and is aimed at promoting the business, e.g. live music or other entertainment at a bar or restaurant.

The cost of delivering promotional offers is deductible as a discount on the sale of goods or services where it is conditional on the customer taking up the offer, e.g. a restaurant offering a "two for the price of one" meal deal.

No deduction is available for hospitality expenditure provided at a promotional event (unless the trade is hospitality related). By concession, HMRC may allow a deduction for minimal hospitality. There is no guidance on the meaning of what is "minimal" for this purpose and how this relates to the overall cost or nature of the hospitality. Examples might include soft drinks offered to the general public at a trade fair, or tea and coffee provided to clients attending a free seminar.

Expenditure incurred on gifts that are unrelated to the business are generally disallowable, although the cost of providing gifts will be deductible if an item includes conspicuous advertising, does not include food, drink or tobacco and does not exceed a cost of £50 per person (see **B19**).

B2.1.3 Sponsorship

Sponsorship is a form of advertising that uses an attachment to another organisation or individual to promote products or brands.

The commercial benefits derived from sponsorship will determine whether it has a business purpose. Commercial sponsorship may take the form of a single payment for a one-off event or a long-term collaboration where the recipient provides a bundle of promotional services.

If there is a sponsorship agreement, this may typically include:

- The prominence and recurrence of advertising the sponsor's business, e.g. on bill boards, hoardings, programmes, websites, logos on team kit.
- Priority tickets and hospitality at a cultural or sporting event.
- Prioritisation of publicity where the recipient has other sponsors.
- Direction of sponsorship funding to specific projects, e.g. for a specific arts production or investing in sporting facilities.
- The rights to use brand images and other intellectual property.

Where part of the sponsorship payment includes hospitality (other than staff entertainment), this may be disallowable as entertainment (see **B13**). If the amount is unspecified, a reasonable apportionment of the cost can be made (e.g. calculated by reference to the value of the tickets and hospitality taken up by the sponsor).

The sponsor may claim capital allowances on a car or other assets that are made available to the recipient, if ownership of the assets is retained by the sponsor.

A lump sum paid for the use of intellectual property rights that belong to the sponsored organisation over the duration of the agreement (e.g. a copyright image of a football club) may be disallowed as capital in nature.

B2.1.4 Duality of purpose

The expenditure may have a dual purpose, where the proprietor of a business or a controlling director shareholder has a personal interest in the sponsored organisation and the business and personal objectives overlap.

The degree of any private purpose is a question of fact. If the commercial benefits and objectives have not been fully assessed and documented, it may be difficult to demonstrate that there is an exclusive business purpose underlying the sponsorship arrangements, e.g. if there is no formal agreement or no cost/benefit analysis has been prepared to justify the effectiveness of the expenditure compared to other types of advertising.

However, expenditure will not fail the duality of purpose test solely on the grounds that the sponsors receive a personal benefit if this is incidental to the overall business purpose.

Sponsorship expenditure might have a dual purpose in the following circumstances:

- There is another connection between the sponsor and recipient, e.g. the proprietor of the sponsor is also a trustee of a sports club (*Southwest Communications Group Ltd v Revenue and Customs Commissioners*).
- The commercial rationale underlying the benefits to the sponsor and connection with its potential customers is unclear, e.g. an international recruitment agency sponsors a local equestrian business operated by a close relative of the sponsor (*Executive Network v O'Connor*).
- The amount of the sponsorship is not commensurate with the level of advertising and publicity that could have been obtained through other media.
- There is no discernible business benefit for the sponsor, e.g. the sponsored organisation is in financial difficulties and the sponsor provides non-contractual payments for no additional benefits or services (*Interfish Ltd v Revenue and Customs Commissioners*).

If the business and non-business expenditure can be clearly identified, the business element may be apportioned and treated as deductible. The non-business purpose must be incidental in order to allow an apportionment of the expense. In the case of *Interfish Ltd*, the Upper Tribunal and the Court of Appeal held that one of the purposes for the payments made to Plymouth Albion Rugby Club was to secure the financial survival of the club. Improving the club's finances was not merely an unintended consequence; neither did it establish an intermediate purpose that could attach it to the main business purpose of the sponsor. Therefore the primary test for deductibility for the sponsoring company was not satisfied, the whole amount was disallowed.

In *Crown and Cushion Hotel (Chipping Norton) Ltd [2016] TC 05492*, the taxpayer operated a chain of hotels. A sponsorship contract was drawn up under which the business agreed to make four annual payments of £160,000 each in return for a 15% share of motor racing earnings (winnings) over a 12 year period. The racing driver was the daughter of the sole shareholder and director of the business; she was 15 years old and showed future promise as a Formula One racing driver.

HMRC argued that the deductions failed on the grounds of duality of purpose as the payments were made due to the personal nature of the relationship with the controlling shareholder of the sponsoring company, rather than to promote the hotel trade.

On balance the motives of the company, to attract customers to the company's hotels, which were located near Silverstone race track, resulted in a successful appeal by the taxpayer. The First Tier Tribunal concluded that the desire to promote the racing career of the driver was found to be an incidental effect of the sponsorship payments. In common with the cases noted above, the facts in *Crown and Cushion Hotel* are specific to the circumstances and may not easily be applied in other situations. This may explain why HMRC did not appeal the Tribunal's decision.

B2.2 REFERENCES

Statutory references

TCGA 1992, s 38(2)(a)

ITTOIA 2005, ss 33, 33A(5), 34, 45–47

CTA 2009, ss 53, 54, 1299, 1300, Part 8

Leading cases

Executive Network v O'Connor [1996] STC (SCD) 29

McQueen v Revenue and Customs Commissioners [2007] STC (SCD) 45

Protec International Ltd v HMRC [2010] UKFTT 628

Southwest Communications Group Ltd v Revenue and Customs Commissioners [2012] UKFTT 701 (TC)

Interfish Ltd v CRC [2014] EWCA Civ 876

Crown and Cushion Hotel (Chipping Norton) Ltd [2016] TC 05492

HMRC manuals

BIM37970, BIM45055, BIM42551, BIM42555–BIM42565, BIM45030–BIM45032, BIM45050

See also

B13, **B19**, **B34**, **B48**, **B50**, **B63**

B3

Bad and doubtful debts

B3.1 COMMENT

The tax treatment of bad and doubtful debts for sole traders, trading partnerships (including limited liability partnerships) and property businesses is covered by specific statutory rules.

Bad and doubtful debts are not relevant for traders and property businesses that use the cash basis as income is not recognised until the time of receipt.

An unincorporated business may claim relief for an unpaid trade debt when:

- the debt is bad,
- the debt is estimated to be bad,
- the debt is released wholly and exclusively for the purposes of the trade as part of a statutory insolvency arrangement, or
- the debt is irrecoverable due to the debtor being bankrupt or insolvent (subject to any reduction for any part recovered as part of the insolvency process).

A statutory insolvency arrangement includes a voluntary arrangement under *Insolvency Act 1986, Schs 4, 5*, *Bankruptcy (Scotland) Act 1985* or *Insolvency (Northern Ireland) Order 1989*, a compromise agreement under *Companies Act 2006, Part 26* or corresponding provisions under the law of a territory outside the UK.

For companies the statutory framework for bad and doubtful debts is governed by the loan relationship legislation (*CTA 2009, Parts 5* and *6*). The corporation tax treatment generally follows GAAP and does not distinguish between capital and revenue in order to determine whether a debt written off or released is deductible or taxable. This contrasts with the rules for unincorporated businesses, where the capital/revenue divide is a key factor in determining a deduction for a trade or property business.

B3.1.1 Relevant debts

Bad debt relief applies to receivables on the sale of goods and services of a trade or rental income of a property business. Losses attributed to loans or advances made to other businesses or individuals are not deductible unless the trade is one of money lending. It is customary for some industries to make loans that are integral to the trading relationship (e.g. the brewing industry) and this type of irrecoverable debt may be allowable. The accumulation of trade debts and extension of terms of settlement may alter the nature of the debt, particularly if the parties are connected. Relief may be denied for all or part of a bad debt between connected parties where sales and further credit would not have been authorised if the transactions had been made on arm's length terms.

An irrecoverable debt arising on an advance payment of undelivered goods or services will not be allowable where the debt represents a loan to fund a supplier's business (*Charles Bay Marsden & Sons Ltd v CIR*).

B3.1.2 Non-relevant debts

Unless exceptionally a taxpayer carries on a trade as a money lender, a loan made by an unincorporated business which proves to be irrecoverable is not related to the trade. It may be possible to claim a capital loss under the relief for "loans to traders", which could be offset against chargeable gains (*TCGA 1992, s 253*).

Irrecoverable loans made by individuals through "peer-to peer" regulated lending arrangements can be offset against interest received on that specific loan or other loans on the same platform. Where interest has been received on other peer-to peer lending platforms in the same tax year the excess can be offset "sideways" against that income. A restricted carry forward is available so any unused losses can be set against interest on peer-to peer loans in the following four tax years. A loss on an assignment of a peer to peer loan is not eligible for relief (*ITA 2007, ss 412A–412J*).

B3.1.3 Settlement of debt other than for cash

On a transfer of assets made in full and final settlement of a trade debt, the deductible amount is the difference between the value of the assets received and the debtor balance. Capital gains realised on a later disposal of a chargeable asset received on the settlement of a former trade debt will be taxed as income up to an amount equivalent to the deficiency on the previous settlement (BIM43725; CG53510).

B3.1.4 Timing of deduction

The statutory provisions governing bad and doubtful debts may override the accounting treatment. In the event that no write-off or provision for debts has been made in the accounts, a deduction may still be claimed where the statutory criteria for specific debts are satisfied.

When assessing the recoverability of debts, hindsight cannot be applied to claim a deduction in an accounting period before the debt was proven to be irrecoverable. No deduction is available for a debt that was recoverable at the balance sheet date but has subsequently proven to be irrecoverable if the conditions for impairment arose after the end of the accounting period. However, where there is evidence after the balance sheet date (and before signing off the accounts) to indicate that a debt was already irrecoverable before the end of the accounting period (e.g. a customer becomes insolvent shortly after the accounting year-end), a deduction is permitted.

A deduction for a provision against debtors who consistently pay late is not necessarily allowable unless there are other factors that suggest the debt will not be settled.

Where a debt is written off for reasons other than it being irrecoverable, the statutory conditions for a bad debt deduction will not be satisfied. For example, businesses under common control may agree to waive and release a trade debt to improve the presentation of the balance sheet of the creditor. A deduction will not necessarily be admissible for the debtor, although the corresponding taxable receipt on a release in the accounts of the creditor will be taxable (*ITTOIA 2005, s 97*), unless arrangements for release of a debt are part of a statutory insolvency arrangement.

An agreement for settlement at a discount may be an allowable expense of the trade under general principles – for example, where this is to facilitate further sales with the customer or avoids costs in pursuing the debt through the courts.

Where a debt is "estimated to be bad" the onus of proof lies with the taxpayer. This is a question of fact, and application of correct accounting principles in making a provision will support the basis for a deduction.

A general provision for bad debt provision is not deductible. For some businesses the valuation of debtor balances and calculation of specific provisions is impractical where there are a large number of small debtors (e.g. a mail order retailer). It may be possible to agree a formula approach to estimate bad debts, particularly if debt recovery is integral to the business model, for example if sales are linked to a personal credit agreement with the customer.

The recovery of a bad debt previously written off will be taxable in the accounting period in which it is recovered. Adjustments to provisions made against specific bad debts will be deductible or taxable in the accounting period when the amounts are recognised.

B3.1.5 Foreign currency restrictions

Where cash cannot be remitted to the UK due to foreign exchange restrictions in the jurisdiction where the debt is settled, a deduction can be claimed for the unremitted amounts (this applies to receipts of overseas trade debts and unremitted rents from an overseas property business).

No deduction is allowed where:

- the debt is unsettled (general rules on bad debts may then apply);
- the unremitted funds are used to finance trade outside the UK or make an investment overseas;
- the business has received insurance proceeds to cover the overseas debt; or
- a claim for relief is available under the general rules for unremittable income which takes priority to deductions for foreign currency restrictions.

B3.1.6 Succession

The transfer of trade debts to another sole trader or partnership, on a sale of a business, that prove to be irrecoverable may be claimed by the successor where the statutory conditions for bad debt relief are satisfied.

B3.1.7 Post-cessation expenses

A deduction is available for bad debts arising after the cessation of a trade subject to satisfying the tests for a "qualifying event" as a post-cessation expense (see **B37**).

B3.2 REFERENCES

Statutory references

TCGA 1992, ss 251(3), 253

ITTOIA 2005, ss 35, 97, 187–191, 272(2), Part 8, Chapter 4

A–Z of Business Tax Deductions

ITA 2007, ss 412A–412J

CTA 2009, Parts 5, 6

Leading cases

Reid's Brewery v Male (1891) 3 TC 279

Charles Bay Marsden & Sons Ltd v CIR (1919) 12 TC 217

Thompson v CIR [2005] SpC 458, [2005] STC (SCD) 320

HMRC manuals

BIM42700–BIM42750, BIM40265, BIM37750

CG53510

SAIM12100

See also

Chapter 2, B37

Revenue Tax Bulletin August 1994

HS296 Debts and Capital Gains Tax (2015)

B4

Car hire

B4.1 COMMENT

Car hire expenses incurred by a sole trader, partnership or property business are subject to a flat rate disallowance of 15% where the following carbon dioxide (CO_2) emissions are exceeded:

From 6 April 2018	110g/km
6 April 2013–5 April 2018	130g/km
6 April 2009–5 April 2013	160g/km

CO_2 limits apply as at the time the car is first registered. The restriction applies to permanently disallow part of the rental costs where the business has incurred the expense under an operating lease, finance lease (other than a hire purchase arrangement) or certain types of short-term car hire agreements. The disallowance is applied when rentals are charged to the profit and loss account. Therefore, when relief is claimed for "depreciation" of capitalised finance lease cars, the restriction will apply in the accounting period in which the expense is charged (see **B29**).

A rebate of hire charges or reduction of debt for hire costs will be reduced by 15% when recognised in the accounts (or, if the trade has ceased, when the amount is taxable as a post-cessation receipt).

The car hire disallowance does not apply to cars that are purchased outright or are subject to a hire purchase agreement; tax relief for the cost of these assets are subject to claims under the capital allowances rules.

The hire charge restriction is intended to apply only to one lessee where a vehicle is sub-leased or part of a chain of leases. Where a car is hired to a connected party, the restriction generally applies to the superior lessor.

Traders and property businesses using the cash basis are not subject to a disallowance on car rental payments.

B4.1.1 Lease commencing on or after 6 April 2009

The hire restriction applies to lease agreements for cars commencing on or after 6 April 2009.

A car is defined as a mechanically propelled vehicle, *except* for:

- a motor cycle;
- a vehicle primarily constructed for carrying goods; or
- a vehicle not commonly used as a private vehicle and unsuitable for that use.

The disallowance does not apply to a car where:

- it is first registered before 1 March 2001;
- emissions do not exceed 110g/km (130g/km and 160g/km for registrations before 6 April 2018 and 6 April 2013 respectively);
- it is electrically propelled; or
- it falls within the definition of a "qualifying hire car".

A "qualifying hire car" means:

- a hire purchase agreement that does not contain an option to purchase; alternatively, if there is an option, the option price is less than 1% of the retail price when new; or
- the car is hired under a long-funding lease agreement (in which case, the lessee is entitled to claim capital allowances).

It is the legal form of the hire arrangements rather than the accounting treatment that determines whether the expenses fall within the car hire provisions. Expenses incurred under a capitalised finance lease (not being a long-funding lease) are within the car hire disallowance.

There is no comprehensive definition of a "car hire charge" for the purposes of computing the 15% disallowance. Case law has established that "hiring" should cover all costs including any amount that might be distinguished as interest for accounting purposes. However, where there is an identifiable charge for maintenance, HMRC accept that this should be excluded when computing the disallowance.

B4.1.2 Short-term hire

For a lessee, cars hired for a period of not more than 45 consecutive days are not subject to a restriction for car hire. Where the hire customer is an employee or connected person, the lessor will be subject to the disallowance regardless of the term of the hire period.

If the provider of a short-term hire car incurs lease expenses associated with supplying the vehicle, the disallowance is borne by the lessor. Conversely, where a lessor makes a car available to a customer for 45 days or more, the lessee will be subject to the disallowance. A qualifying short-term hire car includes all types of cars (except for the exclusions at **B4.1.1**) and there is no longer an exemption for cars used for taxi services or for the short-term hire of disabled cars.

The 45- day period is subject to conditions on linked hire periods and anti-avoidance where one of the main purposes is to avoid the disallowance.

B4.1.3 Leases commencing before 6 April 2009

For hire periods commencing before 6 April 2009, a restriction in the lease charge is applied to a car or motorcycle (excluding qualifying vehicles), where the retail price when new exceeded £12,000. A proportion of the rental charge was allowable by reference to the following formula:

$$\text{Lease rental} \times \frac{\text{£12,000} + \text{Retail Price}}{2 \times \text{Retail Price}}$$

B4.2 REFERENCES

Statutory references

CAA 2001, Chapter 10A, s 70G

ITTIOA 2005, ss 48–50B

ITA 2007, s 998A

CTA 2009, ss 56–58B

SI 2016/984

Leading cases

Britax International GmbH v CIR (2002) 74 TC 662

HMRC manuals

BIM47725–BIM47785

See also

B23, **B29**

B5

Charitable gifts

B5.1 COMMENT

Charitable gifts (donations) are not normally allowed as business deductions. The standard procedure is for cash gifts to be treated as donations made by the individual personally. That is irrespective of whether they are paid from a business bank account or whether they appear as an expense in the business accounts. As a donation made by an individual, the normal rules then follow, including the application of Gift Aid.

Perhaps surprisingly, the deduction is not denied under the basic legislation relating to gifts and entertainment at *ITTOIA 2005, s 45* because *section 47* provides an exception for gifts to charities. The problem arises because of duality of purpose, as BIM45072 makes clear. It is assumed that there is a personal philanthropic motive in making a donation to charity, hence it fails the "wholly and exclusively" test.

There can be exceptions to the above denial as a business deduction, primarily where both of the following criteria apply:

(a) the charity is local to the business geographically; and

(b) there is substantial advertising of the business resulting from the donation.

HMRC's view is that a person carrying on a trade, profession or vocation may deduct the cost of expenses incurred in making any charitable contribution (whether in cash or in kind) so long as the expenditure is not disallowed for any other reason, such as the wholly and exclusively rule.

There can be particular difficulties with partnerships, where the partners agree to support a particular charity. If the above criteria are not met to treat the payment, exceptionally, as a deduction for the benefit of the trade, the only way any tax reduction can be gained is via gift aid. If all partners are to make claims individually, the apportionment of the donation must be in accordance with the partnership profit sharing agreement. A Gift Aid certificate needs to have been made under the normal Gift Aid rules. Until

5 April 2016 only one partner needed to make the Gift Aid declaration on behalf of the other partners, provided they had the power to do so under the partnership agreement. After 5 April 2016 it is necessary for each partner to make their own declaration.

There is a specific exception where a person carrying on a trade gives an article for the purposes of:

(a) a charity, a registered club or a body within a specified list, or

(b) a designated educational establishment,

and the article is one manufactured, or of a type sold, by the donor in the course of the trade.

A registered club is taken to be a community amateur sports club. The specified list shows that a "body" comprises:

(a) the National Heritage Memorial Fund, or

(b) the Historic Buildings and Monuments Commission for England, or

(c) the National Endowment for Science, Technology and the Arts.

The deduction for making a gift out of stock which meets the above criteria is effectively given by not requiring an amount to be brought into account as a receipt in consequence of the disposal of the article. However, if a benefit is received in return, an amount equal to the amount of the benefit must be brought in as a trading receipt.

The treatment for companies differs from that of unincorporated businesses for cash donations. For a company, the payment is permitted as a deduction from profits, but there are loss relief restrictions. The treatment of gifts of trading stock is similar to that for individual trades and partnerships.

BIM45155 clarifies the position relating to relief for gifts of trading stock to charities and other bodies.

B5.2 REFERENCES

Statutory references

ITTOIA 2005, ss 45, 47, 108

CTA 2009, s 105

CTA 2010, s 189

Leading cases

None

HMRC manuals

BIM45072, BIM45155

B6

Compensation and damages

B6.1 COMMENT

A deduction for compensation or damages is determined by the underlying cause of the payment. When payments for compensation and associated costs do no not satisfy the general tests for deductibility (i.e. as an expense wholly and exclusively for the purposes of the trade or where the amount is capital in nature), no deduction is available.

Case law provides a framework for the tax treatment of compensation and damages. For compensation paid to directors and employees, see **B14**. Fines for a breach of the law, such as a parking fine, are generally disallowable (see **B15**).

Compensation encompasses a broad range of payments, including commercial or regulatory penalties and civil damages. A business may risk a financial penalty in order to gain a commercial advantage. When damages are imposed as a punishment, the courts have held that the cost is not incurred wholly and exclusively for the purposes of the trade, as a tax deduction conflicts with the deterrent in the imposition of a financial penalty.

Deductions for non-statutory penalties (for example, a fine imposed by a professional body or sporting regulatory organisation) will depend on the facts. If the penalty has arisen because it falls outside an acceptable way of conducting the trade, it may also be disallowed on the grounds that it is a loss not connected with or arising from the trade.

B6.1.1 Compensation – normal course of trade

A deduction for compensation, cancellation fees or a release from contractual obligations will be allowable where the loss is clearly identifiable with the trade and is not for the enhancement or disposal of a capital asset. In the case of *Anglo-Persian Oil Company Ltd v Dale (1931) 16 TC 253*, it was held that a lump sum payment to a sales agent to release a company from an onerous agreement did not represent a capital payment and was an allowable revenue expense. There was no enduring benefit associated with the contract to employ an agent to manage part of the company's overseas sales, and the arrangements were connected to the circulating capital of the trade rather than fixed capital; consequently, the payment and release from the contract did not result in a structural change to the business.

Similar principles were considered in the case of *Vodafone Cellular & Others v Shaw (1997) 69 TC 396*. Vodafone entered into an agreement to obtain manufacturing licences and know-how for the payment of an annual fee relating to profits. Technological advances made the agreement obsolete and Vodafone paid a one-off cancellation fee for early termination of the contract. The case also addressed the question of duality of purpose, as the contract encompassed the taxpayer company and two of its subsidiaries. It was held that, at the time the payment was made, it was not capital in nature as it did not relate to the "profit-making apparatus" of the business. The licences were no longer valuable and the contract had become onerous and so no enduring benefit or asset was created.

The distinction between fixed and circulating capital has also been considered by the courts to determine the tax treatment of compensation in the hands of a recipient. However, the tax treatment of the recipient does not of itself determine whether the payer is entitled to a deduction; i.e. symmetry of treatment for the payer and recipient does not necessarily apply.

The case of *Van Den Berghs Limited v Clark (HM Inspector of Taxes) (1934) 19 TC 390* considered whether a *receipt* for damages was capital or revenue and held that, as the loss of the contract represented a substantial part of the trade and this fundamentally altered the business structure, the receipt was capital.

It is understood that HMRC regard a substantial part of a business for this purpose as 80% or more of the trade receipts. The application of this non-statutory principle to a payment of compensation or damages is not free from doubt and will depend on the nature and structure of the business.

For example, consider where a sole trader provides consultancy services on a project that secured fees of 90% of income over the previous year. If a successful claim for compensation for negligence is made against the trader by the client, the payment is arguably not capital if future fee income can be replaced by taking on new clients (assuming the claim did not result in regulatory or other restrictions in continuing to carry on the business).

Compensation paid to suppliers or customers that would otherwise be deductible is disallowed when payments are made on the cessation of trade.

B6.1.2 Damages and penalties

Civil damages for breach of contract that are not punitive are generally allowable, but penalties paid for a breach of the law or to defend an individual's personal reputation are not deductible.

In order to secure a deduction for civil damages, the connection between the punishment and the trade must be established. Punitive damages that arise where the plaintiff is seeking to deter others from engaging in similar conduct are not allowable, and this treatment is not limited to statutory fines or penalties.

Fines for criminal behaviour or non-compliance with civil law are not deductible on general principles, as the cost is not a loss connected to the trade but arises from an infringement of the law (*CIR v CE C Warnes and Co Ltd (1919) 12 TC 227*). A deduction cannot be claimed on the basis that the business was not aware of committing the offence.

The case of *McKnight v Sheppard (1996) 171 TC 419* concerned a non-statutory penalty imposed by The Stock Exchange Council on a stockbroker who was found guilty of serious misconduct which was outside the ordinary, proper and lawful conduct of his trade. The fine was disallowed (although legal costs in this case were allowable – see **B30**). *Sheppard* established that, where a penalty is imposed to deter behaviour that is not in the public interest, the burden of the penalty should not be shared with other taxpayers by allowing a deduction.

The *Sheppard* decision contrasts with the outcome in *P Vaines v HMRC [2018] EWCA 45*. In the *Vaines* case the Court of Appeal held that a voluntary payment made by an individual partner to avoid the risk of bankruptcy was not wholly and exclusively related to the trade of the partnership. The payment had to be justified in the context of the partnership trade carried on collectively. The concept of a separate notional trade for each partner (*ITTOIA 2005, s 852*) determines an individual's share of profit for self-assessment purposes but this is not "the trade" and cannot be used to evaluate the deductibility of an expense in isolation which must be considered in the context of the overall partnership.

The capacity in which the penalty is incurred will establish whether the loss is connected to the trade. In the case of *The Herald and Weekly Times Ltd v The Federal Commissioner for Taxation [1932] 48 CLR 113*, a claim for damages for defamation was allowable as a loss of the trade on the basis that this arose from "a regular and almost unavoidable incident of publishing".

The nature of the behaviour, as well as its linkage to the trade, will determine whether the damages are deductible. The question addressed by the courts is whether the liability arose from the trader's normal trade activities when conducted in a lawful manner.

Settlement of damages for a malicious libel was held to be disallowable expenditure, regardless of whether the taxpayer can demonstrate that the purpose of the underlying behaviour was to generate profits of the trade (*Fairrie v Hall (1947) 28 TC 200*).

In *Revenue and Customs v McLaren Racing Ltd [2014] UKUT 269 (TCC)* the McLaren motor racing team signed up to an agreement affirming the team's acceptance of regulations and rules governing Formula One racing. The agreement provided for penalties for non-compliance, including exclusion, suspension or disqualification. McLaren employed engineers that had formerly been working for Ferrari and obtained confidential technical information from them in contravention of the agreement. In order to counteract a perceived sporting advantage, a deduction was made to the points accumulated by the McLaren team in the 2007 racing season and a substantial penalty of £32m was imposed.

The First-tier Tribunal held that the penalty was deductible, as it was incurred as a result of McLaren's strategy to obtain information on its competitors. The taxpayer's argument, that other Formula One teams operated in the same way and this was normal trading practice, was accepted.

The Upper Tribunal overturned the decision on the basis that a deliberate activity contrary to a contractual arrangement was not an inevitable consequence of the trade. It was not accepted that the acts of employees could be separated from the trade. The dissemination of confidential information of competitors was regarded as cheating within the rules of the sport and was not within the remit of a normal trading activity.

If the penalty had not been settled, the McLaren team faced exclusion from Formula One racing which would have brought about the potential destruction of its business, but the fact that the penalty was paid out of commercial necessity was not of itself sufficient to claim a deduction. The purpose of the payment was to meet a contractual obligation – but this was outside its trade. Whether or not the payment might have been capital in nature was not considered.

The *McLaren* decision also considered the distinction between punitive damages and civil damages, and it was held on the facts that the penalty was a punishment, rather than compensation to offset any competitive advantage obtained by McLaren, as the sporting advantage could not be quantified.

Compensation that has a dual purpose will not be allowable under general principles. In the case of *Knight v Parry (1972) 48 TC 580* a solicitor paid compensation to his former employer when his new practice took on a client that had previously been a client of his employer; this was in breach of his employment contract. No deduction was available in computing the profits of the new business, as the payment related to a former employment and Mr Parry's purpose in protecting his professional reputation was not referable to his new practice.

B6.1.3 Compensation – Leases

Compensation payments that relate to a chargeable asset are not deductible as a revenue expense. For example, a payment made by a tenant to a landlord for the early surrender of a lease may have a clear trade propose, but it will be capital in nature as this secures the disposal of the lease.

The terms attaching to a lease and an agreement for surrender will determine whether any element of the surrender payment is a revenue deduction. For example, if a surrender payment allocates part to compensate the landlord for accumulated repairs and dilapidations for which the tenant is responsible under the terms of the lease, this may be deductible (the precise terms of the surrender will influence this).

A payment for restoring the property back into its original condition is likely to be capital, depending on the nature of the works required.

The capital treatment of a surrender payment is distinguished from a provision for future rental expenses, where a tenant chooses to retain a lease that is no longer required for the business. These costs may be treated as revenue expenses if the trade or business is not discontinued.

The Special Commissioners' decision in *Bullrun Inc v Inspector of Taxes [2000] SpC 248, [2000] SSCD 384* held that a lump sum surrender payment to dispose of an onerous lease obligation was capital in nature. The taxpayer's arguments, that the surrender did not affect the structure of the business and was made to extinguish what would otherwise be recurring revenue deductions for future rent, were not sufficient to nullify the legal form of the transaction – which was a disposal of a capital asset.

In *Mallett v The Staveley Coal and Iron Company Ltd (1928) 13 TC 772* the company made payments to divest itself of two mining leases which had become uneconomic, and a deduction was claimed on the basis that no asset or advantage was obtained and the amount represented commutation of the annual rent. This was denied on the grounds that the company did not deal in mining leases and the assets represented fixed capital of the business. This is distinguished from the *Vodafone* decision, where the termination of onerous licences was not considered to be part of the fixed structure of the business.

B6.2 REFERENCES

Statutory references

ITTOIA 2005, ss 33, 34

CTA 2009, ss 53, 54

Leading cases

Strong and Company of Romsey Ltd v Woodifield (1906) 5 TC 215

CIR v CE C Warnes and Co Ltd (1919) 12 TC 227

Mallett v The Staveley Coal and Iron Company Ltd (1928) 13 TC 772

Anglo-Persian Oil Company Ltd v Dale (1931) 16 TC 253

The Herald and Weekly Times Ltd v The Federal Commissioner for Taxation [1932] 48 CLR 113

Van Den Berghs Limited v Clark (HM Inspector of Taxes) (1934) 19 TC 390

Fairrie v Hall (1947) 28 TC 200

Knight v Parry (1972) 48 TC 580

McKnight v Sheppard (1996) 171 TC 419

P Vaines v HMRC [2018] EWCA 45

Vodafone Cellular & Others v Shaw (1997) 69 TC 396

A Consultant v Inspector of Taxes [1999] STC (SCD) 63

Bullrun Inc v Inspector of Taxes [2000] SpC 248, [2000] SSCD

Revenue and Customs v McLaren Racing Ltd [2014] UKUT 269 (TCC)

HMRC manuals

BIM35585, BIM35625, BIM37960, BIM37965, BIM38500, BIM38530, BIM38540, BIM42951

See also

Chapter 3, B14, B42, B15, B30, B39

B7

Counselling and re-training

B7.1 COMMENT

B7.1.1 Counselling

The difference between HMRC's treatment of employees and the self-employed is apparent here, especially within expenditure on counselling. There are circumstances when employees can receive welfare counselling paid for by an employer without it being treated as a taxable benefit. There is a specific exemption on the cessation of the employment or office, with conditions as set out at *ITEPA 2003, s 310*. The *Income Tax (Benefits in Kind) (Exemption for Welfare Counselling) Regulations 2000 (SI 2000/2080)* provide a statutory exemption from welfare counselling being a taxable benefit when certain conditions are met. Particularly, the services must be available to all employees. They must not include: medical treatment of any kind; advice on finance (other than debt problems); advice on tax; advice on leisure or recreation; or legal advice (unless it is associated with an exempt counselling service). Although the Regulations appear to be widely written, HMRC identify the type of matters to which the exemption relates. These focus on, for example, stress, debt problems, personal relationships and workplace-related problems.

There are no equivalent circumstances to give rise to a deduction for the self-employed person receiving counselling.

However, if the self-employed, or any business carrying on a trade, provides for counselling services to be made available to an employee in the defined circumstances, that expenditure will be allowable as a deduction.

The cost of re-training provided to an employee in connection with the termination of his employment is similarly specified in the legislation at *ITEPA 2003, s 311*. Where the conditions are met, the employee will receive the re-training without it being a taxable benefit.

One situation where the cost of counselling provided to a self-employed person could be allowable as a business deduction is where it meets the ordinary definition of expenditure "wholly and exclusively" incurred for the purposes of the trade. A key example is where the trade itself is that of counsellor. Where one of the continuing professional development requirements is that a counsellor should himself receive counselling services, the cost incurred in meeting that requirement would be an allowable deduction.

In a leading case, *Azam*, the costs of counselling were not allowed as a business deduction, despite it being accepted that one of the purposes of the sessions was to help run Mrs Azam's business. However, the personal benefits gained by the therapy sessions were found to be more than incidental, so the deduction was disallowed completely through duality of purpose.

B7.1.2 Re-training

A risk to the owner of a business claiming a deduction from profits arises where re-training is deemed to be capital expenditure rather than revenue. It is HMRC's view that, where a course is intended to give business proprietors new expertise, knowledge or skills that they lack, the course brings into existence an intangible benefit which is of enduring benefit to the trade. A deduction from profits would not therefore be allowed.

In *Dass v R & C Commrs [2006] SpC 570* this principle was followed. The taxpayer traded as a tutor in English and as an adviser in relation to the bringing of appeals before various tribunals. His appeal against HMRC's disallowance of his claim for the cost of the examination fee of a solicitor's qualification was dismissed by the Special Commissioner. He agreed with HMRC that the particular course was one to equip Mr Dass with a new qualification that would have enabled him to venture into new areas of practice, and it was not merely a "refresher" in relation to his existing expertise. Accordingly, it was correct to distinguish between the costs (in relation to courses) that constituted capital as distinct from revenue expenditure.

Alternatively, where attendance at a course is merely to update expertise which the individual already possesses, the expenditure is likely to be considered as revenue in nature. In those circumstances, it will be deductible if it satisfies the test of "wholly and exclusively for the purposes of the trade".

HMRC's "Capital v Revenue Expenditure Toolkit" refers to training and development costs incurred by the proprietor or partner in a business. It explains the rationale that training for a new skill is likely to provide an asset of enduring value. As such, it could not be a revenue item. HMRC give a further reason for disallowance which is that, for such expenditure to be allowed as a deduction, it must be incurred wholly and exclusively for the purpose of the trade or profession at the time the training is undertaken. Thus it cannot be allowed as a business tax deduction if it is to enable a new trade that does not exist at the time of the training.

BIM42526 on specific deductions gives a positive view that, provided it is incurred wholly and exclusively for the purposes of the trade carried on by the individual at the time the training is undertaken, expenditure on training courses attended by the proprietor of a business (either as a sole trader, or in partnership with others) with the purpose of updating their skills and professional expertise is normally revenue expenditure, which is deductible from the profits of the business. The manual continues that, in considering the question of purpose, an unduly narrow view should not be taken of whether the content of any particular course only updates existing skills of the individual. Nevertheless, HMRC also make it clear that, where a completely new specialisation or qualification will be acquired as a result of the expenditure, it should be disallowed as not being wholly and exclusively for the purposes of the existing trade.

B7.1.3 Re-training relaxation?

Changes to the limitation of a revenue deduction to training costs incurred for a trade existing when the course is undertaken are in the air. At the time of publication of this chapter a consultation is in progress on an extension to include supporting individuals needing to upskill or retrain. It is particularly aimed at those wanting to change career or improve their earnings. It focuses on both employees and the self-employed, hoping to align their respective positions more closely than at present. HMRC intend that the design of the extended relief should protect against its misuse on recreational activities and personal purposes. They also want it to be as simple as possible. The consultation period ran from 13 March to 8 June 2018. HMRC publication of the outcome is to follow, but is not available at the time of publication of this chapter.

B7.2 REFERENCES

Statutory references

ITEPA 2003, s 310

ITTOIA 2005, ss 33, 73

Income Tax (Benefits in Kind) (Exemption for Welfare Counselling) Regulations 2000 (SI 2000/2080)

Leading cases

Dass v R & C Commrs [2006] SpC 570

Azam v Revenue & Customs [2011] UKFTT 18 (TC)

HMRC manuals

BIM35660, BIM42526

EIM21845, EIM05005

B8

Crime-related payments

B8.1 COMMENT

A deduction is not allowed for expenditure if making the payment constitutes a criminal offence (or if, in making a payment outside the UK, it would be a criminal offence if made in the UK, from 1 April 2002). Examples include payments for stolen goods, and bribes to win contracts.

In addition, payments in response to demands which constitute blackmail (or extortion, in Scotland) are not deductible in calculating trading profits, such as payments to criminal gangs for "protection".

Any deduction against income is specifically denied by statute. However, in all probability it would also be denied under the general "wholly and exclusively" rule.

This restriction also applies to management expenses of an investment company (under *CTA 2009, s 1219*) and the ordinary basic life assurance and general annuity business (BLAGAB) management expenses of insurance companies carrying on long-term business (for the purposes of *FA 2012, s 76*).

The restrictions also apply to the incidental costs of making that payment (BIM43101).

However, other expenses arising out of blackmail may be allowable on general principles, such as guarding premises and replacing damaged goods, subject to the normal tests that the expenditure is not capital and it is incurred wholly and exclusively for the purposes of the trade and they are not criminal payments (BIM43180).

B8.2 REFERENCES

Statutory references

ITTOIA 2005, s 55

CTA 2009, s 1304

Leading cases

None

HMRC manuals

BIM43100–BIM43185

B9

Defalcations or fraud by employees

B9.1 COMMENT

Losses arising from theft or misappropriation by an employee are normally allowable as a deduction against business income. However, thefts by proprietors (sole traders or partners) or directors are not deductible. The disallowance for theft by directors and proprietors is drawn from *ITTOIA 2005, s 34* which denies a deduction where it is not the trade itself which has directly led to the cost or loss. HMRC clarify this view at BIM45855, focusing on directors at BIM37810.

HMRC use the case of *Curtis v J & G Oldfield* widely to arrive at the above conclusions, despite it being one relating to a company and its director. HMRC's stance is that, in the High Court, Rowlatt J made the following points:

(a) relief for bad debts is confined to items which had they been received would have been taxable receipts;

(b) a trader is taxed on the profits of the trade and not on what they retain at the end of the day;

(c) defalcations by subordinate employees are normally deductible for tax purposes; and

(d) money appropriated by a controlling individual is an application of profits and not an expense of earning profits and no deduction is due.

Accordingly, the principle is that a deduction is allowable for defalcations by subordinate employees. This includes theft and negligence on the part of the employee. Equally, any recoveries (for example, from the employee or insurer) are taxable.

B9.2 REFERENCES

Statutory references

ITTOIA 2005, s 34

Leading cases

Curtis v J & G Oldfield Ltd (1925) 9 TC 319

HMRC manuals

BIM45855, BIM37810

B10

Depreciation and loss on disposal of fixed assets

B10.1 COMMENT

The way to provide relief for wasting assets has been a key issue for much of the history of income tax. It has ranged from "just and reasonable wear and tear", via "depreciation of mills and factories", through the *Capital Allowances Act 1968*, to today's main statute, the *Capital Allowances Act 2001*. In March 2007 the phasing out of Industrial and Agricultural Buildings Allowances marked the end of any revenue deduction for capital investment in buildings.

Capital allowances form the statutory method of providing tax relief for "qualifying business assets". For the business proprietor, this primarily relates to plant and machinery. BIM35030 refers to the divergence of accounting principles from tax law. It gives an example of depreciation, being a proper deduction for accounting purposes; but, for tax purposes, it is not allowed because it is capital. BIM35201 also refers to a deduction under GAAP for the cost of depreciation that is not an allowable deduction in computing trade profits for tax purposes.

BIM35215 states: "Whether expenditure is capital or revenue is not critical for an accountant. The key issue for an accountant is when expenditure is consumed in earning profits." The manual continues that the accountancy treatment "certainly does not conclude the debate". This principle utilised by HMRC could usefully be borne in mind for issues outside that of the treatment of depreciation.

The above states the principle for tax: depreciation and loss on disposal of fixed assets are not allowable deductions for tax purposes. Expenditure per the accounts must be added back in the tax computations and replaced by allowances determined by tax legislation. Equally, a capital profit on disposal is deducted. This principle is primarily represented by the capital allowance legislation for plant and machinery.

The overriding of accountancy treatment for expenditure on capital assets for tax purposes is equally true where renewals accounting has been applied under 'old GAAP' FRS 15 and under FRS 102 (which has superseded FRS 15).

Where there is a change in the basis of depreciation in the accounts, *ITTOIA 2005, s 235* provides that the adjustment should only apply for tax purposes when there is a relevant disposal, rather than in the accounting period of change.

One situation where an adjustment for the accounting treatment of depreciation or a loss on disposal of fixed assets can prove beneficial for the business proprietor is where his capital account has become overdrawn. As a consequence, relief for loan interest must be restricted. However, HMRC accept that an adjustment should be made for accumulated depreciation when assessing the true value of the balance sheet in these circumstances. Case law supports this premise, with *Silk v Fletcher*.

B10.1.1 Potential for change

The complexity of the capital allowance system for providing tax relief on capital expenditure to businesses has been recognised by HMRC. Consequently, the Chancellor has asked the Office of Tax Simplification (OTS) to explore the challenges of using accounts depreciation instead of capital allowances. The project relates to tangible fixed assets only.

The basic idea is that allocating assets to various pools would no longer be necessary, replaced by the accounts treatment of assets flowing through to the tax return.

A consultation was set up by the OTS in September 2017, asking for the opinions on a wide range of questions from businesses, representative groups and professional advisers. It closed on 30 November 2017. The OTS published its report on 15 June 2018, see www.gov.uk/government/publications/ots-review-on-simplyfying-tax-relief-for-fixed-assets. Broadly, its findings are that, although using depreciation as a basis could be made to work, the complexities of the change from the present system of capital allowances are likely to outweigh the advantages.

B10.2 REFERENCES

Statutory references

ITTOIA 2005, s 235

Leading cases

Silk v Fletcher (HMIT) [2000] SpC 262

HMRC manuals

BIM35030, BIM35215, BIM34110, BIM45705 onwards

See also

HMRC Toolkit: Capital allowances for plant and machinery

B11

Dilapidations (leases)

B11.1 COMMENT

The terms of a lease may impose an obligation on the tenant, at such time as the tenant vacates the property, to pay to the landlord an amount to cover the cost of reinstating the property to its standard at the start of the lease. The case of *Fitzgerald v CIR* analysed the re-building of leased property, and BIM43255 particularly comments on capital expenditure aspects.

For tax purposes, those payments, i.e. dilapidations, may be capital or revenue depending on the nature of the reinstatement. A business trader might be acting in the capacity of tenant or landlord, but the principle behind the tax treatment is the same.

The general rule in *ITTOIA 2005, s 33* – setting out that no deduction is allowed in calculating the profits of a trade for items of a capital nature – applies. HMRC accept that expenditure on dilapidations that are of the nature of deferred repairs is admissible as a deduction to the trader incurring it, to the extent that it would have been allowable had it been incurred direct by the trader whilst he held the lease of the property.

Particularly, hypothetical repairs are not treated as a revenue deduction (or receipt). Thus, if dilapidations are so significant as to require, for example, the re-building of leased premises and accordingly the expenditure is deemed to amount to capital, there is no deduction for tax purposes of an amount that could have represented an element of repair. This was highlighted in the *Jacksons v Laskers* case. In that case, Danckwerts J distinguished accumulated repairs and alterations from current repairs, with the former category being treated as capital expenditure, therefore disallowable as a deduction against income. He also considered the position had the contract been written differently, but stated that there was no justification for saying that a taxpayer who had adopted one method should be treated as one who had adopted a different one.

Nevertheless, if a composition payment is made to reflect a mixture of capital and repair expenditure, it can be apportioned between the two for tax purposes. A composition payment is one agreed between the landlord and tenant that replaces the tenant's obligation to make good the dilapidations. The repair element is allowed as a deduction for tax purposes in the accounting period as determined by GAAP. This applies even if the landlord does not subsequently carry out the repair work.

Furthermore, if repairs have been delayed for whatever reason and consequently are carried out after the lease has expired, tax relief on the expenditure would still be allowed for such genuine repairs.

Mining leases have a different treatment (see BIM62025). There is a distinction where a payment for compensation is made or provided for in respect of an ascertained past damage to a person's property. That is allowed as a deduction from the profits of the mining entity that made the payment.

B11.2 REFERENCES

Statutory references

ITTOIA 2005, s 33

Leading cases

Fitzgerald v CIR [1926] IR 585

Jacksons v Laskers Home Furnishers Ltd (1956) 37 TC 69

HMRC manuals

BIM43250 onwards, BIM43260, BIM35620, BIM62025

B12

Employer deductions for employee benefits

B12.1 COMMENT

B12.1.1 Wide ranging benefits provided to employees

When considering the provision of benefits by employers in respect of their employees, the tax position first considered is usually that of the employee receiving the benefit. Yet the extent to which it is an allowable deduction from the employer's profits is a separate consideration and of key importance to the employer.

The rules governing employer deductibility of employee benefits have the same starting point as any other trade expenses. Allowable expenditure must comply with the contents of *ITTOIA 2005, Part 2* (trading income). Particularly, it must not fall within *Chapter 4* "Rules restricting deductions".

Whether the benefit provided should correctly be reported on a P11D or payrolled and subject to PAYE is not relevant in determining its deductibility against the employer's income. Employment expenditure is allowable as a deduction, whether it is the funding of the benefit itself or Class 1 or Class 1A NICs.

Equally, it is not possible to deny that a benefit was paid to the employee, thus avoiding the benefit tax charge on the employee, simply by deducting it in the business tax computations. If, as a fact, a benefit has been provided, the only way to prevent it from being taxable on the relevant staff is by a PAYE Settlement Agreement (PSA). Note that the PSA process has changed from 6 April 2018, in order to simplify it.

If a reimbursement made to an employee is categorised as a benefit for P11D purposes, but is subject to a claim under *ITEPA 2003, s 336* because it is a business expense and consequently not deemed a taxable benefit, the cost remains deductible for the employer.

One type of expense that might fall outside that pattern is that of entertainment expenses paid for or reimbursed to employees. If the entertainment is a direct benefit to the staff, such as a party, the cost will be allowable as a deduction to the employer. Alternatively, if it can be justified as a business expense by the employee because he was present at an occasion primarily to assist in entertaining clients, such as a hospitality event, the position differs. Entertainment comes within the category of restricted deductions (see *ITTOIA 2005, s 45*) and, as such, will generally be a disallowable expense for tax purposes.

B12.1.2 Employee benefit contributions

This is more commonly found with corporate employers because it is usually only larger businesses which set up such arrangements. Nevertheless, there is nothing to prevent smaller and unincorporated businesses embarking on the relevant schemes. Indeed, key legislation relating to the contributions is found not only in in *CTA 2009, s 1290*, but also in *ITTOIA 2005, ss 38–44*.

The fundamental principle is to restrict the timing of deductions in the employer's business to match the tax charge on the employees who receive a benefit (see *MacDonald v Dextra Accessories*). The meaning of an employee benefit scheme for these purposes is set out at *ITTOIA 2005, s 39(2)*. It is defined as "a trust, scheme or other arrangement for the benefit of persons who are, or include, present or former employees of the employer or persons linked with present or former employees of the employer".

The most usual structure to which this code applies is the employee benefit trust (EBT), although the legislation is written widely so as to encompass any employee benefit schemes. Since its heyday around 2000–2001 the use of an EBT as an aggressive tax planning tool has been persistently curtailed by HMRC, starting with legislation enacted from 27 November 2002. The latest addition to the anti-avoidance armoury was in *F(No 2)A 2017*. Nevertheless, there remain valid uses for an EBT, and the rules relating to deductions must be observed.

The restriction, at *ITTOIA 2005, s 38*, broadly states that no deduction is allowed in the accounting period when the employer makes an employee benefit contribution unless the relevant employee benefits are paid out of those contributions within the same period or within nine months of the end of the period.

If the cash basis were being used by the employer, the nine-month extension after the end of the period is omitted.

The amount disallowed as a deduction is allowed in a subsequent period to the extent that qualifying benefits are paid out. However, one of the effects of the further criteria introduced by *F(No 2)A 2017* is that a deduction for an employer's contribution to an EBT may be permanently denied, rather than deferred under the "matching" approach. The new rules have been inserted into *ITTOIA 2005, s 38* and they apply on or after 6 April 2017. An in-depth examination of the EBT rules is outside the scope of this chapter. However, if an unincorporated business does consider using an EBT, he should examine the legislation in detail before proceeding. Where the nine-month rule will make a contribution allowable in the accounting period when it is made, if the employer files his tax return before that payment has actually been made, i.e. he files it less than nine months after the end of the period, he can only include in his deductible expenses the amount that has at that date been paid out and become taxable on the employee. He can make an amended return later in that nine-month period when the benefit has fully crystallised for tax purposes.

ITTOIA 2005, s 38(4) provides exemptions from this restriction, primarily being contributions under a registered pension scheme or under an accident benefit scheme.

The legislation recognises that, where a third party (e.g. an EBT) is responsible for the administration of the scheme, part of the employer's contributions will be funding those costs. Accordingly the full amount contributed can never be paid to the employees. This is dealt with by allowing employer contributions to the extent that they are used for "qualifying expenses".

Further restrictions apply to those costs to bring them in as "qualifying" to ensure that they would have been allowable had the employer paid them direct. That is designed to prevent anything that would, for example, have been judged as capital rather than revenue.

The benefit being provided to the employee might take the form of a transfer of an asset rather than cash. The way the value of the asset must be assessed covers a situation where the asset has fallen in value since its acquisition.

B12.2 REFERENCES

Statutory references

ITTOIA 2005, ss 38–44, Part 2, Ch 5

F(No 2)A 2017

Leading cases

MacDonald v Dextra Accessories Ltd [2005] BTC 355

HMRC manuals

BIM44500, BIM44575, BIM44580, BIM44590

B13

Entertainment

B13.1 COMMENT

No deduction is allowed for business entertainment when computing the taxable profits of a trade or business. The statutory disallowance also includes gifts (see **B19**). The disallowance also applies to taxpayers who use the cash basis (*ITTOIA 2005, ss 32A, 272ZA*).

The amount of disallowable entertaining includes the associated non-recoverable input VAT. The basis used for restricting input VAT recovery is similar but not identical to the rules for direct taxes and outside the scope of this publication.

The following types of entertainment are *not* treated as disallowed:

- entertainment provided in the ordinary course of a trade; and
- entertainment for staff at an event for employees and where the cost incurred is not incidental to entertaining third parties.

The disallowance applies to direct payments made by a business or "sums at the disposal of an employee" and includes specific or round sum allowances used for the purposes of entertainment. An employee includes a director or anyone involved in the management of a company.

The meaning of entertainment is not specifically defined in statute that refers to "hospitality of any kind". The ordinary meaning of the terms "entertainment" and "hospitality" should be applied in determining the nature of the expenditure. The following are characteristics of business hospitality:

- it is provided free of charge to the recipient (BIM45012);
- there is no reciprocity – the expenditure is a speculative gesture of goodwill; and
- the relationship is between the business as a host and its customers, suppliers or others who receive the entertainment, as guests.

B13.1.1 Incidental entertainment

The statutory rule for applying the disallowance includes incidental expenses incurred in providing entertainment, e.g. the travel and accommodation of guests attending an event.

The question of whether expenditure is incidental is not entirely free from doubt. For example, HMRC accept that, if an employee travels alone to meet a customer for lunch, the cost is not incidental to the entertainment, but the travel cost is disallowed if the customer and employee travel together (BIM45015).

If the purpose of the expenditure is not to entertain, so that the hospitality is incidental to another event, the disallowance is restricted to the cost of the hospitality (*Netlogic Consulting Ltd v Revenue and Customs Commissioners [2005] STC (SCD) 524*).

If the entertainment expenditure provides an incidental benefit for the business, such as advertising, no apportionment of the cost can be made to treat part of the costs as allowable (see **B2**).

B13.1.2 Staff entertainment

Entertainment costs relating to employees are disallowed when part of the overall cost in entertaining others. The costs of a function open only to employees (and their partners) will generally be allowable for the business. There may be a taxable benefit for the staff depending on the cost and nature of the event. By informal concession, HMRC allow functions that include retired and past employees to be included as staff (BIM45033). A deduction for employee entertainment will still depend on whether the expense satisfies the general rule as wholly and exclusively for the purposes of the trade or business.

When a customer joins an employee for lunch in the staff canteen, the cost of providing hospitality to the guest will be disallowed but the employee's meal will be an allowable deduction. If, instead, the customer is taken out to lunch, the total cost will be disallowed (BIM45034).

B13.1.3 Capital expenditure

Plant and machinery capital allowances are not available for assets used by a business for entertainment.

B13.1.4 The dividing line between allowable and disallowable entertainment

Surprisingly, the nature of entertainment has been considered in only a handful of direct tax cases, and HMRC use VAT cases to define entertainment (BIM45011).

The following are examples of hospitality that may be allowable:

- *Not provided free of charge:* Hospitality provided as part of a bundle of services, such as food and accommodation in attending a residential course, will be paid for by the customer and is not free of charge. For example, training provided to a franchisee will not be hospitality if the franchise holder is required to attend a course as part of granting a franchise and is covered by franchise payments. Other examples of this include drinks offered by a leisure spa or casino where the entrance price includes the price of the refreshments (*Celtic Football & Athletic Club Ltd v Commissioners for Customs and Excise [1983] STC 470*; BIM45047).
- *Quid pro quo:* Where the recipient provides services or goods in return for hospitality, the cost will be allowable. No contractual obligation is necessary and the hospitality may be provided voluntarily but something of equivalent value is given in return by the recipient, otherwise the whole cost will be disallowable (*Customs and Excise v Kilroy Television Company Ltd [1997] STC 901*; BIM45014).
- *Hospitality provided in conjunction with other services:* Food and accommodation provided by a business to its suppliers as part of a training event for existing or prospective sales agents is disallowable (*Netlogic Consulting Ltd v Revenue and Customs Commissioners [2005] STC (SCD) 524, Customs and Excise v Shaklee International [1981] STC 776*; BIM45047, BIM45012). Hospitality was incidental to the main purpose; other costs associated with the training, such as room hire, are allowable.
- *Subsidised expenditure:* A financial contribution towards the cost of entertainment from the recipient (or another party) will reduce the amount of the disallowance but, to the extent that this does not cover the full amount, the net cost will be disallowed (*BMW (GB) Ltd v Customs and Excise [1997] STC 824*; BIM45012).
- *Reciprocal arrangements:* Hospitality provided as part of a reciprocal *contractual* arrangement between the provider and recipient is allowable (*Celtic Football & Athletic Club Ltd v Customs and Excise [1983] STC 470*). Where there is no formal obligation or no direct linkage between the hospitality and what is given in return by the recipient, the expense is disallowed (*Associated Newspapers Group Ltd v Fleming (1972) 48 TC 382*; BIM45013, BIM45031).

- *Reward for services:* Entertainment provided as a reward for services is allowable, e.g.:
  - awards to third party suppliers or customers, such as incentives given to sales agents for hitting sales targets or hospitality given to suppliers as a non-cash settlement of invoices (BIM45080); and
  - subsidised meals or refreshments for self-employed or sub-contracted workers who are providing services directly to the business (BIM45045).
- *Sponsorship:* Sponsorship payments will be partially disallowed if an element of entertainment is provided by the recipient, such as tickets to a sporting or cultural event.
- *Ordinary course of a trade:* The costs of promotional events, where the business provides hospitality as part of its ordinary trade, will not be treated as disallowable. For example, a meal offered by a restaurant under a "two for the price of one" is a discount, as the customer is required to make a purchase. Free samples of goods or services that relate directly to the business are allowable (see **B2**; BIM45071).

B13.2 REFERENCES

Statutory references

CAA 2001, s 269

ITTIOA 2005, ss 32A, 45, 46, 272ZA

CTA 2009, ss 1298, 1299

Leading cases

Bentleys, Stokes and Lowless v Beeson (1952) 33 TC 491

Associated Newspapers Group Ltd v Fleming (1972) 48 TC 382

Customs and Excise v Shaklee International [1981] STC 776

Celtic Football & Athletic Club Ltd v C&E [1983] STC 470

C&E v Kilroy Television Company Ltd [1997] STC 901

BMW (GB) Ltd v C&E [1997] STC 824

Netlogic Consulting Ltd v Revenue and Customs Commissioners [2005] STC (SCD) 524

HMRC manuals

BIM45000–BIM45062, BIM45012, BIM45013, BIM45014, BIM45020, BIM45030, BIM45080

See also

B2, **B19**, **B60**

B14

Ex-gratia payments

B14.1 COMMENT

Although the term is widely used and understood, it is not defined in general tax legislation. It is used in the legislation relating to tax credits and also appeared in SP 13/91 (now withdrawn) in the context of employment termination awards.

Ex-gratia payments are distinguished from contract payments by being made voluntarily and by not being legally enforceable. The proprietor might nevertheless consider that they benefit the business. The reason behind the payments will help to determine the tax treatment. Factors to be considered are:

- was there a personal element driving the payment?
- if entirely a business motive, is the payment capital or revenue?
- if a business expense and it relates to a payment to an employee, should it be subject to PAYE/NIC?

B14.1.1 Personal element

This aspect has not been the subject of leading case law in the context of deductibility of ex-gratia payments. Nevertheless, the possibility that a payment has been made in part for personal reasons will always affect its qualification as a business deduction. Particularly, consider whether there is a family link with the recipient of the ex-gratia payment, such as in the role of a seemingly disgruntled customer who is also a relative.

For companies, this is apt where a payment is made to a director of his personal company, maybe on employment termination. HMRC tend strongly toward denying it as an ex-gratia payment and instead treating it as general earnings (which would still be likely to qualify as a deductible expense). Yet the company might then prefer to lose its deductibility in favour of arguing it as a personal expense of the director and debiting his loan account.

B14.1.2 Capital or revenue?

Where an ex-gratia payment is clearly made for business reasons, the distinction between capital and revenue must be determined. As expected, the logic to use is whether or not there is long-term benefit to the business. However, the circumstances can be borderline, as shown by the number that form case law.

The case of *Cooke v Quick Shoe Repair Service* involved the purchaser of a business paying off the vendor's debts to suppliers. The reason was to preserve the good name of his new business so that supplies would continue. This was held to be a revenue expense, because retaining the supply of goods was the driver; accordingly, it was deductible.

A different conclusion was formed in *Watney Combe Reid & Co Ltd v Pike*, where the taxpayer wished to remove some tenants from tied properties, yet did not want to suffer adverse publicity. Accordingly, he made some ex-gratia payments to the tenants. Although the taxpayer argued on the basis that the payments were made to preserve the goodwill and were therefore deductible, Walton J ruled that the payments were made for the long-lasting benefit of the business, and were consequently capital.

Switching the other way again, in *Lawson v Johnson Matthey*, a £50m capital injection to rescue a subsidiary from insolvency was considered to be deductible as a revenue expense. Without it, the demise of the subsidiary would probably have caused the parent company's trade also to fail.

B14.1.3 Subject to PAYE/NIC?

A full analysis of whether a payment to an employee, usually on the termination of employment, is taxable as earnings under *ITEPA 2003, s 62* or within *ITEPA 2003, s 401* (this includes the well-known £30,000 exemption from tax) is outside the scope of this publication. However, it is so important a distinction that it is valid to remind here that, merely because the employer applies the term "ex-gratia" to a payment made on the termination of an employment, that alone does not place it outside the scope either of tax or of the PAYE system.

To be treated as a termination payment under *section 401*, there must have been nothing in the relevant employment contract which led to the payment, nor must it have been customary for such a payment to have been made to equivalent employees. An ex-gratia payment that meets the appropriate criteria is likely to be (but see below) a deductible expense, and it would not be subject to PAYE. A payment that fails under *ITEPA 2003, s 401* and instead is subject to *section 62* would still be deductible but with the additional tax and NIC of PAYE.

Furthermore, NIC legislation interprets the liability of earnings on termination of employment even more strictly than for tax purposes. HMRC manuals express the view that, even if the employee has no legal or contractual right to the payment, it will still be earnings for NIC purposes if the payment can be held to derive solely from the employment and for no other reason.

The deductibility of ex-gratia and redundancy payments on the termination of employment can be treated differently if they occur because of the cessation of the business itself. There is established case law that distinguishes situations where payments are made, not in order to enable a proprietor (or company) the better to carry on the trade, but to enable it to go out of business. In those cases, the courts have held that the money so paid was not deductible as an expense wholly and exclusively laid out or expended for the purposes of the trade.

B14.1.4 Finally

Remember that the treatment of ex-gratia payments for tax purposes can affect the taxable profits of a business as a receipt as well as an expense. Particularly, HMRC in limited circumstances will make an ex-gratia payment to a taxpayer where it has made an error, either technically or in its administration of his affairs. The payments would be made as a result of HRMC applying their own "Complaints and Remedy Guidance".

Fortunately, HMRC make it clear – in their Complaints and Remedy Manual (CRG) – that payments for financial redress made under that policy would not be taxable, except where they pay an agent direct; in those circumstances the payment should be treated as normal trading income by the agent.

B14.2 REFERENCES

Statutory references

ITTOIA 2005, s 34

Leading cases

Cooke v Quick Shoe Repair Service (1943–1949) 30 TC 460

Watney Combe Reid & Co Ltd v Pike (HM Inspector of Taxes) [1982] BTC 288

Lawson (HM Inspector of Taxes) v Johnson Matthey plc [1992] BTC 324

HMRC manuals

BIM38390

CRG5100

EIM12805

NIM02610

B15

Fines

B15.1 COMMENT

A principle when considering whether a particular expense is deductible against profits is that it should not be for anything that is a result of a breach in the law.

HMRC explain, at BIM38500, that this is because the fine is not incurred wholly and exclusively for the purpose of the business. As a general rule, damages incurred as a result of normal trading operations are allowable. Penalties for infraction of the law are not.

HMRC acknowledge that the cost of a fine on an employee may be deducted where it is the employee's liability yet paid by the employer. Here the employee is taxed on the payment made by the employer as a benefit in kind. This treatment is liable to dispute if the fine is that of a director, e.g. a parking fine reimbursement by a company, especially where it is his personal company and it might not have been reimbursed for all employees in similar circumstances.

HMRC concede that a revenue payment made by a taxpayer in settlement of a civil action arising out of their business can be deducted where the allegations were neither admitted nor proved. Where liability was admitted or proved, a deduction is due if the payment was restitutionary (that is, made good the loss to the other party), but not if it was punitive (that is, in the nature of a fine or penalty).

Where a trader incurs a liability to a regulatory body on revenue account that is broadly intended to cover the regulator's costs of performing its duties in relation to the trading activities, such costs will normally be allowable even where the trader has committed a breach of regulations. However, should a regulatory body impose a penalty for breach of regulations, or should a penalty or fine become payable as a result of a prosecution for a trader's breach of regulations, this will not be an allowable expense (see *McKnight v Sheppard* below).

HMRC set out their comments in both the business income and the property income manuals. The same principles apply to both types of income and, in general, to the expenditure of companies.

There are further circumstances when the treatment of fines needs detailed consideration and the uneasy distinction between deductible and otherwise is exemplified by case law.

In *McKnight v Sheppard*, which was both appealed and cross-appealed before finally being won in part only by the taxpayer (Sheppard), the fines imposed by the stockbroker disciplinary board and the legal costs of defending the position were both in point. Despite his defence, Mr Sheppard had been fined by the disciplinary board and suspended for six months. He then appealed against that decision and gained a slight mitigation by the board. He claimed both the fine and the legal costs as expenses in his trade as stockbroker. It was this with which HMRC disagreed and which led to the tax case. The Special Commissioner in the first instance determined against Mr Sheppard in respect of the fine but agreed the deductibility of the legal fees. In the appeal in 1996 against the Special Commissioner's decision by HMRC (and cross-appeal by Mr Sheppard), Lightman J decided that neither costs nor fine were allowable against profits. He did so on the basis that trying to prevent a fine and suspension were too far from the nature of the stockbroker trade itself for the fine to be deductible. He had, however, accepted that Mr Sheppard had been motivated by the preservation of his business and not his personal reputation.

When, in the above cases, Mr Sheppard appealed in 1997, the decision was reversed and the legal expenses were determined as deductible. It was decided that the closeness of the cause of the expenses to the direct trade was not relevant. It was sufficient that the motivation was for the trade and not Mr Sheppard's personal reputation. However, importantly, the position on the fine was unchanged and not appealed by Mr Sheppard.

Finally in this yo-yo of a tax case, HMRC in 1999 appealed to the House of Lords against the High Court decision on allowing the legal costs to be deductible. This, too, was decided in favour of Mr Sheppard. It hinged on the fact that, although he might have had a wish that his personal reputation should not be adversely affected by the decision of the stockbroker disciplinary board, his purpose in incurring legal fees to defend his position was to save his business. However, the non-deductibility of the fine remained, as determined at the original Special Commissioner hearing, on account of a fine not being expended for the purpose of the trade.

A further example given by HMRC uses the costs of a libel action. Thus, civil damages awarded against a publication for libel, arising as a result of normal trading operations, are generally allowable. However, civil damages arising outside the normal course of the trade are not allowable. That was shown in *Fairrie v Hall*, where the libel action related to remarks made in a personal capacity.

In *CIR v Alexander von Glehn Ltd* the company had paid a fine and incurred legal costs in transgressing trade sanctions imposed in the war. It sought to claim both as deductions in computing its profits. It was held that, although there had been no criminal proceedings as the company agreed to pay to forestall them, the payment was nevertheless in response to an infraction of the law. As such, it was not admissible as a deduction and, accordingly, the associated legal costs also failed.

In *Golder v Great Boulder*, civil actions were brought against the company in connection with the formation of other companies. Rather than continue with the case through the courts, the company settled for damages of £25,000, without having admitted any fault. On appeal, the Commissioners held that the *£25,000 and the attendant costs were disbursements made wholly and exclusively for the purposes of the trade*. This decision was unsuccessfully appealed by HMRC.

In *G4S Cash Solutions (UK) Ltd [2016] TC 05015* the FTT held that parking fines incurred by the taxpayer were not wholly and exclusively incurred for the purposes of the trade, on the basis that they were also incurred because of a breach of parking restrictions. This was despite special circumstances claimed by the company, including driver and customer safety. Its trade was that of providing secure cash transportation and delivery services to and from customers' premises and the replenishment of ATMs. The company argued that this could not be carried on safely without parking infringements being incurred. There are exclusions from certain parking restrictions available to such circumstances. Applications can also be made for dispensations where access to customers' premises is particularly difficult and consequently potentially dangerous. However, on analysis of the company's parking infringements, the FTT concluded that the instances cited did not come within those categories. Other factors led to the company's decision to instruct its employees to park such as to incur those penalties. They were primarily commercial ones, to minimise costs. Accordingly, the fines were in the nature of punishments for breaking the law and were not necessitated wholly and exclusively to carry out the trade itself.

B15.2 REFERENCES

Statutory references

ITTOIA 2005, s 34

Leading cases

CIR v Alexander von Glehn Ltd (1920) 12 TC 232

Fairrie v Hall (1947) 28 TC 200

A–Z of Business Tax Deductions

Golder v Great Boulder Proprietary Goldmines Ltd (1952) 33 TC 75

McKnight (HM Inspector of Taxes) v Sheppard; Sheppard v McKnight (HM Inspector of Taxes) [1996] BTC 355

McKnight (HM Inspector of Taxes) v Sheppard [1997] BTC 328

G4S Cash Solutions (UK) Ltd [2016] TC 05015

HMRC manuals

BIM42515, BIM38500

PIM2068

B16

Fixed rate deductions

B16.1 COMMENT

These were introduced into the legislation on the back of the "cash basis" rules of *FA 2013* and related to sole traders and partnerships. Although the cash basis applies within strict criteria, the element of fixed rate deductions (originally termed "simplified expenses") was replicated to apply to the businesses of all sole traders and partnerships. It does not apply to companies, LLPs or partnerships which include a corporate member. Their use has been available from 6 April 2013.

The relevant expenses are:

- cars and motor cycles;
- use of home as office; and
- private use of business premises.

From 6 April 2017 the availability of fixed rate deductions in respect of vehicles has been extended to property businesses. The criteria are the same as those for trading unincorporated businesses. Property rental businesses are examined at **A5**.

The detail is as follows.

B16.1.1 Cars and motor cycles

Expenditure on these vehicles can be deducted using an allowance based on HMRC's authorised mileage allowance payments (AMAPs) and the business mileage incurred. Although this has been permitted in the past for businesses below the VAT registration limit, it has now been extended to all unincorporated businesses within the criteria set out above.

There are conditions relating to the relevant vehicle. It must be one that qualifies for a business deduction under the normal rules, or would be if it were not capital. It must not be an excluded vehicle.

An "excluded vehicle" is a vehicle that is used for the purposes of the trade but which is either:

- a vehicle on which the person carrying on the trade has at any time claimed capital allowances; or
- a motor cycle or goods vehicle on which any expenditure incurred in acquiring the vehicle has been allowed as a deduction in calculating profits of any relevant trade or business under the cash basis.

It is specified that "relevant trade or business" means any trade or property business carried on by the aforesaid person.

Once a fixed allowance for business mileage has been used for a particular vehicle, this method of calculation must continue to be used for as long as the vehicle remains in the business.

The mileage rate covers the costs of buying, running and maintaining the vehicle, such as fuel, oil, servicing, repairs, insurance, vehicle excise duty and MOT. The rate also covers depreciation of the vehicle. However, it does not include incidental expenses incurred in connection with a particular journey, such as tolls, congestion charges and parking fees. These will be allowable as a deduction where they are incurred solely for business purposes.

The business proportion of the finance element of a hire purchase or finance lease may also be claimed as a deduction.

At the date of this publication the rates are:

- cars and goods vehicles: 45p/mile for the first 10,000 miles, and 25p/mile thereafter; and
- motor cycles: 24p/mile irrespective of the amount of travel.

B16.1.2 Use of home as office

This flat rate allowance is based on the number of hours worked in the home for business purposes. It is a monthly rate and it can be varied each month if the number of hours has changed to a different rate band. The annual allowance is defined as the sum of each of the 12 monthly ones within the period of account. The "number of hours worked" means the number of hours spent wholly and exclusively on work done by the person, or any employee of the person, in the person's home, wholly and exclusively for the purposes of the trade.

The type of expenses included are household running costs on heat, light, power, cleaning and metered water.

Use of the flat rate deduction for household running costs does not prohibit a separate deduction for fixed costs such as council tax (or domestic rates in Northern Ireland), insurance and mortgage interest, where an identifiable proportion can be attributed to business use.

Use of the flat rate deduction also does not prohibit a separate deduction for telephone and broadband/internet connection costs. HMRC manual BIM47820 provides information on how to work out the business proportion of these costs. Note that if the private use is not significant the full cost of the telephone and broadband service can be claimed as a business expense.

The *Finance Act 2016* introduced an amendment to the legislation in respect of partnerships and use of home as office. Its purpose was to clarify the way the deductions work for partnerships. It inserted new *ss 94H and 94I* into *Chapter 5A, Part 2* of *ITTOIA 2005*. It ensures that, when considering a home used for the purposes of a trade, the provision now applies to a partner's home, or that of an employee of the firm, where the deduction is to be made against the partnership profits. It operates in the same way as it does for an individual's home. The basis of calculation is also the same, as set out above.

In particular, the partnership amendments ensure that:

- where more than one person works in the same home, any hour spent wholly and exclusively for the purposes of the trade is counted only once;
- where a partnership has more than one premises that are used both for business and as a home, any claim to use the simplified expense deduction must be applied to all such premises; and
- when a firm makes a claim to use a simplified expense deduction for a partner's home, it must consistently use the same rules for deductions for any other partner's homes.

At the date of this publication, the rates per month are:

– Working 25 to 50 hrs/month in the home	£10
– 51 to 100 hrs/month in the home	£18
– More than 100 hrs/month in the home	£26

B16.1.3 Private use of business premises

This situation is appropriate where, for example, premises such as hotels are primarily used for business purposes, but where there is also personal occupancy. The fixed rates represent the private use add-backs where entire actual running costs appear in the accounts. It is based on the number of relevant occupants.

A "relevant occupant", in relation to a month or part of a month, means an individual (including a child) who, at any time during that month or that part of a month, occupies the premises as a home or stays at the premises otherwise than in the course of the trade. On this basis, it means that, if a relative or friend comes to stay for a single night on a non-fee paying basis, the private add-back amount could increase for the relevant month by £150.

This fixed rate add-back operates equally for occupants where the premises are used by a partnership that trades, as it does for sole traders. This is made clear in *ITTOIA 2005, s 941*.

If a person chooses not to use the standard adjustment, they can claim an allowable portion of actual expenses in accordance with the well-established legislation.

The flat rate amount includes all household goods and services, food, non-alcoholic drinks and utilities. It does not include mortgage interest, rent, council tax or business rates. Therefore, further calculations are necessary to apportion these expenses between private and business use.

Prior to the introduction of the simplified expenses rules, a number of local agreements existed between HMRC officials and representatives of owners of guesthouses and hotels in order to minimise the administrative costs of establishing an appropriate level of non-business expenditure. All local "board and lodging" agreements have now been withdrawn and no business can use them for the first time for the 2013–14 tax year. Transitional arrangements permitted the continuation for 2013–14 only where they were already in use for a particular business.

At the date of this publication the rates per month are:

– For one occupant	£350/month
– For two occupants	£500/month
– For three or more occupants	£650/month

B16.1.4 Finally

There are other statutory fixed (or flat) rate expenses that HMRC permit, but not in the context of determining the profits of an unincorporated business. Particularly, they can apply to employment expenses such as subsistence, but do not in law translate to allowable deductions for the self-employed. It might well be that, in the absence of any vouchers supporting actual costs, HMRC would permit, say, an equivalent rate for subsistence as that for employees. However, it is not automatic and, if such estimates are included within the figures submitted on the business pages of a tax return, it would be wise to disclose this in the additional information box.

B16.2 REFERENCES

Statutory references

ITTOIA 2005, ss 94D, 94F, 94H, 94I

Leading cases

None

HMRC manuals

BIM75001, BIM75005, BIM75010, BIM75015, BIM47820

B17

Foreign exchange losses

B17.1 COMMENT

There is no specific statutory framework for the taxation of foreign exchange differences for unincorporated businesses and the tax treatment usually follows the treatment of the underlying transaction.

For traders foreign currency difference may arise on:

- settlement of sales and purchases in a currency other than sterling;
- translation of foreign currency bank accounts and working capital;
- realisation of fixed assets for foreign currency;
- long-term foreign currency borrowing; and
- hedging transactions, including forward contracts and currency futures.

There are no foreign exchange differences on transactions for taxpayers who use the cash basis as the profit or loss on foreign currency will be translated at the time foreign currency is received or expended.

Foreign exchange differences are not included within the definition of incidental costs of obtaining loan finance; this type of expense is subject to a separate statutory relief (see **B24**).

For unincorporated businesses, the tax treatment of foreign exchange losses and gains are governed by the underlying transaction:

- Foreign exchange differences on current assets and liabilities are deductible or taxable and follow the accounting treatment, i.e. an accrual basis applies (with no distinction in the tax treatment of realised or unrealised foreign exchange differences).
- Where expenses denominated in a foreign currency are disallowed, e.g. legal costs or settlement of overseas tax liabilities, the related foreign currency differences will also be disallowed (or non-taxable).
- The disposal of chargeable assets denominated in a currency other than sterling is taxed on a realised basis.

- Foreign exchange differences on long-term liabilities are non-deductible/ non-taxable.
- For foreign exchange losses on long-term liabilities, a deduction may only be available if the funding is applied for hedging foreign currency exposure relating to assets used for working capital (*Pattison v Marine Midland*).

B17.1.1 Accounting for monetary assets and liabilities

Foreign exchange rates used to compute sterling equivalents in compliance with GAAP are also acceptable for computing the result for tax purposes. Acceptable foreign exchange conversion rates include:

- London closing rates;
- main clearing banks set rates; or
- average monthly rates published by HMRC.

For a trader that prepares its accounts in a functional currency other than sterling an average exchange rate for the accounting period can be used unless exchange rates "fluctuate significantly" (FRS 102, paragraph 30.19).

Realised or unrealised foreign exchange losses (or gains) on the translation of working capital balances, comprising monetary assets and liabilities, are deductible (or taxable) when computed in accordance with generally accepted accounting principles.

Non-sterling monetary assets and liabilities of a trade or property business include:

- bank current accounts used for working capital, and trade debtors;
- trade creditors and bank overdrafts or other short-term funding; and
- forward currency contracts used to hedge foreign currency exposure on trade transactions.

If the functional currency of the business is a currency other than sterling, translation differences arising on the opening and closing monetary assets and liabilities may be accounted for via reserves (based on the closing rate/ net investment accounting method). Foreign exchange differences will not be deductible or taxable even where these are derived from the working capital of a business. This follows the general rule that the starting point for computing taxable profits should be the accounting profit calculated in accordance with generally accepted accounting principles and these types of foreign exchange differences do not exist in the accounts of the presentation currency.

When accounts are prepared in a local currency, the accounting result after adjustments to arrive at taxable profit or loss is translated at the closing rate or average rate of exchange for the period. No foreign exchange differences will arise from the translation of the profit or losses to sterling.

B17.1.2 Fixed assets

Additions and disposals of assets qualifying for capital allowances are translated into sterling at the date of purchase or sale. The foreign currency translation differences (if any) calculated during the period of ownership of the asset are ignored when computing trading profits.

B17.1.3 Long-term borrowing

Realised or unrealised foreign exchange losses on long-term borrowings are not allowable as a revenue deduction and foreign exchange gains are non-taxable. This contrasts with the position for companies where the corporate loan relationship rules generally tax foreign exchange differences on an accruals basis without distinguishing between the underlying capital or revenue source.

Foreign exchange differences on chargeable assets used by the business will be taxable as part of the overall capital gain or loss when realised on eventual sale. The exchange rate at the date of the transaction applies to determine the extent of the currency gain or loss (*Bentley v Pike (1981) 53 TC 590*).

Long-term liabilities are, by definition, not chargeable assets; therefore, realised or unrealised foreign exchange losses on borrowings cannot be relieved as a revenue deduction or as a capital loss (*Firestone Tyre & Rubber Co Ltd v Evans (1976) 51 TC 615, Ch D*).

The application of long-term foreign currency borrowing for the purposes of working capital is not, of itself, sufficient to permit a deduction for foreign exchange losses (or to tax gains): *Beauchamp v F W Woolworth plc (1989) 61 TC 542*.

A payment made to indemnify the lender for foreign currency differences arising on a long-term debt is also disallowed (*Kato Kagaku Co Ltd v HMRC [2007] SpC 598, [2007] SSCD 412*).

An exception to the general rule for long-term borrowing is where it is used to hedge trading assets or working capital in the same currency (*Pattison v Marine Midland HL (1983) 57 TC 219*). HMRC guidance on this is given in SP 2/02, which provides examples of where foreign exchange losses that are matched with foreign exchange profits on trade assets can be offset (similar principles apply to foreign exchange gains). To the extent that foreign currency liabilities are unmatched, foreign exchange losses or gains arising on the excess long-term borrowing are ignored.

B17.2 REFERENCES

Statutory references

ITTOIA 2005, ss 25, 25A

CTA 2009, ss 328, 447–452

CTA 2010, ss 4–17

Exchange Gains and Losses (Bringing into Account Gains or Losses) Regulations 2002 (SI 2002/1970)

Leading cases

Firestone Tyre & Rubber Co Ltd v Evans (1971) 51 TC 615, Ch D

Pattison v Marine Midland HL (1983) 57 TC 219

Beauchamp v F W Woolworth plc (1989) 61 TC 542

Kato Kagaku Co Ltd v HMRC [2007] SpC 598, [2007] SSCD 412

HMRC manuals

BIM39500, BIM39515, BIM39530, BIM39580

See also

Chapter 1, **B24**

Accounting Standard SSAP 20

Section 30 of FRS 102

IAS 21 (as applied by FRS 101)

Statement of Practice SP 2/02 Exchange Rate Fluctuations

"Tax implications on application of New UK GAAP, FRS 102 – FRS 102 Overview Paper – Tax implications" (22 January 2014), Part 17, available at www.gov.uk/government/publications/accounting-standards-the-uk-tax-implications-of-new-uk-gaap

B18

Franchise payments

B18.1 COMMENT

There is no body of tax law specific to franchising. Consequently, it is necessary to apply established law to the facts of each case and to the terms of the particular agreement. Typical franchises require the payment of an initial fee for use of the franchisor's business structure, trademark or goodwill, followed by a series of payments which are akin to consideration for goods and services supplied by the franchisor on an ongoing basis. Alternatively, the ongoing payments might represent royalties for permission to use the franchisor's business systems during the period of the franchise agreement.

The amount of detail set out will vary between agreements. Particularly, it might be clear as to the elements of a payment which represent consideration for the acquisition of goodwill, know-how, or for training, management support, IT resources and equipment, or maybe for the use of premises.

The tax treatment of the payments in the hands of the franchisee does not necessarily align with the treatment of the receipts for the franchisor. This is indicated in CG38720, where HMRC state:

> "An initial payment on the grant of a franchise will usually be treated as capital expenditure on the acquisition of franchise rights in relation to the franchisee even though it may be treated as an income receipt in the hands of the franchisor."

It will generally be agreed by HMRC that annual fees are deductible business expenses.

In accordance with HMRC's view above, the initial payment, whether payable in one sum or instalments, is usually capital, as are any related legal fees. This will remain the same even if the instalments are payable over several years. HMRC's "Capital v Revenue Expenditure Toolkit" explains this, as follows:

> "Generally the annual fees payable in respect of a franchise agreement will be an allowable revenue expense. The initial payment however, together with any related legal fees, is usually capital expenditure for tax purposes

and not allowable as a revenue deduction. An initial fee for the acquisition of a franchise will still be capital expenditure even if it is paid by instalments over a number of years."

Despite the above, the capital treatment of the initial payment might be mitigated by an apportionment between revenue and capital expenditure, depending on the facts, especially those reflected in the detail of the agreement. Apportionment would not be feasible if it is apparent from the agreement that all services of a revenue nature were separately charged for in the annual fees.

Case law has determined that, to the extent that the initial payment is wholly or mainly for "substantial rights of an enduring nature", it is to be treated as capital. Similarly, where the payment is made for the initiation or extension of the franchisee's business, it will be treated as capital. The cases of *Atherton v British Insulated and Helsby Cables* and *IR Comms v Granite City Steamship Co Ltd* support the capital treatment.

To the extent that the initial payment represents consideration for revenue items, such as trading stock or services such as training of staff (but not of the franchisee where this puts him in a position to run the business), it will be a deductible trading expense for the business proprietor. For the situation where training costs are likely to be of a capital nature, see **B7**.

Particularly if the initial payment is to be apportioned between capital and deductible revenue expenses, it should follow precisely the franchise agreement, and not an estimate. Furthermore, the following conditions should be met:

- the specific services should actually be provided by the franchisor in accordance with the franchise agreement;
- the agreement should stipulate that those particular services are paid for by reference to the initial payment and not the annual fees; and
- the amount allocated to revenue expenditure should be commensurate with the services provided.

B18.1.1 Capital allowances

Where the initial payment has been determined as capital not revenue, this does not prevent other tax rules from being in point. Thus, where items qualify under the capital allowance regime, a deduction can be made accordingly. In particular, this might be relevant to "know-how", which is dealt with specifically in the capital allowance legislation.

Nevertheless, HMRC contend that, in the majority of cases, know-how paid for by a franchisee does not qualify for capital allowances. They base this on the premise that the payment is for a licence to operate a business including know-how and, as such, it is commercial and not industrial know-how. It is industrial know-how acquired as a piece of property that is within the capital allowance regime. Whilst this does not mean there could never be a franchise agreement which gave the opportunity for a capital allowance claim under the know-how legislation, it does mean that the circumstances are rare.

The possibility that capital items to which the initial payment refer might include plant and machinery which qualify for capital allowances should not be discounted. Again, the agreement would need to be perused carefully to ensure that all conditions were met, especially those relating to title of the asset.

B18.1.2 A different slant

In *Balloon Promotions Limited*, the franchisee disposed of its restaurant business to the franchisor, after having run it successfully for several years. It then claimed rollover relief on the sale of goodwill. HMRC disputed this, primarily on the basis that the value of the goodwill remained with the franchisor.

The Special Commissioners decided that the taxpayers had established that, on the balance of probabilities, they sold goodwill to a franchisor in specified amounts within the meaning of *TCGA 1992, s 155, Class 4*, thereby allowing the gain on any such disposal to qualify for rollover relief, subject to the requirements of *ss 152–154*.

Accordingly, in particular circumstances where the franchisee's goodwill can be identified, capital treatment on disposal might be beneficial to the taxpayer.

B18.1.3 Finally

The above rules apply for income tax only. For a company, the rules relating to intangible fixed assets are relevant. In that context, although the acquisition represented by the initial payment would be classed as an asset, the amortisation rules are likely to provide tax relief in accordance with the appropriate write-off period. All other qualifying conditions, such as connection between the parties, would need to be considered.

B18.2 REFERENCES

Statutory references

CAA 2001, Part 7, s 11

Leading cases

Atherton v British Insulated and Helsby Cables (1925) 10 TC 155

IR Commrs v The Granite City Steamship Co Ltd (1927) 13 TC 1

Balloon Promotions Limited (Appellant 1) and Alonso Vela-Castro, Edward Kidney and Natale Lucibello (Appellant 2) v Wilson and Rodin [2006] SpC 524

HMRC manuals

BIM57600–BIM57620

CA70030

CG68270

See also

HMRC Capital v Revenue Expenditure Toolkit

B19

Gifts to customers

B19.1 COMMENT

The statutory disallowance that applies to entertainment also extends to the cost of gifts provided by unincorporated traders and property businesses (see **B5**, **B13**).

Exceptions to the disallowance of gifts are as follows:

- Items that the business provides in its ordinary trade – if given to advertise to the public generally (see **B2**).
- Gifts that include conspicuous advertising, *except*:
  - a gift is food, drink, tobacco or a voucher that can be exchanged for goods; or
  - other types of gifts, where the cost or combined cost for a single recipient exceeds £50.
- Gifts provided to employees, unless similar gifts are incidental to providing gifts to others (BIM45030).
- Gifts to a registered charity, the Historic Buildings and Monuments Commission for England or the Trustee of the National Heritage Memorial Fund.

Prizes given by a trader to the winner of a competition are not regarded as a business gift and will be an allowable expense where the promotion results in publicity for the business. HMRC regard this as a commercial transaction, as consideration is given for the prize under the "quid pro quo" principle (BIM45014, BIM45075; *C&E v Kilroy Television Company Ltd [1997] STC 901*; see **B13**).

Certain items described as gifts are not gratuitous and may be treated as allowable, for example:

- catalogue sales schemes, where "gifts" are discounts on costs of goods sold; and

- incentives offered by timeshare promoters to potential customers in return for attendance at sales events.

The cost of gifts of trading stock to, or for use by, registered charities, community amateur sports clubs, designated educational establishments and other designated national funds are deductible. An adjustment receipt will apply to include the value any benefit received by a donor or a connected person derived from the donation (see **B5**).

B19.2 REFERENCES

Statutory references

ITTOIA 2005, ss 45, 47, 108, 272(2), 272ZA

CTA 2009, ss 105, 1298, 1300

Leading cases

None

HMRC manuals

BIM45070, BIM45075, BIM45080–BIM45090

See also

B2, B5, B13, B55

B20

Goodwill and know-how

B20.1 COMMENT

B20.1.1 Goodwill

No deduction is allowed for unincorporated traders on the amortisation of goodwill under GAAP. This rule applies equally to purchased goodwill, goodwill recognised on business acquisitions (fair value accounting adjustments) and internally generated goodwill.

The profit and loss account charge for goodwill is disallowed when computing taxable profits, and any credit on sale or revaluation is treated as non-taxable. No relief is available for goodwill under the capital allowances regime.

The cost of purchased goodwill forms part of the capital gains base cost and may be deducted when computing capital on a future disposal of the business.

B20.1.2 Know-how

Know-how is defined for tax purposes as industrial information or techniques (excluding patents) that are associated with:

- the manufacture and production of goods or materials;
- searching a source of mineral deposits (including geothermal energy); or
- an agricultural, forestry or fishing trade.

The acquisition of know-how by an individual trader is treated as a capital expense and relief is obtained by claims for capital allowances. Know-how is allocated to a separate pool, with allowances calculated at 25% p.a. writing down (in a similar way to patent rights).

Qualifying expenditure for know-how may only arise on the acquisition of a trade. A claim cannot be based on internally generated know-how. Proceeds on sale are included in the pool (but not restricted to original cost) to calculate a balancing adjustment. If the vendor and purchaser are under common control, no capital allowances are available.

Traders or property businesses using the cash basis from 6 April 2017 may be eligible for relief on an acquisition of know-how but no relief is available under the capital allowances rules.

The tax treatment of goodwill and know-how for companies is dealt with under the corporate intangibles legislation (*CTA 2009, Part 8*), and these rules do not apply to unincorporated businesses.

B20.1.3 Cash basis

Changes brought in by *F(No 2)A 2017* for the cash basis for traders and property businesses may allow relief for capital expenditure on intellectual property. The cash basis requires a taxpayer to first consider whether a payment is "of a capital nature". It then prescribes what type of capital items can be treated as deductible (see **Chapters 2** and **5**).

Intangibles will qualify if the rights fall within the definition used in the "Financial Reporting Standard applicable to the Micro-entities Regime", FRS 105, Section 13 which covers "Intangible assets other than goodwill".

No deduction can be claimed for any type of goodwill as this is excluded by Section 13.

Tax relief is potentially available for other types of internally generated intangibles or acquired intellectual property.

Intellectual property is defined under FRS 105 as:

- patents, trademarks and registered designs, plant breeder rights (UK registered or similar rights registered overseas);
- unregistered information or techniques with industrial, commercial or other economic value; and
- licences in connection with the above rights.

An intangible is "non-qualifying", unless it is an asset, or right to an asset, which must cease to exist within 20 years.

Intangible expenditure that would otherwise be regarded as eligible for a deductible is also treated as "non-qualifying" if the trader or property business grants a licence in respect of the intangible asset to another person.

A deduction for know-how may be claimed by taxpayers using the cash basis, subject to satisfying the statutory tests.

B20.1.4 Deduction of income tax at source

There is a requirement to deduct income tax at the basic rate from periodic payments for certain types of intellectual property where the usual place of abode for the owner is outside of the UK. This follows an extension to the UK withholding tax rules highlighted by the OECD Base Erosion and Profit Shifting project and EU review of cross-border payments.

An income tax withholding may apply to certain types of "know-how" if the rights fall within the definition of "Information on industrial, commercial or scientific experience".

The deduction of income tax is subject to reduction available under a double tax treaty with the UK and the jurisdiction of the recipient.

B20.2 REFERENCES

Statutory references

CAA 2001, Chapter 2, Part 7

ITTOIA 2005, ss 33A, 191A–195, 307B

ITA 2007, ss 906, 907

Leading cases

None

HMRC manuals

CA71000–CA71400

See also

B46, **B48**

B21

Guarantee payments

B21.1 COMMENT

A payment made under a loan guarantee is deductible only if:

- the guarantee, when it was made, was wholly and exclusively for the purposes of the trade; and
- a capital advantage is not secured by it.

B21.1.1 Wholly and exclusively for the trade

To clarify, the key point is whether there is an allowable deduction for the person being forced to make the payment for the guarantee that he gave. It is therefore his trade that is in issue, and not that of the debtor. It follows that a payment made by a guarantor following the principal debtor's default is deductible if the giving of the guarantee was a normal incident of the guarantor's business. BIM45301 examines this aspect.

To achieve this, there is likely to be a connection between the respective trades of the guarantor and the debtor who has defaulted. Examples, taken from successful cases, are:

- A payment under a guarantee to the promoters of an exhibition was held deductible where the guarantor had hoped to obtain work as a result of the exhibition (see *Morley v Lawford*). BIM45305 refers to this case.
- A firm of solicitors guaranteed a payment by a client who was later declared bankrupt. The guarantee payment was held deductible because, in those circumstances, it would be common for solicitors to proffer such a guarantee (see *Jennings v Barfield*).
- A payment by an accountancy partnership under a guarantee entered into by a deceased partner was held to be wholly and exclusively for the purposes of the partnership's profession (see *Bolton v Halpern*). This focused on an obscure point because the debtor's guarantee had been arranged by one particular partner (the deceased partner) and it was his capital account upon which the called-up guarantee payment would fall.

Nevertheless, the arrangement was made in the partnership's name and as part of its business (the debtor was a client of the accountancy firm). Accordingly, it was determined that the partnership's profits and losses had to be computed ignoring the fact that the burden of that payment must (as between the continuing partners and the deceased's estate) fall on the deceased partner.

An example of the opposite can be found in corporate cases, but the principle holds good for unincorporated entities as well. Thus:

- In *Redkite Ltd v CIR*, it was held that the guarantee to a recently acquired subsidiary company was advanced to protect the trade of the subsidiary, and not that of the parent which offered the guarantee. The latter contended that it provided the guarantee and, ultimately, the payment to the bank when the subsidiary collapsed, in order to protect the reputation of its own trade by paying its suppliers without default. However, the court found that, at best, that was only part of the motive so it failed on the duality of purpose test.

B21.1.2 A capital advantage

A guarantee payment is likely to be a revenue expense if the guarantee is for a short period, and is made to help acquire or keep income-producing contracts.

Alternatively, a guarantee payment is likely to be capital in nature if it was provided in respect of a capital asset or investment, whether that purpose was to acquire, dispose of, improve or modify the asset.

Similarly, if the guarantee was in place for a lengthy period and it helped secure an enduring business advantage for its own trade, it could be viewed as capital. Even if the guarantee assisted an enduring improvement to the whole profit-making structure of the business, it could be an advantage of a capital nature, according to HMRC.

All the basic criteria for judging expenditure to be deemed either capital or revenue by nature apply in the same way here, without special reference to the payment in question being called upon under a loan guarantee agreement.

B21.1.3 Export Credits Guarantee Scheme

This is a specialised and uncommon category. A specific trading deduction is allowed for sums paid under the above. It is, effectively, an arrangement for insuring overseas investments pursuant to *Export and Investment Guarantees Act 1991, s 2*. Such payments are allowable as revenue expenses, whether or not the amounts would be allowable based on normal principles.

B21.2 REFERENCES

Statutory references

ITTOIA 2005, ss 33, 34, 91

Leading cases

Morley v Lawford & Co (1928) 14 TC 229

Jennings v Barfield (1959–1963) 40 TC 365

Bolton v Halpern & Woolf (1980) 53 TC 445

Redkite Ltd v HM Inspector of Taxes [1996] SpC 93

HMRC manuals

BIM45301, BIM45305, BIM35000

B22

Herd basis

B22.1 COMMENT

B22.1.1 Overview

This is one area where taking a deduction against trading income often has a less desirable tax outcome than an expense being charged as a fixed asset.

If a farmer who does not calculate his profits on the cash basis elects for the herd basis to apply to a production herd, the animals in that herd form part of his fixed capital for tax purposes. The end result is that, to the extent that a disposal of the herd gives rise to a gain over its cost, that gain will be free from all taxes. The converse is also true – if a loss occurs, that will not be allowable as a relief.

B22.1.2 Practicalities for the accounts

There are several rules and procedures to contend with. Their effect should be taken into account when deciding whether or not to elect for the herd basis to apply.

At BIM 55410 HMRC explain their basis of valuing farming stock. They confirm that the "Fair value model" refers to the stock valuation approach applicable under either IAS 41 or FRS 102, Section 34, in which stock is recognised in the accounts at its fair value less costs to sell. They indicate that both IAS 41 and FRS 102, Section 34 distinguish between biological assets (a living animal or plant) and agricultural produce (the harvested product of a biological asset). Further, HMRC say that where the fair value model is applied, biological assets are measured initially and at each reporting date at fair value less costs to sell. Agricultural produce is measured at fair value at the point of harvest and this is considered to represent its cost at that date. Accordingly, the accounting principles applied to the herd basis should be acceptable both to "old GAAP" and to "new GAAP" under FRS 102. Thus:

- The initial cost of the herd is not deductible in arriving at the computation of taxable profits.

- The cost of additions is not deductible, so the value is not brought into the trading account.
- When an animal is added by transfer from trading stock, a trading receipt equal to its cost is included. The cost is that of acquisition (or breeding) plus that of rearing. Where actual cost cannot be assessed, a deemed cost basis may be used. That equates to a set percentage (currently 60% for cows, and 75% for sheep and pigs) of the market value of the animal.
- Animals acquired by gift are treated as acquired at market value.
- When a herd animal is disposed of, whether by sale or death, and is replaced by another animal, the sale proceeds of the original animal are included as a trading receipt. Similarly, the cost of the animal replacing it is deductible as a trading expense. However, no further deduction is due if the cost of the replacement has already been deducted, typically because it has been home bred.
- If a replacement animal is of better quality, the additional cost reflecting the improvement is not deductible from trading profits.
- If there is a minor reduction in the herd size because an animal is disposed of without replacement, the profit or loss on comparing proceeds to that animal's original cost on entering the herd is included in the trading account.
- HMRC regard "minor" as being less than 20% of the whole herd.

The above transactions, where they do affect the trading account rather than the fixed assets on the balance sheet, are usually posted to a single heading within direct costs such as "Production herd movement".

B22.1.3 Effect of a major disposal

As indicated above, "major" is considered to be a reduction of 20% or more in the herd size (i.e. number of animals) without replacement.

If there is a major disposal of the herd within a period of 12 months, such that the animals are not replaced within five years by a new herd of the same class, neither profit nor loss is included in the trading account. The profit/loss is calculated by comparing disposal proceeds to the cost of the herd as reflected on the balance sheet (or that major part of the herd which has been disposed of). In turn, the cost of the herd asset will have been computed in accordance with the rules set out above (see "Practicalities for the accounts"). This profit adjustment is likely to be made in the tax computations, if the net sale proceeds have been included in the trading account under GAAP.

Anti-avoidance legislation, at *ITTOIA 2005, s 127* prevents abuse of the tax advantages where there is a sale to connected parties. It ensures that market value would be used in calculating the tax position.

B22.1.4 What is a herd?

The herd basis can apply to a variety of farm animals. It is defined as a herd of animals of the same species maintained by a farmer wholly or mainly for the products obtainable from the individual animals within the herd (or flock etc). In this instance, the "products" referred to include the young of the animal as well as any other product that can be obtained from the animal without the need to slaughter it. For example, dairy herds, suckler cow herds, ewe flocks, pigs, poultry, thoroughbred horses kept for breeding (but not horses for racing) – and even bees – all meet the criteria.

As well as being of the same species, each herd must be kept for the same class of product. Therefore, a dairy herd and a suckler cow herd are two separate entities and would require two separate elections if the herd basis is required for both. This also means that one herd could be subject to the election and one not.

Before deciding to take up the opportunity, however, consider the way the calculations work (see above). Remember that:

- An end result of disposing of the herd at a substantial profit makes the whole system worthwhile.
- The likelihood of attaining very little profit on herd disposal is probably not worth the record keeping (and additional accountancy costs?).
- A loss at the final disposal is a tax disaster.
- A herd basis election is irrevocable.

Clarifying further, the following categories of farm animals do not qualify for herd basis election:

- Animals produced primarily for slaughter or for onward sale before maturity.
- Flying flocks, i.e. cattle or sheep bought and kept for a short term prior to resale.
- Animals kept specifically for competitive or show purposes (as opposed to those, such as dairy cows, which might be shown as pedigree animals but that is incidental to the main, qualifying, purpose of keeping them for milk production).

Young stock do not meet the criteria for being in the herd basis. They could qualify when they reach maturity, i.e. when they produce young. At that stage, they can be transferred into the herd, subject to the accounting rules set out above (see "Practicalities for the accounts").

B22.1.5 Share farming

Share farming is a useful part of today's farming scene. It permits persons who have differing farming interests to join together in a single farming activity. Typically, there will be a "landlord" holding the fixed assets and a "working farmer" to carry out the practical activities. They agree at the outset fixed proportions of costs and income applicable to each person.

The legislation allows that a farmer who has only a share in a herd may elect for the herd basis provisions as if that share were for whole animals. That means that each share farmer can decide separately whether he wishes to elect for the herd basis to apply to his proportion of the breeding animals. The procedures and calculations are the same as for an individual farmer, but the relevant apportionment is applied. Thus, for a farmer with a 70% share in a dairy herd where circumstances dictate that he should use a deemed cost basis: he first establishes the market value of the animal in question; he takes 60% of that for the deemed cost; and, finally, he applies 70% to represent his ownership.

B22.1.6 The election

An election to apply the herd basis has to be made – it is not automatically available. There is a time limit for making the election and, once that deadline has been missed, there is no opportunity to opt for the herd basis unless circumstances change appropriately (see below).

The election must be made on or before the first anniversary of the filing date for the relevant tax year, i.e. for individuals the 31 January two years after the end of that tax year. The relevant tax year is the one in which falls the first period of account when the farmer kept a production herd of the class relevant to the election.

For corporation tax purposes, the election must be made within two years of the end of the first accounting period in which the company kept a herd of the class to which the election relates.

For the purposes of the herd basis election, each farming entity is a separate one. Therefore, if a sole trader who was out of time for making the election merged his business into a partnership, or incorporated it, a fresh period for election commences for the new trading entity.

The time limit is extended by 12 months where a new farming business has been established by a sole trader, as opposed to merely being the first time that the particular species of animal was established as part of the trade. The same facility is not available to partnerships. However, every time there is a change in the partnership members, a new election opportunity becomes available.

In view of a herd basis election being irrevocable, pausing to check the long-term plans of the farmer, as well as long-term price trends, could be useful – provided the deadline is not then missed inadvertently.

The format of an election is not set out in the legislation and there is no special form available. A separate letter, or a clear note in computations or on a tax return, should all suffice. It must specify the class of production herd. Consequently, if both a dairy herd and a suckler herd are to be elected, each must be separately made. Similarly, if one class of herd later changes to a different one (e.g. dairy to suckler herd), using the same animals rather than by selling one herd and buying in another, an election on the first herd no longer applies, and a fresh election opportunity arises for the new type of herd.

B22.1.7 Compulsory slaughter

A farmer has a fresh right to elect for the herd basis to apply to a particular class of animals, if the whole or a substantial part of that same production herd is slaughtered under a disease control order and he also receives compensation for the slaughter.

The time limit given in those circumstances is as if the event causing the slaughter took place in the "relevant tax year" as set out above. Thus, for individuals it would be the 31 January two years after the end of the tax year reporting the accounts in which the slaughter took place.

The election then has effect for so long as the farmer keeps a production herd of that class, as with an election made in normal circumstances.

B22.2 REFERENCES

Statutory references

ITTOIA 2005, ss 111 onwards, 124(2)(a), (3), 126, 127, 175(3)

Leading cases

None

HMRC manuals

BIM55410, BIM55500 onwards

B23

Hire purchase

B23.1 COMMENT

Payments made for an asset acquired under a hire purchase agreement are capital amounts and are not allowable revenue deductions, except for the finance element which is deductible as an expense of the business when charged to the profit and loss account. The treatment of hire purchase assets applies equally to unincorporated businesses and companies. The key characteristic of hire purchase finance is that typically the agreement provides an option to purchase the asset outright at the end of the hire period, usually for a nominal sum, so that the hirer would be expected to make the payment at the end of the contract to take legal ownership of the asset.

Tax deductions for a hire purchase asset comprise:

- capital allowances based on the capital element of the hire charge; and
- finance costs charged as an expense account in accordance with generally accepted accounting policies.

The permanent disallowance of 15% for leased car rentals with CO_2 emissions above 130g/km does *not* apply to hire purchase cars if the option price is more than 1% of the retail price when new (see **B4**).

B23.1.1 Capital allowances

Capital allowances may be claimed on the whole capital cost of plant acquired under a hire purchase arrangement, subject to the following:

- The time when the expenditure is incurred is the point at which the asset is brought into use, and not (if earlier) the date of entering into an unconditional contract for the hire purchase finance.
- Where the hirer is no longer entitled to the contract and does not become the owner of the asset, the plant is treated as disposed of. The disposal value recognised will be the sale proceeds plus the outstanding capital expenditure under the terms of the hire purchase agreement.

- Where the asset is used for a qualifying leasing business, additions for capital allowances purposes are restricted to the actual capital payments made under the hire purchase agreement during a chargeable period; that is, the entire cost of the asset is not brought into account at the date the asset is first brought into use.

B23.1.2 Accounting for hire purchase assets

The economic substance and accounting treatment of an asset under a hire purchase agreement and a finance lease may be identical, although the legal form and tax treatment of each type of finance are distinct. Under a hire purchase agreement, the legal ownership of the asset remains with the finance provider for the duration of the agreement but passes on the payment of option by the hirer; whereas, under a lease arrangement, the lessor retains ownership throughout (see **B29**).

The hire charges of both hire purchase and leased assets are treated as a finance expense but may be described as interest in the accounts.

For accounting purposes, a hire purchase asset is usually capitalised as a fixed asset, with a corresponding liability recognised for the hire purchase finance obligations. The cost of the asset is written off through depreciation charges.

B23.1.3 Cash basis

Where a trader uses the cash basis, deductions of interest costs and incidental costs of obtaining loan finance are limited to £500 p.a. This restriction does not apply to hire purchase expenses where the cash basis permits a deduction for the full hire cost in respect of depreciating assets, e.g. plant and equipment. Traders and property businesses using the cash basis should be able to obtain relief for expenditure on qualifying assets when payments are made. However, cars on hire purchase arrangements remain in the capital allowances regime and the element relating to the finance charge is deductible over the period of the agreement, when paid (see **Chapters 2** and **5**).

B23.2 REFERENCES

Statutory references

CAA 2001, ss 1A, 67, 229

ITTIOA 2005, ss 33A, 48–50B, 57B, 3017B

Leading cases

Darngavil Coal Co Ltd v Francis (1913) 7 TC 1

HMRC manuals

BIM45350–BIM45365, BIM70040, BIM70035

See also

B4, **B29**

B24

Incidental costs of obtaining loan finance

B24.1 COMMENT

Under general principles, the costs associated with raising long-term borrowing or permanent capital is disallowed as capital expenditure, but relief is available for specific categories of costs where these are incidental to obtaining loan finance.

Financing costs connected with raising short-term finance, such as bank overdrafts, lease or hire purchase finance and debt factoring costs, may be allowable under general principles and do not fall within the specific relief.

Incidental expenses are allowed if the interest on the loan is deductible for the business, and relief is available whether or not the business is successful in obtaining the loan.

The following categories of incidental costs are allowable for traders and property businesses (*ITTOIA 2005, s 58*):

- fees, commissions, advertising and printing and other incidental matters; and
- expenses incurred for obtaining finance, providing security, or repaying it.

If costs of raising finance have been capitalised, relief is available when costs are charged to the profit and loss account over the period of the loan, if this complies with accounting principles (BIM45801).

For businesses that use the cash basis see **B24.1.3**.

B24.1.1 Allowable incidental costs

The following types of expenses are allowable as incidental expenses:

- legal, brokerage, introduction fees and similar professional costs for negotiating the loan and preparing legal documentation;

- valuation, search and Land Registry fees associated with security for the loan;
- guarantee fees;
- costs of varying or extending the terms of an existing loan; and
- costs of arranging life insurance cover (but not the premiums).

The First Tier Tribunal decision *Ayeni [2016] TC05329* considered the deductibility of life insurance premiums and held on the facts that a proportion of these costs were deductible as incidental expenses on the ground that these were incurred as a pre-condition to secure funding.

B24.1.2 Excluded costs

The following are not allowable:

- foreign exchange losses;
- fees for hedging or protecting against foreign exchange losses;
- repayment of a loan at a premium;
- additional cost of repaying a loan issued at a discount;
- stamp duty; and
- costs relating to loans convertible into equity.

When the terms of the loan carry a right for the borrower to convert into shares or "other securities" and the right is exercised within three years from the date the loan was made, relief is not available for the incidental costs of the original loan (*ITTOIA 2005, s 59*).

At first glance, this limitation on relief is not relevant to an unincorporated business where there is no legal framework to issue share capital. However, the restriction might apply in circumstances if debt is novated on an incorporation of a business and the company subsequently converts the debt to share capital.

The purpose of the restriction is to prevent the relief from being used to issue equity by first issuing convertible stock (BIM45810). The term "other securities" excludes loan stock where interest is deductible in computing profits of a trade. This would not seem to restrict incidental costs of a loan that was subsequently converted to something other than a security (such as a capital contribution in a partnership or a member's interest in an LLP), but this interpretation of the legislation has not been tested in the courts and is not entirely free from doubt.

Whether or not a payment made by the borrower as compensation for early termination of a loan can be treated as an incidental cost of obtaining loan finance will depend on the terms of the loan agreement. A premium on the repayment of a loan is not an allowable incidental cost. Often the distinction between a break payment and a premium is not clear. HMRC have provided some guidance on the characteristics at BIM45820 (based on the Special Commissioner's decision in *Kato Kagaku Co Ltd v HMRC [2007] SpC 598, [2007] SSCD 412*).

B24.1.3 Allowable incidental costs – cash basis

For traders using the cash basis, relief for the combined costs of interest and incidental costs of loan finance is capped at £500 p.a. (**B31**).

For property businesses using the cash basis a deduction for "costs in relation to a loan" include incidental finance expenditure and may be restricted if the overall loans exceed the initial market value of the properties. Where costs relate to a "dwelling related loan" for a residential property business (other than a furnished holiday letting activity) relief will be restricted to the basic rate of income tax in line with the adjustment required for interest (**B31**).

B24.2 REFERENCES

Statutory references

ITTOIA 2005, ss 57B, 58, 59, 272ZA, 307C

Leading cases

Kato Kagaku Co Ltd v HMRC [2007] SpC 598, [2007] SSCD 412

Ayeni [2016] TC 05329

HMRC manuals

BIM45800, BIM45801, BIM45810, BIM45815, BIM45820, PIM2105

See also

B17, **B25**, **B31**

B25

Insurance

B25.1 COMMENT

The nature of the insurance payment must be analysed before deciding whether or not the expense is deductible in calculating trade profits. Such payments can be grouped into main categories as follows:

- keyman insurance (see **B27**);
- fee protection; and
- other insurances.

B25.1.1 Fee protection

This type of cover is now commonly taken out by accountancy firms in one of the various forms offered by specialised insurance companies. It is also provided by different organisations to businesses and individuals, usually under the umbrella of a larger, main-purpose type of cover.

Where the cover is provided by accountancy firms, a fee is then charged to the client. The decision on the cover option chosen by the firm has significant effects in that the broad options are:

- to provide a service to the client, whereby the firm is the insured entity and it provides a "service" out to its clients, which means that VAT is applicable at its current rate; or
- the firm provides insurance to its clients which means that insurance protection tax (IPT) is applicable (at 12% from 1 June 2017 and at writing of this chapter) but no VAT. Within this category the firm is either regulated by the Financial Conduct Authority (FCA, formerly FSA) or it has a designated professional body (DPB) licence to offer insurance, with the client being the insured entity.

Whichever of the above two routes is taken by the accountancy firm, when preparing business accounts it will find that the client has tucked away the cost somewhere in its trading expenses. The client probably assumes that it will be an allowable expense, especially if he has not been the target of an HMRC "check" during the relevant period. What is the accepted position?

When this type of insurance was first available on the market, the accepted principle was that, provided no HMRC enquiry had found anything amiss, the cost would be deductible. That was on the basis that the insurance had not been found to cover anything which was contrary to tax law. The cost would be disallowed if anything untoward had been found in an enquiry.

In more recent times, this has been reviewed by HMRC. Their view is now generally implemented by accountants (even if without total conviction as to the validity of HMRC's contention).

The argument is that the cost is not allowable in any circumstances, on the basis that it is cover taken out, at least in part, to guard against any action by the taxpayer that might result in an adjustment to their self-assessment tax return. The implication is that such adjustment would have resulted from an action by the taxpayer that was contrary to the law. HMRC contend that, in consequence, there is duality of purpose between the correct and the incorrect. Furthermore, although an enquiry might have resulted in no adjustment at all, it is impossible to apportion costs when the position is hypothetical. HMRC's stance is set out at BIM46452 and in Tax Bulletin 65 June 2003 (*IRInt 247*).

Note that this conclusion relates to the cost of fee protection cover. Accountancy fees incurred where an enquiry is involved are based upon the outcome of that enquiry (or business check). Thus, accountancy fees are allowed where no adjustment to the tax return results. They are not allowable if adjustments are found necessary.

Whilst VAT topics are outside the scope of this publication, brief reference to VAT in the context of fee protection cover is appropriate here. Of the two broad options open to accountants offering this type of cover to their clients, referred to at the outset of this section, one type is effectively a service to clients. That results from the accountancy firm being the insured entity (the classic group policy, where all clients are covered irrespective of whether they pay to take out "cover"). In that case, VAT must be charged by the accountancy firm. Although the cost of the cover itself is not allowable to the client business, for the above reasons, the input VAT is reclaimable. That is because, within VAT legislation, a business service offered by the accountants is a valid cost leading to a valid reclaim of the VAT charged.

B25.1.2 Other (allowable)

The costs of general insurances which are clearly of a business nature are allowable under first principles of business deductions. These include:

- Premiums on policies providing indemnity cover for current assets, such as trading stock or trade debts owed to the business.
- Use of home as office. HMRC accept that, where the business operates from the taxpayer's home and the trade use is covered by a separate policy, that cost is allowed in full, with no part of the household policy being deductible. Otherwise, an appropriate part of the household premium can be allowed.
- Loss of profits.
- Employee indemnity. HMRC accept that premiums on a policy paid by the employer to indemnify employees against legal action taken against them personally relating to actions in the course of the employment are allowable as a deduction in computing the employer's trading profits. HRMC refer to their key principles that the payments are not capital expenditure, and they are incurred wholly and exclusively for the purposes of the trade. Note that the cost of the premiums paid by the employer in those circumstances is not a taxable benefit on the employee.

  Furthermore, *F(No 2)A 2017* introduced clauses into *ITEPA 2003, s 558* to widen the deduction available to an employee against his earnings where he incurs expenses in connection with employment related proceedings, even where there is no allegation against him personally. A typical example would be where the employee has been called as a witness. The position regarding the employer's costs where the employee is reimbursed remains that they are allowable as a deduction against profits.
- Locum and fixed practice expenses policies. By contrast with permanent health insurance policies (see below), the premiums on certain sickness insurance policies are allowable deductions. These insurance policies indemnify the policyholder against business costs, such as payments to a locum temporarily to carry out the policyholder's professional activities, or the cost of other fixed overheads, in the event of the policyholder's incapacity to carry on the business during a period of illness. Policies of this type are held mainly by medical professionals such as doctors and dentists who practise alone or in partnership. The premium costs are specifically allowed as business deductions. Note that these special circumstances do not extend to other business proprietors generally, however indispensable the owner might seem to be. HMRC's view is set out at BIM45565.

Insurance receipts

The corollary, when an insurance policy pays out on the occurrence of a relevant event, must be accepted. The monies received from the insurers are treated as trading receipts. That the full amount of insurance proceeds received should be treated as a trading receipt, even where part of the proceeds were not expended, was set out in the 1929 *Glikstén* case in the House of Lords. There, a fire destroyed the company's trading stock of timber, and the insurers duly compensated for the loss incurred. However, because the current demand was for timber of a different nature, the company spent on replacement timbers only about 25% of the total received from the insurers. The company attempted to include only the same amount as a taxable trading receipt. Ultimately, it failed in the highest court, although it had met with some success along the way.

Thus, if the sum is of a revenue nature, it will be brought into account on ordinary principles. However, if the insurers' pay-out is in relation to a capital sum, the receipt remains taxable as a trading receipt by virtue of a specific statutory provision, but only to the extent that any deduction was allowed (*ITTOIA 2005, s 106*).

Health and employment insurance payments paid out by insurers are exempted from being taxable income by *ITTOIA 2005, s 735*. There are conditions to be met for this to apply. Particularly:

- the payment is a benefit provided under so much of the policy as insures against a health or employment risk, and
- no part of any premiums under the policy has been deductible in calculating the income of the insured for income tax purposes.

B25.1.3 Other (disallowable)

- Premiums paid by a sole trader or partner to provide life, accident or sickness insurance cover for himself or a partner are not allowable deductions in computing trading profits. These are primarily the ones known as permanent health insurance policies. Similarly, the benefits payable under such policies are not trading income.
- Life cover and endowment policy premiums for a policy taken out by a sole trader or partner to cover borrowings are not allowable as deductions, even where the policy is insisted upon by the lender. Again, it fails on the duality of purpose argument. The cost of the premiums is not an incidental cost of the financing. In contrast, the costs of taking out such policies are allowable as being incidental to a business loan (provided it meets the requirements of revenue not capital). This position is confirmed by HMRC at BIM45815.

Seemingly at odds with this position, in *Ayeni [2016] TC 05329* the FTT did permit as a deduction the cost of premiums during two relevant years, where the life assurance policies were necessarily incurred to obtain bank finance for Mr Ayeni's business, an accountancy practice. The Tribunal concluded that the premiums were allowable as incidental costs of obtaining finance under *ITTOIA 2005, s 58*.

See **B27** for guidance on specialised keyman insurance policies.

See **B24** for further detail on incidental costs of obtaining loan finance.

B25.2 REFERENCES

Statutory references

ITTOIA 2005, ss 34, 58, 106, 735

Leading cases

Green (HM Inspector of Taxes) v J Gliksten & Son Limited (1929) 14 TC 364

Ayeni [2016] TC 05329

HMRC manuals

BIM42051, BIM46452, BIM37965, BIM46450, BIM45500, BIM45505, BIM45565, BIM47820, BIM45815

IRInt 247

B26

Interest on overdue tax and penalties

B26.1 COMMENT

B26.1.1 Main provisions

The basic position for interest, surcharges and penalties on overdue tax is that such a cost is not allowable as a deduction in computing the profits of a business. There is a specific exception connected with corporation tax (see below).

TMA 1970, s 86 provides for interest to be charged where payment of tax is delayed. However, the process of harmonising the penalty and interest regime across taxes continues, as heralded by *Finance Act 2009*, but has not yet been concluded.

As a consequence, the different regimes have their own statutes which determine that interest on overdue tax will not be allowed as a deduction. Thus, *ITEPA 2003* (see below) states that not only is interest on overdue PAYE disallowed as a deduction, but there is also a specific disallowance of interest paid by employers in respect of:

- late payments of tax under the construction industry deduction scheme;
- National Insurance contributions; and
- student loan repayments.

ITTOIA 2005, s 54 sets out a useful table that expressly disallows the listed interest and penalties. Effectively, there are none, including VAT surcharges, that can be deducted in calculating the profits of a trade subject to income tax. At time of writing this chapter, the latest update to *s 54*, relating to *sub-s (2)*, was inserted by *F(No 2)A 2017*.

Interest charged can be mitigated where an assessment in respect of which interest had been paid is subsequently reduced or discharged because of reliefs due to the taxpayer. Typically, this would happen where a tax return is amended. The interest previously charged is then waived or repaid as appropriate. An overpayment can only be set against an underpayment of the same tax. Nevertheless, that is not permitting the interest to be a deduction against profits.

Following the same principle, interest will be charged where an amended return indicates additional tax should have been paid and as a consequence of the amendment it was paid late. HMRC say, at SAM112030, that any repayment supplement which was found to have been over paid as a result of the amendment is lost and will not be recovered.

Note that there is no jurisdiction for section 86 interest to be waived where it has been validly charged. This was found in *Gratton v HMRC [2012] BTC 1656* when Herrington J concluded that: "There is no discretion on the part of the First-tier Tribunal to determine that interest should not be payable". The later case of *Catal [2016] TC 05080* came to the same conclusion. This perhaps heightens the importance of the non-deductibility of such interest.

There is some relief for trusts where trust management expenses (TMEs) are concerned. In narrow circumstances, where it can be shown that paying the interest charge on an overdue income tax liability under *TMA 1970, s 86* was in the best interests of the beneficiaries, it can be included as a TME. Penalties and interest thereon are not permitted as TMEs.

For those keen to find an overview of HMRC's current position on interest and penalty charges generally, CH140100 is extremely helpful, providing a comprehensive listing and including links to other key legislation.

B26.1.2 Interest on late paid corporation tax

For company accounting periods ending on or after 1 July 1999, interest on overdue corporation tax chargeable under *TMA 1970, s 87A* is deductible. It is treated as such within the non-trading loan relationship rules. The timing of the deduction follows the accounting treatment, provided that the accounts are prepared in accordance with GAAP.

Similarly, interest on late and inadequate instalment payments of corporation tax is also a deductible expense under the loan relationship rules. This type of interest is charged at a lower rate than that on late paid "normal" corporation tax, being known as debit interest.

The balancing provision to the deductibility of interest on late paid corporation tax is, of course, that any credit interest paid by HMRC on overpaid, or paid early, corporation tax is taxable. Again, it is charged within the non-trading loan relationship rules.

B26.2 REFERENCES

Statutory references

TMA 1970, ss 86, 87A

ITEPA 2003, s 684(4)

ITTOIA 2005, s 54

CTA 2009, s 1301

Leading cases

Gratton v HMRC [2012] BTC 1656

Catal [2016] TC 05080

HMRC manuals

BIM42520, BIM45740

CH140100

CTM92190

TSEM8735

SAM112030

B27

Keyman insurance

B27.1 COMMENT

A business owner will often take out a policy insuring against loss of profits resulting from the death, critical illness, sickness, accident or injury of an employee, director or other "key person". The costs of these policies should be deductible, provided the sole purpose of taking out the insurance is a trade purpose without a personal motivation.

Thus, the thrust of the policy should be to meet a loss of trading income that may result from loss of the services of the key person. This includes the cost of replacing the key person so that a reduction in trading income does not arise.

Such loss should not be a capital loss if the premium is to qualify as a revenue deduction. The latter circumstance is more likely to arise in a corporate situation where the policy targets protection of the shareholding, such as by enabling the acquisition of shares by a surviving shareholder. HMRC consider that it can also arise for premiums on whole life or endowment policies, or critical illness or accident policies with an investment content. The effect would be that the premiums were contributing to a capital investment and were thereby not deductible.

As regards life assurance of employees and directors, premiums are deductible provided:

- the insurance is term insurance only;
- the policy provides cover only against the risk that one or more of the lives insured dies within the term of the policy;
- the policy has no other benefits; and
- the term does not extend beyond the period of the employee's usefulness to the company.

Where a sole trader or partner is the target for the policy, the cost would not be allowable as a business deduction, whether for critical illness or life. See **B25**.

HMRC also perceive that a non-trade purpose can arise for a company funding a policy where it benefits a controlling director or shareholder. In such instances, the potential for direct loss to the company's trade if the director is unavailable to carry out his normal duties should be demonstrable if deductibility is sought. The decision in *Beauty Consultants Ltd v Inspector of Taxes [2002] SpC 321* upheld HMRC's non-trade argument in respect of policies paid through the business. Although a company rather than an unincorporated business is at the centre of the case, the issues would be similarly treated for partnerships or sole traders.

B27.1.1 Key person policy associated with loan finance

Endowment policies on the life of a key person may be taken out as a condition of the provision of long-term finance. As has been covered in **B25**, the cost of the premiums is not allowable where it relates to the lives of sole traders and partners.

In the case of companies, the incidental costs of loan finance are covered by the loan relationships rules. However, the net effect in HMRC's view – which is generally accepted – is that premiums paid on endowment policies are not deductible by the company as they are not considered to be incidental costs of obtaining loan finance.

Criteria for qualification as incidental costs are particularly set out at *ITTOIA 2005, ss 57 and 58,* with a monetary amount of £500 to be met for cash basis users, identified at *s 57B(3)*.

An alternative position from disallowance in the company's profits is where the policy clearly provides a benefit direct to the employee or director. In that case, it would be treated as a taxable benefit in kind on the director, but allowable as a deduction from the company's profits.

B27.1.2 Keyman policy receipts

As also set out in **B25**, the receipt of policy proceeds is expected to follow that of the cost of the premiums. Thus, where the premiums have been allowed as trading deductions, so would a pay-out be a trading receipt.

However, HMRC consider that the converse is not always the position, i.e. that where the cost of premiums has been disallowed, the proceeds from the policy could be a trading receipt. This is on the basis that the treatment of receipts is a separate matter of law from the deductibility of expenditure. The circumstances quoted by HMRC are largely those where receipts have been claimed as unsolicited and are therefore not a part of trading income. The circumstances where HMRC might consider policy receipts should be taxable where the premiums were not deductible could be where they were disallowed as being of a capital nature, e.g. paid to enable the company or a surviving shareholder to acquire the shares of a stricken shareholder. However, the proceeds instead might be used by the company direct for its own trade and working capital.

The case of *Greycon Ltd v Klaentschi* was decided as a capital case in respect of policy pay-out, although there were complex circumstances and it should not be taken as a precedent. The policies had been taken out as part of an agreement with an investor, indeed as a condition of it. Accordingly, the purpose of taking out the policy was not to protect profits but to enable capital investment.

B27.2 REFERENCES

Statutory references

ITTOIA 2005, ss 34, 57, 58, 106

Leading cases

Greycon Ltd v Klaentschi (HMIT) [2003] SpC 372

Beauty Consultants Ltd v Inspector of Taxes [2002] SpC 321

HMRC manuals

BIM45525, BIM45530, BIM40751

B28

Lease premiums

B28.1 COMMENT

The treatment as to whether or not the payment of a premium to a landlord by a trader is deductible in calculating his profits differs depending on a number of factors. In particular, no trading deduction at all is allowed in respect of a payment which the tenant is required to make to the landlord for assets qualifying for capital allowances (a rare occurrence).

B28.1.1 Granting of a short lease

Where the period of the lease is for 50 years or less, it is treated as a short lease. In those circumstances, where a premium is charged in addition to the rent, a proportion is taxed on the landlord as rental income. Special provisions attach to the calculation (see below).

The tenant may then obtain a form of tax relief for the payment of the premium, even though it would on normal principles be treated as a capital payment. For this tax relief to be due to the tenant, it is a requirement that the landlord must first be liable for an income tax charge on the same payment. However, the relief is not denied to the tenant if the landlord has not paid tax on the premium simply because other tax relief was available to him.

Note: It is not usually expected that a tenant should enquire into his landlord's tax position. It is more that, assuming there is no connection between landlord and tenant that might lead to a tax avoidance situation, there is nothing in the lease agreement that could lead the tenant to any conclusion other than the landlord would be subject to notional rental income based upon the premium that the trading tenant paid.

The requirement for the landlord to be taxed on the receipt of the premium can be met by a corporate landlord just as by an individual landlord; in other words, being subject to corporation tax rather than to income tax does not alter the position of the tenant.

The calculation of the amount of the lease premium which gives rise to the additional notional rent is set out by formula. It is based on the principle that it accrues on a daily basis over the entire period of the lease. Furthermore, to be entitled to the deduction from his profits, the person claiming it must occupy the land for the purposes of his business. The same person must also hold the entitlement to the lease during the period for which he claims the trading deduction.

B28.1.2 Calculating the notional rent

Stage (1): The amount of the lease premium on which the landlord will be taxed as an income receipt in his rental business must first be calculated. The rule is that the amount of the premium taxable as income is found by reducing the premium by 2% of the cost of the premium for each complete year of the lease after the first. Thus:

- a 25-year lease is granted
- the premium paid is £130,000
- the reduction to £130,000 to arrive at deemed rent is (2% × (25 – 1) × £130,000) = £62,400
- notional rent is (£130,000 – £62,400) = £67,600.

Stage (2): The above notional rent is converted into the relevant deductible charge for the tenant according to the length of his relevant trading accounting period. Thus:

- annual deduction = £67,600/25 (i.e. tenant's full trading lease period) = £2,704 per annual accounting period.
- if the relevant trading period is less than a year (perhaps because the start of the trade creates a shorter accounting period), the £2,704 would be reduced proportionately.

Note that HMRC examples calculate on a daily basis rather an annual one (see BIM46255). This is not normally a material consideration, but HMRC's version is considered to be technically correct.

B28.1.3 Further apportionment of notional rent as a deduction

If only part of the premises subject to the lease premium is occupied or used for trade purposes, the amount of the deductible trading expense is reduced according to the proportion of the land so occupied or used, calculated on a just and reasonable basis.

B28.1.4 Tenants with a property business

Where the property subject to the lease premium is used for the purpose of a property business by the direct tenant, but without it being occupied by him for a trade (i.e. he sub-lets it), it is treated as if he did occupy it for the allowable purpose. He is therefore entitled to a deduction. Consequently, the end user of the property is not entitled to a deduction in his own trade.

B28.1.5 Special circumstances

- Where a trading deduction has been available for part of a premium paid on a lease, the deduction continues to be available where, during any part of the receipt period, the trader stops using the land for the purposes of his trade but particular circumstances such as those in *Hyett v Lennard* apply. There, the direct tenant commenced using the premises for his trade. Two years later, his losses were such that he ceased his trade. Thereafter he sub-let the premises, albeit at a lower rent than he himself was paying. It was held that the rent he paid could be deducted from the rent he received, despite his not continuing to occupy the premises himself.
- Allied to the above case (and quoted in reaching the decision in *Hyett*) is that of *IR Commrs v Falkirk Iron Co Ltd*. There, the company took a lease of a warehouse which turned out to be larger than was required. Parts of it were sub-let and the remainder was unoccupied for two years. The difference between the rent paid and the rents obtained from sub-letting was held to be deductible. The deduction for the rent paid out on the premises, reduced by the rents received, was allowed on the basis that allowable business expenditure had been expended for the purpose of trading profitably.
- Whilst the detail is outside the scope of this publication, where a tenant operates a property letting business and in turn becomes a landlord because he duly sub-lets onwards, charging a lease premium to his own new tenant, calculation rules apply to ensure that there is no double counting of the tax relief (see further PIM2320).

B28.1.6 Long leases

Where the period of a lease entered into by a tenant exceeds 50 years, no deduction against his annual profits is available. The expenditure is one of a capital nature. As such, it would come within the relevant capital gains tax regime.

B28.1.7 Cash basis

From 2013–14 a person who is, or has been, carrying on a trade may elect for the profits to be calculated on the cash basis rather than in accordance with

GAAP, provided he meets the relevant criteria. (See **Chapter 2** for detail on the "cash basis").

Under the cash basis rules, certain deductions against trading income determined under GAAP are not allowable. One of those is the deduction in respect of notional annual rent detailed in this section. Accordingly, the provisions outlined above have no relevance to the calculations of profits for an individual for whom the cash basis is currently operative.

B28.2 REFERENCES

Statutory references

ITTOIA 2005, ss 61, 63, 277, 296

Leading cases

CIR v Falkirk Iron Co Ltd (1933) 17 TC 625

Hyett v Lennard (1940) 23 TC 346

HMRC manuals

BIM46255

PIM1205, PIM2320

B29

Lease rental payments

B29.1 COMMENT

When an asset is leased for the purposes of a trade or business, the expenses are deductible as charged to the profit and loss account, in accordance with generally accepted accounting practice. The principles for the deductibility of leases apply equally to unincorporated traders or businesses and companies.

Special tax rules are applicable for lump-sum lease premiums for property leases and this is covered in **B28**.

For traders and property businesses that operate on the cash basis, a deduction may be available for lease expenditure as incurred but this depends on the legal form of the transaction. Short-term hire costs where no ownership of the asset is transferred will be deductible when paid. Payments for hire purchase assets are covered at **B23**. Further details on the classes of fixed and intangible assets that are eligible as deductible capital expenditure under the cash basis can be found at **Chapters 2** and **5**.

Lease hire expenses for cars are subject to a flat rate disallowance of 15% where CO_2 emissions exceed 110g/km (see **B4**).

B29.1.1 Legal form and accounting treatment

There are broadly two types of lease:

- *Operating lease:* Rentals are charged to the profit and loss account as incurred. These leases are often short-term arrangements (less than five years) and typically the lessor retains responsibility for service and maintenance of the asset.
- *Finance lease:* The economic substance of a finance lease is similar to that of the purchase of an asset by way of loan finance. The accounting treatment under Section 20 of FRS 102 prescribes that the lease is capitalised as a fixed asset, with a corresponding recognition of the liabilities during the lease period.

The accounting distinction between an operating and a finance lease is described as follows: "A lease is classified as a finance lease if it transfers substantially all the risks and rewards incidental to ownership. A lease is classified as an operating lease if it does not transfer substantially all the risks and rewards incidental to ownership" (paragraph 20.4 of FRS 102).

If a business uses international accounting standards new accounting rules apply from 1 January 2019 under IFRS 16 which adopts a single lessee accounting model to determine whether a lease should be recognised on the balance sheet. If IFRS 16 is used by an unincorporated business then operating lease assets will be accounted for in a similar way to finance lease assets (unless the lease term is less than 12 months or the asset value is immaterial). For tax purposes the timing of deductions would then correspond to the rules for finance leases.

B29.1.2 Finance leases

The distinction between a finance lease and a hire purchase is often not clear from the accounts, and the agreement for the hire arrangements should be reviewed to establish the exact legal form (tax relief for hire purchase assets is given through the capital allowances system – see **B23**).

A deduction for finance lease assets comprises depreciation and finance costs (less rental rebates). The statutory disallowance for depreciation does not apply to lease assets. The accounting classification of lease rentals as "depreciation" represents a write-off of hire charges. The charge to profit and loss determines the timing of the deduction (rather than when payments are made under the terms of the lease).

B29.1.3 Long-funding leases

The general rule for leased assets is that the lessee is not entitled to claim capital allowances, as the legal ownership of the asset is retained by lessor. An exception to this is where the lease falls within the definition of a "long-funding" lease, in which case the commercial substance (rather than the legal form) of the arrangement determines the tax treatment.

Legislation introduced in *Finance Act 2006* transfers claims for capital allowances from the lessor to the lessee where the economic substance of the lease is that of a loan (*CAA 2001, ss 70A–70YI*), subject to the statutory tests being satisfied.

It is particularly important to establish which party has entitlement to capital allowances when leases are entered into between connected parties.

The provisions potentially apply to any size or type of lease transaction. The rules also apply to fixtures and may prohibit a claim for capital allowances by a landlord who provides "non-background" plant or machinery.

The effect of a long-funding lease is that:

- The lessor's expenditure will not qualify for capital allowances, and relief is given for providing the asset on hire through the accounting treatment as a net return on investment.
- For the lessee, a deduction is available for the finance expenses when charged to the profit and loss account, and capital allowances are available to relieve the capitalised part of the hire cost.

Long-funding lease – definitions

A "funding lease" is identified by one of the following characteristics:

- a finance lease for accounting purposes;
- where the present value of the minimum lease payments under the lease is equal to or greater than 80% of the fair value of asset; or
- the term of the lease covers more than 65% of the remaining useful economic life of the asset.

A funding lease will *not* be a long-funding lease if it is a "short" lease, which is broadly defined as:

- a lease of no more than five years; or
- a lease between five and seven years and all of the following apply:
  - it is treated under GAAP as a finance lease;
  - the residual value of the finance lease is less than or equal to 5% of the market value of the plant at the commencement of the lease term; and
  - rentals are not fluctuating within certain defined limits.

Finance leases entered into after 11 March 2008 under a sale and leaseback transaction are treated as long-funding leases (regardless of the lease term), so that the lessee retains entitlement to capital allowances.

The term of the lease includes any period for which the lessee has an option to continue to lease the asset if, at the inception of the lease, it is reasonably certain that the lessee will exercise that option. There are anti-avoidance provisions to prevent the creation of artificial short leases between connected persons.

By applying the above criteria, it is possible that valid accounting treatment applied by both the lessor and lessee may result in both parties having an entitlement to claim capital allowances. If so, the lessor has priority and the lessee will claim a deduction for rentals.

"Background" plant or machinery leased as part of a building does not fall within the long-funding lease rules, and entitlement to capital allowances claims remains with the landlord.

Background plant is not restricted to fixtures and fittings, and includes plant of a type that might reasonably be expected to be installed in a particular type of building, if the sole or main purpose is to contribute to making the building usable as an environment for the tenant (*SI 2007/303, arts 2, 4*).

"Non-background" plant and machinery provided by the landlord under a lease for a period of five years or more will be within the long-funding lease rules, and the tenant has entitlement to claim the capital allowances on these items – subject to certain de minimis rules.

Long-funding lease rules do not apply to non-background plant that is "low value", falling within the following limits:

- less than 10% of the overall background plant leased with the land; and
- less than 5% of the market value of the land including buildings, fixtures and fittings.

B29.1.4 Anti-avoidance

There are a number of complex anti-avoidance rules to counter tax advantages on lease transactions targeted at the timing of deductions for lease and leaseback transaction, and a brief summary follows.

Sale and leaseback: Anti-avoidance measures designed to restrict the amount or timing of deductions for expenditure incurred by a lessee on a sale and finance leaseback transaction have generally been superseded by the long-funding lease rules. This is because all leaseback arrangements (including short leases of five years or less) are treated as long-funding leases. Consequently, the lessee will retain entitlement to claim capital allowances as the previous owner of the asset (*CAA 2001, ss 221, 228A–228J*).

If the parties to a sale and leaseback jointly elect to disapply the long-funding lease rules, the lessee is restricted to relief for a "permitted maximum" deduction, being the finance charge in the accounts and the amount of any depreciation that would have been charged.

Leased trading assets: Deductions for lease expenses on assets that have previously been used for a trade are restricted if the amounts exceed a commercial rental. Where necessary, the timing of the deduction is adjusted to comply with generally accepted accounting practice. This provision does not apply to long-funding lease assets (*ITA 2007, ss 681D–681DP*; *CTA 2010, Part 19, Chapter 4*).

Disposal of lease for a capital sum: Where a trader has obtained relief for lease rentals in the early years of a lease and then disposes of his interest for a capital sum, the previous deductions may be clawed back in the tax year of the receipt. This provision does not apply to long-funding lease assets (*ITA 2007, ss 681C–681CG*; *CTA 2010, Part 19, Chapter 3*).

B29.2 REFERENCES

Statutory references

CAA 2001, ss 70A–70YI, 221, 228A–228J

ITTOIA 2005, ss 25, 48, 148A, 148G–148I

ITA 2007, ss 681C–681CG, 681D–681DP

CTA 2009, ss 46, 56, 377–379

CTA 2010, ss 377–379, Part 19, Chapters 3, 4

Capital Allowances (Leases of Background Plant or Machinery for a Building) Order 2007 (SI 2007/303), arts 2, 4

Leading cases

None

HMRC manuals

BIM61200

BLM10000–BLM00001, BLM20000, BLM30000, BLM40000, BLM60000

See also

Chapters 2, 5, B4, B23, B28

Statement of Practice 3/91 – Finance lease rental payments

FRS 102, Section 20

IFRS 16

HMRC summary of discussion document responses and consultation, 1 December 2017 – “Leasing: Tax response to accounting changes”

B30

Legal and professional costs

B30.1 COMMENT

There is no comprehensive statutory rule governing the deductibility of legal and professional expenses. The underlying purpose of professional fees has been considered by a large body of case law, the principles of which may be applied to all types of business entities.

For unincorporated businesses, specific relief is available for professional fees for raising loan finance (see **B24**).

Where a trader opts to use the cash basis, capital expenditure and associated legal fees are not allowable, except where this relates to the purchase of an asset (other than a car) which would have been eligible for capital allowances.

Legal costs in dealing with trading disputes are allowable, and so costs associated with the recovery of trade debts or settlement of trade creditors are deductible expenses. Fees connected to the disposal of debtors and creditors on a sale of an entire business are not deductible, as the costs are not wholly and exclusively for the purposes of the ongoing trade where there is a cessation.

Legal costs in dealing with proceedings for defending illegal trading activities are not allowable, as this is a loss that is not connected with the trade (*CIR v EC Warnes & Co Ltd (1919) 12 TC 227*, *CIR v Alexander von Glehn & Co Ltd (1920) 12 TC 232*; see **B6**).

B30.1.1 Duality of purpose

Where there is a duality of purpose, all or part of the fees for professional advice may be disallowed. Legal fees in defending against a criminal prosecution arising from an accident involving a lorry operated by a trader were not allowable, as the expenditure was incurred to defend a charge of manslaughter against the individual (*Duckmanton v Revenue and Customs Commissioners [2011] UKFTT 664 (TC), [2012] SFTD 293*).

The reasons for seeking professional advice may be wholly and exclusively for the purposes of the trade or business, notwithstanding that the outcome of legal proceedings results in a payment of a fine or compensation that is disallowable. Legal fees incurred by a stockbroker on a disciplinary hearing were held to be allowable expenses, as the purpose of the action was to preserve the business (*McKnight v Sheppard (1996) 171 TC 419*, see also *Cattermole v Borax & Chemicals Ltd (1949) 31 TC 202*).

The legal costs of defending personal reputation are not allowable (*Knight v Parry (1972) 48 TC 580*). However, if the main purpose of pursuing or defending a claim is to protect the business, any incidental benefit for the business proprietor or director, who may also a plaintiff, will not necessarily taint the expenditure (*Key IP Ltd v Revenue and Customs Comrs [2011] UKFTT 715 (TC), [2012] SFTD 305*).

B30.1.2 Professional fees – capital

The following professional expenses are disallowable:

- Fees in connection with raising equity finance for a company, including the costs of incorporation or a purchase of own shares.
- Liquidator and other professional fees on a winding up.
- Purchase of share capital.
- Costs of loan finance for unincorporated businesses where the conditions for relief under incidental costs of raising loan finance are not satisfied.
- Altering the capital structure of a partnership, including a merger, change of partners or dissolution.
- Fees incurred by unincorporated businesses for pursuing non-trade debts or compensation of a capital nature.

Incidental legal and professional costs relating to the acquisition or disposal of fixed assets, including land and buildings and goodwill, are disallowed as capital (and part of the base cost on the eventual disposal of the asset when computing the capital gain).

For a property-trading or dealing business, legal and professional costs relating to land and buildings held as trading stock will be allowable trade expenses.

For unincorporated businesses, expenses in acquiring or removing the rights to a licence are disallowed, but the costs of licence renewal may be deductible.

Specific statutory relief is available for unincorporated businesses to allow expenses in registering, renewing or abandoning a patent, design or trade mark right (see **B34**).

Fees for the purchase of assets that qualify as plant and machinery are also capital in nature but may be eligible for capital allowances. Where legal and professional expenses are incurred on the acquisition of a business, a reasonable apportionment of costs between different categories of assets can be made so that a deduction is available where the expenditure is allocated to working capital.

The dividing line between capital and revenue expenditure may be unclear where fees are incurred to assess the viability of reorganising or expanding a business. The costs involved in appraising the potential to acquire a new business may be deductible if the advice includes the impact on the existing trade.

Costs for establishing and preserving rights over an asset of the business are revenue in nature. The fees for the enhancement to an existing right are disallowed (*Pyrah v Annis & Co (1957) 37 TC 163, Southern v Borax Consolidated Ltd (1940) 23 TC 597, Markets South West (Holdings) Ltd v Revenue and Customs Commissioners [2011] UKUT 257 (TCC), [2011] STC 1469*).

Legal costs incurred by partners in successfully defending against a claim for an interest in a partnership are allowable as the expenditure of the trade if the outcome of litigation does not alter the structure of the partnership (*Linslade Post Office and General Store v HMRC [2012] UKFTT 457 (TC)*). This contrasts to legal costs associated with changes in partnership interests generally, where alteration of the capital structure would characterise the expenses as disallowable (*C Connelly & Co v Wilbey (1992) 65 TC 208*).

In *Hanif and Anor [2017] TC05940* the joint owners of a property business incurred legal fees in a dispute with a bank that had placed the business in the hands of a receiver. Legal advice was sought on obtaining an injunction to prevent the bank forcing a sale of the properties, advice on making a claim against the bank and defending against the bank's recovery of the receiver's fees. The taxpayers contended that the costs were deductible as incidental capital expenses in computing the gains on the sale of the properties. The Tribunal pointed out that these were not incidental capital expenses on sale (*TCGA 1992, s 38*) and using income tax principles to support a capital deduction was rejected. The Tribunal did not consider the income tax treatment of the expenditure in depth but referred to the *Linslade Post Office* decision and suggested that the legal fees might be deductible against property rental income.

The purpose of the expenditure is not altered if a transaction does not proceed; for example, the costs of an unsuccessful planning application will be disallowed as capital in nature.

B30.1.3 Property businesses

Fees for the grant of a new lease or licence to occupy a property are disallowed as capital.

Professional fees for renewal of a lease of less than 50 years may be allowable where the replacement lease is identical or nearly identical and no premium is paid by the tenant. Legal fees or other costs relating to the payment of a premium are not deductible, whether or not these relate to a new lease or a renewal.

Recurring fees for rent reviews are allowable deductions of the tenant or landlord, but legal disputes to enforce the terms of a lease are generally disallowed.

B30.1.4 Preparation of accounts, tax enquiries and appeals

Accountancy fees for preparing financial statements are allowable expenses under general principles, and this includes the cost of preparing tax provisions and professional valuations of property or other assets for accounting disclosures.

Costs in preparing a tax return for a business are disallowable under the principle established in *Smith's Potato Estates Ltd v Bolland (1948) 30 TC 267*, where it was held that costs in establishing a tax liability have no trade purpose but relate to an obligation to pay tax. By concession (see BIM46450), fees for recurring tax compliance of a business, including a partnership return, are deductible. However, the following costs are disallowed:

- Completion of personal tax returns of the partners or the directors of a company.
- Dealing with an HMRC enquiry, except where there is no adjustment to the return or if the inaccuracies or additional liabilities are not due to careless or deliberate behaviour.
- Premiums for fee protection insurance that entitles the taxpayer to recover professional fees incurred in negotiating further tax liabilities due to careless or deliberate behaviour (HMRC do not accept any apportionment of premiums).
- The costs of an appeal to the First-tier Tribunal or a higher court, regardless of the outcome for the taxpayer.

Where a business requires certainty on the tax treatment of a contentious issue, the purpose of making an appeal may not be clear and it might be argued that establishing the correct tax liability is not the main purpose. The outcome of an appeal may influence planning decisions for the business (e.g. the decision may impact on future employment status issues or the recovery of input VAT).

B30.1.5 In-house legal expenses

Staff costs of in-house legal and tax departments are disallowed where the duties of the employees include projects of a capital nature or dealing with tax investigations or appeals. Similarly, time spent by directors or management in dealing with non-trade matters (e.g. investigating illegal activities) may also be disallowable.

B30.2 REFERENCES

Statutory references

TCGA 1992, s 38

CAA 2001, s 11

ITTOIA 2005, ss 33, 33A, 58, 89

CTA 2009, s 33

Leading cases

CIR v EC Warnes & Co Ltd (1919) 12 TC 227

CIR v Alexander von Glehn & Co Ltd (1920) 12 TC 232

Southern v Borax Consolidated Ltd (1940) 23 TC 597

Smith's Potato Estates Ltd v Bolland (1948) 30 TC 267

Cattermole v Borax & Chemicals Ltd (1949) 31 TC 202

Morgan v Tate & Lyle Ltd (1954) 35 TC 367

Pyrah v Annis & Co (1957) 37 TC 163

Knight v Parry (1972) 48 TC 580

Hammond Engineering Co Ltd v IRC (1975) 50 TC 313

C Connelly & Co v Wilbey (1992) 65 TC 208

McKnight v Sheppard (1996) 171 TC 419

Duckmanton v Revenue and Customs Commissioners [2011] UKFTT 664 (TC), [2012] SFTD 293

Key IP Ltd v Revenue and Customs Comrs [2011] UKFTT 715 (TC), [2012] SFTD 305

A–Z of Business Tax Deductions

Markets South West (Holdings) Ltd v Revenue and Customs Commissioners [2011] UKUT 257 (TCC), [2011] STC 1469

Linslade Post Office and General Store v HMRC [2012] UKFTT 457 (TC)

Philip McMahon v Revenue & Customs [2013] UKFTT 403 (TC)

Hanif & Anor [2017] TC05940

HMRC manuals

BIM35540, BIM37965, BIM38545, BIM46410, BIM46415, BIM46420, BIM46450, BIM46452

PIM2120

See also

B6, **B8**, **B15**, **B24**, **B34**

RInt 256 (23 June 2003): Fee protection insurance

B31

Loan and overdraft interest

B31.1 COMMENT

Interest is allowable as a trading deduction where it arises on an overdraft, loan or other finance (such as an alternative finance arrangement) and the funds are applied for the purpose of the trade. Where a trader uses GAAP to prepare accounts, interest expenses are deductible on an accruals basis as charged to the profit and loss account.

A separate regime applies to establish the deductible amount and measure of income tax relief available for interest and finance costs incurred by an unincorporated property business.

With effect from 6 April 2017 property businesses are subject to specific rules restrictions:

- where the value of loans exceeds the value of let properties at the end of the tax year; and
- by limiting tax relief to the basic rate of income tax for finance costs on residential letting (see **B31.1.9**). This restriction does not apply to commercial properties or furnished holiday lettings.

A deduction for interest is not influenced by the usual principles of the capital or revenue divide (*ITTOIA 2005, s 29*). Interest expenses are therefore allowable on:

- short-term debt (e.g. applied for working capital); and
- long-term loans, such as borrowings used to acquire trading premises or plant and machinery.

This differs from the tax treatment of foreign exchange differences, where the underlying purpose and use of the borrowing determines the tax treatment of foreign exchange losses or gains (see **B17**).

There is no definition of "interest" in the *Taxes Acts*. Interest has been described by the courts as "… payment by time for the use of money" (*Bennett v Ogston*

(HM Inspector of Taxes) (1930) 15 TC 374) and "… just recompense to the creditor for being deprived of the use of his money" (*Schulze v Bensted (1916) 7 TC 30*).

HMRC refer to Halsbury's Laws of England which describes interest as "… the return or compensation for the use or retention by one person of a sum of money belonging to or owed to another. Interest accrues from day to day even if payable only at intervals, and is, therefore, apportionable in respect of time between persons entitled in succession to the principal" (SAIM2030).

Businesses incur interest costs on a variety of debts, including short- or long-term funding loans, bank overdrafts, credit cards, promissory notes, settlement of compensation claims, or overdue trade creditors. A premium on the repayment of debt, where this represents a commercial return to the lender, is treated as interest (*Lomax (HM Inspector of Taxes) v Peter Dixon & Sons Ltd (1943) 25 TC 353*).

Hire purchase or lease costs that are often described as interest are part of the hire cost but may nevertheless be deductible (see **B23**, **B29**). Similarly, charges to factor debts or expenses incurred under interest rate swap agreements do not derive from an underlying debt but may be allowable as a finance expense under general principles.

The deductibility of penalties for the early redemption of a loan may be described as additional interest, and the formulation of the penalty may have the characteristics of an interest expense. The precise terms of the loan agreement will determine the nature of the payment. Typically, a break clause penalty is compensation to the lender for early release from the agreement and is not payment for the use of the funds over time; consequently, no deduction as interest will be available when computing the profits of a trade or business (*Arizona Copper Company v Smiles (CES) (1891) 3 TC 149*; see **B24**).

Interest paid on loans made to an individual to acquire an interest in a partnership, trading LLP or shareholding in a close company are not expenses of the business, and no deduction is available in computing taxable profits or losses. However, relief for interest paid may be claimed by the individual when calculating net income – subject to satisfying statutory rules for interest relief (*ITA 2007, Part 8*).

HMRC accept that, where individuals who are partners or shareholders incur interest costs on borrowings to acquire property used by a partnership or a close company, the interest may be treated as deductible in computing the profits of the business (BIM82075, BIM45744, formerly SP 4/85). The statutory basis for this treatment is unclear. A deduction is conditional on the interest being charged in the business accounts and paid in lieu of rent. Interest paid by a partnership on behalf of a partner for use of other assets may also be eligible for relief (see PM30500).

Interest arising on a joint mortgage should be allocated between the borrowers in proportion to the amounts paid by each individual. If the whole interest expense is recharged to the business, a deduction can be obtained for the full interest expense – subject to the loan being applied for the purposes of the trade. Otherwise, only interest incurred by the individual carrying out the trade will be deductible.

"Peer to peer" lending arrangements allow individuals and businesses to lend to each other through the intermediary of an internet platform.

No interest relief is available where rent-a-room relief is claimed.

Interest on overdue tax is generally disallowable (see **B26**).

For companies, the tax treatment of interest and related transactions is dealt with under the loan relationship rules which have no application to unincorporated businesses.

B31.1.1 Non-deductible interest

The following types of interest paid by a partnership or LLP are disallowed in computing trade or business profits:

- interest paid as a return on a partner's current or long-term capital account (i.e. a fixed profit share); and
- interest that must be paid under deduction of basic rate income tax, i.e. "yearly" interest.

B31.1.2 Interest payable – corporate partners

Interest payable by a partnership or LLP on a loan made by a corporate partner or corporate member will be taxed under the loan relationship rules, by reference to the recognised credits and debits in the company's accounts. The company will be taxable on the full amount of interest receivable less its allocated proportion of the interest deductible on computing the trading profits or losses (*CTA 2009, s 381*). Interest deductions for non-corporate partners are allocated in proportion to the agreed profit-sharing ratio (i.e. as part of their separate notional trades).

B31.1.3 Requirement to deduct income tax from yearly interest

Income tax must be withheld at the basic rate (20%) on payment of interest for certain types of loans.

Deduction applies to loans that carry "yearly" interest. There is no statutory rule to distinguish between short-term and yearly interest but the courts have interpreted this as loans with a measure of permanence and a deduction is likely to apply if interest arises on loans that are capable of exceeding one year.

There are a number of exemptions in the requirement to deduct income tax from yearly interest. For unincorporated businesses deduction of income tax should be considered for:

- "mixed" partnerships, i.e. which include a corporate partner; or
- interest paid by any person to a non-resident whose usual place of abode is outside of the UK, (subject to any available reduction under the UK double tax treaties or if the recipient is a company or permanent establishment in another EU Member State).

Main exceptions to the requirement to deduct income tax include the following classes of recipients:

- interest paid to a bank or building society;
- interest paid to a non-resident that arises from a non-UK source;
- statutory interest on late payment of commercial debts;
- interest paid in respect of "peer to peer" lending arrangements where authorised by the Financial Conduct Authority.

B31.1.4 Loans – duality of purpose

Relief for interest incurred by a business may be restricted where:

- loans are applied wholly or partly for a non-business purpose;
- a proprietor's loan account becomes overdrawn;
- borrowing is obtained against revalued assets and applied for non-business use; or
- there is no clear application of the funds for a business purpose.

In order to determine if interest is allowable, the application of the funds must be ascertained. When funds are used to acquire business assets that have been disposed of before the loan is repaid, interest costs will continue to be allowable, subject to any proceeds on sale not being applied for private use (BIM45675).

The use of private assets as security for a business loan does not influence the deductibility of interest. Similarly, securing debt on business assets will not necessarily mean that the interest is deductible if the funds are applied for private purposes. In both cases, it is the use of the funds by the business that determines whether the interest is allowable.

The following are examples of factors that restrict the amount of deductible interest:

- Interest expenses on borrowings used to fund drawings are disallowed if the amount exceeds the proprietor's contribution plus retained profits (*Silk v Fletcher [1999] STC (SCD) 220*; BIM37680, BIM45715).
- Where a capital account has become overdrawn due to accumulated losses of the business, this will not restrict the interest deduction on borrowings, unless the drawings are in excess of original capital contributed by the proprietor (BIM45715).
- Assets contributed to a business represent the proprietor's capital contribution. HMRC's view on a drawdown of capital and replacement with debt has recently been reviewed. HMRC previously accepted that interest on loans used to replace the proprietor's capital could be treated as deductible up to the amount of the initial value assets contributed, regardless of whether the funds were withdrawn for the business for private use. The guidance was temporarily amended during 2017 and this rejected interest relief on replacement borrowing where the funds were applied for non-business use. Guidance has now been amended again to reinstate the original view that the application of the drawdown capital is irrelevant so long as the amount does not exceed the original value of assets contributed or acquired. This is supported by new examples in BIM45700.

Example – Restriction of interest expense: excess borrowing

Alistair purchased a commercial property for £300,000 on the commencement of his new sole trade in 2014. At that time, there was no mortgage on the property. All of the fixed assets are currently valued at £480,000 and Alistair borrows £350,000 from the bank at an interest rate of 5%. The accumulated reserves of the business are £5,000.

Alistair uses the mortgage to purchase a holiday home for personal use. The balance sheet of the business is as follows:

	£
Revalued property and working capital	480,000
Current assets	5,000
Less: Loan	(350,000)
Net assets	135,000

	£
Represented by:	
Revaluation reserve	180,000
Drawings	(45,000)
Equity	135,000

The "excess" drawings of £45,000 is represented by the value of the original value contribution to the business of £300,000 plus accumulated profits of £5,000 less the new loan of £350,000. This restricts the interest deduction as follows:

Total interest expense p.a. = £17,500 (£350,000 @ 5% p.a.)

multiplied by 45,000/350,000 = £2,250 disallowed

The example is based on the revised BIM45700, as at January 2018. Example 3 of the guidance includes an adjustment to exclude depreciation on available drawings to adjust for assets at original cost when considering the level of capital withdrawn.

See also BIM45730 for further examples.

The allocation of interest costs on borrowing used to purchase assets with a mixed private and business use will depend on the legal form and structure of the lending arrangements (*Dixon v Revenue and Customs Commissioners [2006] STC (SCD) 28*; BIM45670).

When a mortgage is used to partly fund a business and partly for private purposes an allocation of interest must be made between the private and business use of the funds.

B31.1.5 Cash basis

For traders using the cash basis a deduction for interest is restricted to a maximum of £500 p.a. The cap applies to interest and costs incurred in obtaining loan finance. However, there is no restriction for non-trade interest (that would otherwise be disallowable if GAAP applied) so interest on a "mixed use" loan is permitted up to £500. The finance charges associated with hire purchase or finance leases, credit cards or interest charged by suppliers are not restricted as these amounts are not classified as interest (**B23**). A deduction for these types of finance charges will be subject to apportionment for any private element.

For landlords using the cash basis, interest relief is not capped but instead is subject to the restrictions outlined at **B31.1.7**.

B31.1.6 Relief for interest costs against net income

An individual may claim relief for interest paid on a loan used for the following purposes:

- investment in a partnership or LLP by a capital contribution, members' interest or loan;
- purchase of plant or machinery used by a partnership; or
- acquiring shares or making a loan to a close company.

The rules to allow a claim for relief for interest by an individual are complex and may be subject to general restrictions for sideways losses against income generally (*ITA 2007, s 24A*).

Interest costs on borrowings by an individual to fund investment in a business are restricted in the following circumstances:

- Interest arising on short-term borrowing, including overdrafts or credit cards.
- Interest paid in excess of a reasonable commercial rate.
- When a proportion of the debt is used for a qualifying purpose, only the relevant proportion of the interest may be claimed.
- No relief is available where a partner has elected to use the cash basis.
- No interest relief is available for funds borrowed by:
  - a limited partner of a limited partnership; or
  - an individual member of an investment LLP (i.e. one whose business consists wholly or mainly of making investments and the principal part of the income is derived from those sources).

Interest on a loan used to fund a trade may be treated as part of the trading loss where there is insufficient income to relieve the expense against net income. The interest may then be carried forward as a trade loss for offset against future trading profits of the same trade, or included as part of a terminal loss relief claim on a cessation of trade.

A deduction for interest cannot be claimed twice, i.e. as a deduction of the business and again by the individual partner as relief against taxable income (*ITTOIA 2005, s 52*).

B31.1.7 Property businesses

The statutory framework for relieving interest and finance costs for property businesses has substantially changed from 6 April 2017. *Finance (No 2) Act*

2015 introduced restrictions for interest relief for residential property letting to the basic rate of income tax on "dwelling-related loans". The restrictions are phased in from 2017/18 and take full effect in the tax year 2020/21. Finance expenses in connection with furnished holiday lets are not within the new rules.

In addition to the above, *Finance (No 2) Act 2017* included a separate restriction from 2017/18 that applies to all types of residential and commercial property letting where the cash basis is used and the total loans in the business exceeds the total market value of the properties at the time it was first introduced to the business ("loan to value" restriction).

From 6 April 2017 the restrictions for finance costs apply to different types of property businesses and depend on whether the cash basis is available or whether the taxpayer elects out of, or is required to use, GAAP. Individuals can choose to elect out of the cash basis for each property business in which they have an interest. Joint owners of property who are spouses or civil partners must both calculate property income on the same basis – unless they have made a declaration of unequal beneficial interests. Other types of joint owners, for example individuals who are partners in a property investment partnership can adopt different bases.

Type of property business	"Loan to value" restriction		Relief restricted to basic rate of income tax	
	Cash basis	GAAP	Cash basis	GAAP
Commercial property	Yes	No	No	No
Residential	Yes	No	Yes	Yes
Residential – Furnished holiday letting	Yes	No	No	No

Businesses using the property cash basis that are potentially subject to restrictions on deductions of interest under the "loan to value" rule may wish to elect to prepare accounts under GAAP. The general computational principles under GAAP that apply to traders will then operate – however the further restriction limiting tax relief to the basic rate of income tax for residential properties continue to apply, regardless of the accounting method adopted by the taxpayer.

Where a property is let for only part of a year or is used partly for a non-business purpose, an allocation of interest should be made on a just and reasonable basis by reference to the proportion and duration of business use (PIM2056, PIM2060). Interest can be claimed for periods when the property is unoccupied where the property is available for letting or being prepared for letting prior to commencement of the property business (see **B38**).

B31.1.8 Loan to value restriction

Taxpayers using the property cash basis are subject to a "loan to value" restriction on relevant loans, when the total outstanding amount of the principal ("L") immediately before the end of the tax year (or before the business permanently ceases), is more than the value of all relevant properties "V" at the end of the tax year.

V is equal to the sum of the market value of the properties at the time these were first used in the business plus any further capital enhancement expenditure. The value of V includes properties that continue to be owned at the end of the tax year, plus one or more properties which have been sold during the year – but does not include the value of any properties disposed of in previous tax years.

Where a loan is used partially for non-business purposes the principal of the loan is adjusted to arrive at the amount of the relevant loan L, before comparing this to V.

Example – Cash basis: loan to value restriction

Lisa purchased a property in August 2015 for £600,000 which comprises a ground floor shop and first floor flat. The flat is occupied by Lisa as her main residence and she lets the shop to a local business on a short-term lease, renewable annually. The flat was originally valued at £450,000 and shop premises at £150,000.

The original acquisition of the property was part-funded by bank borrowing of £300,000. HMRC have agreed that 1/3rd of the interest costs are allowable as a deduction against rental income.

Significant improvements were made to the flat in early 2017 and this was financed by re-mortgaging the whole property on 6 April 2017. In total the mortgage is now £600,000, carrying interest at 6% p.a.

Interest of £36,000 was paid in the tax year 2017/18. Following completion of the works, the total property value had increased to £750,000 with the flat valued at £600,000 and shop remaining at its original value of £150,000.

The "outstanding business loan" is:

$$\frac{\text{Business related interest before restriction}}{\text{Total interest}} \times \text{Loan principal} =$$

13,000/36,000 × £600,000 = £200,000 ("L")

L, the relevant loan at 5 April 2018 is £200,000

V is £150,000, being the original value attributed to the shop

As V is < L the interest deduction is restricted as follows:

V/L	×	Business related interest:		
£150,000/£200,000	×	£13,000	=	£9,750

Note: If the let property had been residential (other than a furnished holiday let), the adjusted interest figure of £9,750 would be used as the starting point to compute the basic rate restriction for finance costs (see **B31.1.9**).

B31.1.9 Residential property businesses – restriction of relief to basic rate of income tax

From 6 April 2017 interest on "dwelling related loans" is subject to tax relief to the basic rate band by:

- calculating the restriction of the gross interest allowable under the loan to value rule;
- adding back interest expenses that would otherwise be claimed in arriving at taxable property profits; and
- making a reduction to income tax payable at the basic rate (20%).

The restrictions apply to:

- interest including premiums, discounts, returns under sharia-compliant arrangements and incidental costs of loan finance in respect of a dwelling related loan;
- a UK or overseas property businesses;
- individuals in their capacity as sole owners, joint owners or members of a property investment partnership or LLP and also to trustees and personal representative;
- businesses taxable on the cash or accruals basis.

If an individual has an interest in a property business in a different capacity the restriction is calculated separately for each business.

A "dwelling-related loan" is defined as a loan for generating income from land that comprises a dwelling house (or part) including land used for enjoyment of the dwelling. Borrowings for the acquisition, construction or adaptation of a dwelling house are included within the definition but a just and reasonable apportionment is made if part of the borrowing does not relate to a dwelling.

The new rules do *not* apply to commercial properties, furnished holiday letting, property development trades and residential property used as part of a trade (e.g. staff accommodation), for which the general rules on interest deductions continue to apply.

The restrictions do not apply to companies, including corporate members of a partnership or LLP (these entities are not subject to income tax).

Furthermore the restriction for interest on what would otherwise be a dwelling-related loan does not apply to income from property that may be taxable as part of a trade including: wayleaves; caravan parks; receipts from surplus business accommodation; receipts derived from tied premises.

HMRC guidance (PIM2054) states that the restriction of relief does not apply to residential mobile home parks or caravan parks which are treated as a trade.

The restriction of interest relief to the basic rate of income tax takes full effect from tax year 2020/21. The methodology used to compute the restriction of relief may result an effective rate of tax in excess of 100% of the taxable income.

Example – Residential property businesses: restriction of relief to the basic rate of income tax

Tommy purchases a residential buy-to-let in June 2020 for £500,000 with a mortgage of £400,000 carrying a fixed interest rate of 5%. Interest of £15,000 was paid during the tax year to 5 April 2021. Letting commenced in October 2020 and the rental income net of expenses but before interest, was £16,000. The accounting profit for the first period of letting is £1,000. Tommy is self-employed and has taxable trading profits of £48,000 for tax year 2020/21.

		£
Trading income		48,000
Net property income	1,000	
Add non-allowable finance costs -100%	15,000	
		16,000

	£
Total income (before personal allowance)	64,000
Income Tax	
£11,850 @ 0% (personal allowance*)	0
£34,500 @ 20%	6,900
£17,650 @ 40%	7,060
Less finance cost reduction for non-allowable finance £15,000 × 20%	(3,000)
Income tax payable	**10,960**

*Assumes 2018/19 personal allowance and income tax rate bands

Tax relief of £3,000 is lost, £15,000 on the difference between the higher and basic rate of income tax; i.e. an effective income tax rate on property income of 300% (£3,000/£1,000).

Transitional rules apply so that the restriction is phased in over three tax years as follows:

Tax year	Proportion of finance costs deducible against rental income	Restricted relief at basic rate of income tax "relievable amount"
2017/18	75%	25%
2018/19	50%	50%
2019/20	25%	75%
2020/21	0%	100%

The calculation of "basic rate reducer" is complex. The proportion of the relievable amount that qualifies for tax relief at the basic rate may include amounts from the current year and also amounts that did not qualify for income tax relief brought forward (for tax years from 2017/18).

The proportion of interest costs which are restricted to relief at the basic rate is found as follows:

(1) Establishing the finance costs for dwelling-related loans for each separate property business ("L"), being the lower of:

- the total finance costs for the current tax year, plus unrelieved finance costs brought forward; and
- taxable profits of the property business, less any losses brought forward;

(2) The sum of L for each separate property business is added together to arrive at "S";

(3) Comparing S to Adjusted Total Income – "ATI", being the taxpayer's total taxable income, after deducting personal allowance (and blind person's allowance, where relevant), and excluding savings or dividend income.

Where:

(i) S is < ATI then S is the relievable amount, i.e. qualifies for income tax relief at @20%;

Alternatively if:

(ii) S is > ATI the relievable amount of interest for each relevant property business is based on the following formula:

ATI/S × L @20%

Example – Residential property businesses: restriction of relief to the basic rate of income tax

Mavis has interests in two residential property businesses. In tax year 2018/19 Mavis also has employment income of £35,000.

Property business A is owned solely by Mavis and has rental profits of £40,000, after accounting for interest costs of £20,000.

Property business B is a house Mavis inherited jointly with her brother in 2016/17. The net rental profits for 2018/19, after interest costs, are £10,000 of which her share is £5,000. The house was inherited without the encumbrance of a mortgage however Mavis and her brother refurbished the property and this was funded by a "dwelling-related loan" on which total interest of £3,000 was paid in 2018/19.

Mavis has restricted relief for finance costs of £12,000 carried forward from 2017/18 arising from property business A.

2018/19 – Calculation of income tax liability

	£	£
Salary		35,000
Net property income A and B (£40,000 + £5,000)	45,000	
Add non-allowable finance costs property business A – £20,000 × 50%	10,000	
Add non-allowable finance costs property business B – £1,500 × 50%	750	
		55,750
Total income (before personal allowance)		90,750
Income Tax		
£11,850 @ 0% (personal allowance)*		0
£34,500 @ 20%		6,900
£44,400 @ 40%		17,760
Less finance cost reduction for non-allowable finance £22,750** × 20%		(4,550)
Income tax payable		20,110

*Assumes 2018/19 personal allowance and income tax rate bands

**Calculation of relievable amounts:

1. *Property business A:*
   - Non-allowable current year finance costs plus brought forward finance costs

     50% of £20,000 = £10,000 + £12,000 = £22,000;
   - Taxable property profits: business A = £50,000 (i.e. £40,000+£10,000)

Lower amount, L1 = £22,000

2. *Property business B:*
   - Proportion of non-allowable current year finance costs = £1,500 × 50% = £750.
   - Proportion of taxable property profits = £5,750 (£5,000 + £750).

Lower amount, L2 = £750

3. *Compare S and ATI:*

S = the sum of Ls £22,000 + £750 = £22,750**

Adjusted Total Income "ATI" = £78,900 (taxable income £90,750 less the personal allowance £11,850).

The relievable amount "S" = £22,750 and this is < ATI being = £78,900. Therefore the relievable amount is based on S.

Mavis has obtained relief at the basic rate for all the restricted finance costs of £12,000 brought forward from 2017/18.

B31.2 REFERENCES

Statutory references

ITTIOA 2005, ss 25, 29, 34, 51A, 52, 57B, 271A–E, 272A–B, 274A–C,307C, 307D, 869

ITA 2007, ss 24A, 96, 383, 398, 399, 874, 888E

CTA 2009, s 381

F(No 2) Act 2017, Sch 2, Pt 2

Leading cases

Arizona Copper Company v Smiles (CES) (1891) 3 TC 149

Silk v Fletcher [1999] STC (SCD) 220, [2000] SpC 239

Dixon v Revenue and Customs Commissioners [2006] STC (SCD) 28

HMRC manuals

BIM37680, BIM45725, BIM45690, BIM45695, BIM45700, BIM45710, BIM45715, BIM45730, BIM45735, BIM45755

PM30500

PIM2050, PIM2052–PIM2060, PIM2064

SAIM2030, SAIM9070

Other

EU Interest and Royalties Directive 2003/49/EC

See also

Chapter 5, B17, B23, B24, B26, B29, B38

B32

Management charges

B32.1 COMMENT

Management charges arise where managerial or technical services are recharged to an entity for using the facilities provided by another business. The most common situations for recharges are shared cost centres, where businesses are under common control, or where a trader collaborates with other businesses to source supplies and obtain bulk-buying discounts.

The following expenses are commonly recharged as between connected businesses:

- centralised salaries and pension costs;
- rent and accommodation services;
- finance costs;
- commission and agents' fees;
- use of intangibles;
- centralised purchases of stock and production overheads (e.g. fuel and power).

Recharges may include an element of indirect costs or overheads and a profit margin the basis of which may be determined by the nature of the service and relative risks of the parties in the transaction.

Deductions for management recharges may be claimed, subject to satisfying the basic criteria that the expense is wholly and exclusively for the purposes of the business, and this will be determined by the nature of the underlying costs and whether the amount is set at a commercial level (*Stephenson v Payne, Stone Fraser & Co Ch D (1967) 44 TC 507*). A recharge may include an additional charge for administrative overheads plus a profit margin. For connected parties the charge should be benchmarked to a third party transaction. A management charge that has no commercial basis is disallowable under general principles.

B32.1.1 Transfer pricing

Where an unincorporated business falls within UK transfer pricing rules, a statutory adjustment may be made to impute an arm's length price where a tax advantage is obtained under an existing pricing structure used for management recharges or other transactions between entities under common control.

Transfer pricing legislation applies to transactions where one party directly or indirectly participates in the management, control or capital of another entity and:

- the parties are classified as "large" (or, in certain cases, medium-sized), as defined by *European Recommendation 2003/361/EC*; or
- the transaction is with a business that is resident in a territory where the UK does not have a double tax treaty with an appropriate non-discrimination article.

An unincorporated business resident in the UK that falls within the above definition will be required to assess and document an acceptable policy for management service charges it supplies or receives. The appropriate transfer pricing method will depend on a function of risk. Usually core administrative services will be recharged on a basic cost-plus method, based on a profit mark up on a share of centralised costs. Recharges for the use of intangibles may require a more complex method of value-chain analysis. Establishing the amount of the recharge does not alter the requirement under general principles for the payer to establish whether a deduction is allowable.

Subject to a relieving provision under a double tax treaty, a UK business that pays for a technical service may be required to withhold income tax at the basic rate if the payment comprises a technical service and its nature is that of a royalty.

B32.1.2 Sole traders, partnerships and limited liability partnerships

No deduction is available for the salary or management fees charged for the services of a proprietor, partner or member, as this is an appropriation of profits and disallowable as drawings. However, management services charged from a limited company to an unincorporated business, which are under common control, may be an allowable expense. This is subject to the recharge being made on a proper commercial basis and the correct accounting treatment being applied by each entity (*Craig v HMRC [2012] UKFTT 90 (TC)*).

A statutory deduction is available for "disguised salary" payments made to individual members of a limited liability partnership where anti-avoidance provisions apply to reclassify a fixed profit share as remuneration (i.e. when the fixed entitlement to profits does not reflect the economic risks and rewards of the business, the individual has no significant influence, and the capital contribution to the business is less than 25% of the expected disguised salary).

B32.2 REFERENCES

Statutory references

ITTOIA 2005, ss 92, 863A–863G

ITA 2007, s 907

CTA 2009, Part 12

TIOPA 2010, Part 4

Leading cases

Stephenson v Payne, Stone Fraser & Co Ch D (1967) 44 TC 507

Earlspring Properties Ltd v Guest (1995) 67 TC 259

HMRC v Lansdowne Partners Limited Partnership CA [2012] STC 544

Craig v HMRC [2012] UKFTT 90 (TC)

HMRC manuals

BIM37740, BIM38230, BIM46020, ESM60000

INTM440070, INTM440090

See also

OECD: Aligning transfer pricing outcomes with value creation, Actions 8–10, 2015 final reports

B34, **B42**, **B43**, **B46**

B33

Mileage allowances

B33.1 COMMENT

Allowable deductions for car travel for unincorporated businesses, which are the focus of this section, are spared the raft of legislation and HMRC output that attaches to travel expenses incurred by employees. That will be familiar to sole traders and partnerships who have staff but will be of little assistance when reviewing their own mileage claims. Note that travel expenses in a wider sense are considered in **B57**.

B33.1.1 Defining the journey

The choices for mileage rates which are available to the unincorporated business are important. Arguably of greater importance is the way a business journey is defined, being especially difficult with certain trades.

We can say that a business journey means any journey that is made wholly and exclusively for the purposes of the trade. However, the "wholly and exclusively" rule means that no deduction will be given where an expense is incurred partly for business and partly for non-business purposes. In tax terms, that is the classic "duality of purpose" trap. However, *ITTOIA 2005, s 34(2)* now assists. It specifies that:

> "If an expense is incurred for more than one purpose, this section does not prohibit a deduction for any identifiable part or identifiable proportion of the expense which is incurred wholly and exclusively for the purposes of the trade."

Accordingly, we can add to the business journey definition so as to include one where any identifiable part or proportion of a journey is made wholly and exclusively for the purposes of the trade.

A key part of the above wording is that an allowable deduction is for an *identifiable* proportion of the expense. Therefore, where a self-employed person uses a car for both private and business purposes, it requires adequate records to be kept to demonstrate which part of the mileage was for business purposes.

B33.1.2 Measuring the journey

A self-employed person will usually maintain that his office is at home, therefore every journey which includes an element of business is measured from home. HMRC will always consider whether or not the home really is the correct place from which to start measuring. To achieve it, a self-employed person must show that the home is his true base of operations.

There is a significant amount of case law on home being the start point for business mileage.

The *Samadian* case has become a benchmark in this context. Dr Samadian initially appealed to the First-tier Tribunal (FTT) against HMRC's refusal to accept his mileage claims in his self-employed accounts. The FTT decided that Dr Samadian's journeys from home to either of the private hospitals or the NHS one (he was both a self-employed consultant and an NHS-employed consultant) were private and not business journeys. The FTT accepted that Dr Samadian had a place of business at home and that it was needed for his professional practice. However, they also found that, because of a "pattern of regular and predictable attendance" at the two private hospitals, the latter also formed places of business.

Dr Samadian appealed against the FTT decision to the Upper Tribunal (UT). The UT upheld the FTT decision, ruling that the cost of journeys by the consultant between private clinics and NHS hospitals and between private clinics and his home were not incurred 'wholly and exclusively' for the purposes of his private practice and were therefore not deductible expenses. That the journeys between the hospitals were deemed not deductible is perhaps the most surprising decision. However, the FTT found that the object of Dr Samadian's travel between the NHS hospitals and private hospitals was so that he could carry on his business away from where he was employed and the travel was thus 'not an integral part of the business itself'.

A subsequent case, *Jain [2015] TC 04788*, used the guidelines laid down in Samadian to arrive at a similar decision. It was determined that Dr Jain – a private medical consultant in addition to being employed by the NHS – also had two centres for his business, therefore his home to hospital mileage costs were not allowable as business deductions. This had ramifications on Dr Jain's subsistence claims – see **B50**.

In *Horton v Young* the taxpayer was a bricklayer who entered into contracts with a builder and, as a consequence, worked at several widely separated sites. He had no office other than his home. It was there that his business records were maintained. It was concluded that business mileage could be measured from his home.

In *Sargent v Barnes*, a dentist had a laboratory located between his surgery and his home. He called in there on a daily basis when travelling from home to his surgery, and claimed the mileage costs between the laboratory and the surgery. However, despite the laboratory visits, it was determined that the journey between home and surgery retained a dual purpose which disqualified the expenditure. HMRC cite this case, as well as others, at BIM37630, where they are reviewing the broad issue of whether a journey is allowable as a deduction or not.

B33.1.3 Rate per mile

There are two options for the self-employed to use:

- fixed rate deductions; and
- actual costs.

Fixed rate deductions

These facilities have been available from tax year 2013/14. The legislation was brought in at the same time as the cash basis rules (see **Chapter 2**).

Unincorporated businesses, whether or not they use the cash basis, have the choice of using the fixed rate deductions (see **B16**, and **B16.1.1** should be reviewed to determine the conditions and the rates). Broadly, the latter uses the HMRC's authorised mileage allowance payments (AMAPs), provided all the conditions are met. Summarising the latter, at the date of this publication the rates are:

- car and goods vehicles: 45p/mile for the first 10,000 miles, 25p/mile thereafter; and
- motor cycles: 24p/mile irrespective of the amount of travel.

Note that the previous use of AMAPs in calculating their business mileage allowances by the self-employed was permitted where turnover did not exceed the VAT registration limit. That facility has now been removed, and all the conditions relating to motor fixed rate deductions must be met for AMAPs to be used.

Actual costs

HMRC recognise that *ITTOIA 2005, s 34(2)* assists when determining the costs of a business journey. They refer to the running costs of a car used partly for the purposes of the trade and partly for other purposes. In addition to actual costs of any trade journeys (e.g. fuel, tolls, parking fees), a proportion of the motoring overheads – such as licence, insurance (provided the insurance covers business use), repairs, finance costs – should also be allowed. Further, HMRC accept that there is no need to argue that motor overheads would be incurred in any event and that only the marginal additional costs attributed to trade use are allowed.

The apportionment between business and private use extends to capital allowances on the purchase of a vehicle.

Where a hire car is used, there is a restriction applied to the allowable deduction if the CO_2 emissions exceed 160g/km. The restriction is calculated as 15% of the actual hire cost. It is aimed at leased cars and does not apply to short-term hire (less than 45 consecutive days). The logic is that it compares with the threshold for special rate pool expenditure in the capital allowances regime. Other conditions remove from the regime:

- hire purchase cars which cannot be owned by the hirer;
- those where an option to purchase is based on a sum of not more than 1% of the retail price of the car when new; and
- hire cars under a long-funding lease.

HMRC provide detail of the hire car restriction at BIM47730.

B33.2 REFERENCES

Statutory references

ITTOIA 2005, ss 32A, 34(2), 272ZA

Leading cases

Horton v Young (1971) 47 TC 60

Sargent v Barnes (1978) 52 TC 335

Samadian v Revenue and Customs [2013] TC 02533

Samadian v Revenue and Customs Commissioners [2014] BTC 504

HMRC manuals

BIM37600, BIM37630, BIM47730, BIM47750

B34

Patent rights and expenses

B34.1 COMMENT

A registered patent gives the owner the right over the intellectual property in the jurisdiction in which it is registered and provides exclusive rights over the production and sale of an invention. Patent rights registered under the *Patents Act 2004* can be used by the original inventor, by the grant of a licence to a third party or by acquiring the patent outright. Patents may be registered in the UK, European Patent Office or other jurisdictions.

For accounting periods ending before 5 April 2007, relief for patent royalties was given when royalties were paid as a charge on income. From tax year 2007/08, patent royalties are deductible on an accruals basis where the cost relates to products manufactured or sold by the business.

For companies, the tax treatment of patents is dealt with under the corporate intangibles regime (*CTA 2009, Part 8*), and these provisions do not apply to unincorporated businesses.

B34.1.1 Expenses

Expenses incurred in creating a patented innovation may be deductible under general principles where the inventor carries on a trade. If there is no trade activity, expenditure relating to developing the patent, making a patent application and any associated expenses are deductible when paid against patent income received, with any excess expenses carried forward for offset against patent income in a future tax year.

Costs in development of a trademark may be capital in nature and – unlike invention costs for patents – no statutory relief is available, except for registration expenses (see below).

B34.1.2 Capital allowances – patents

A purchase of patent rights is capital in nature, and no deduction is available as a revenue expense, unless the trade is one of dealing in patents or similar intellectual property.

Deductions for expenditure on acquiring patent rights can be obtained by claiming capital allowances where the patents are used for a qualifying trade. Non-qualifying patent expenditure may also qualify if non-trade income is derived from those rights.

Capital allowances are available on unexpired patents, with separate pools for each qualifying activity. Allowances are computed on the pool value comprising expenditure incurred (plus acquisition costs) the value of the pool brought forward, less any proceeds on sale. Writing down allowances are claimed at 25% p.a. Net sale proceeds are restricted to the original cost, and a balancing charge will arise where this exceeds the residual pool value. A balancing allowance may crystallise in the final period of trade. Anti-avoidance applies to sales between connected parties.

The outright purchase of a trademark is capital in nature, and this type of asset is not eligible for capital allowances.

B34.1.3 Registration expenses

Costs of the grant, registration, extension and renewal of patent rights are specifically allowable for a trader, and a deduction can be claimed if applications are abandoned or rejected (*ITTOIA 2005, s 89*). This statutory relief does not extend to an unincorporated business where the individuals carry out a profession or vocation. The costs of assignment of an existing patent will be capital in nature and the purchaser may be entitled to capital allowances.

The registration, extension or renewal costs of designs or trademarks are also specifically allowable (*ITTOIA 2005, s 90*). As for patents, this does not apply to professional trades.

B34.1.4 Cash basis

Traders and property businesses using the cash basis can claim a deduction for patents and trademarks where the payments are revenue in nature and relate to the trade or business. Capital sums for intellectual property may also be deductible under specific rules for intangibles that apply to taxpayers using the cash basis (from 6 April 2017). No relief is available under capital allowances rules.

Capital payments for intangibles will qualify where these comprise:

- rights which fall within the definition used in the accounting standard for micro-entities, FRS 105, Section 13; and
- internally generated intangibles or intellectual property.

Intellectual property is defined as including patents and trademarks or other rights in connection with those types of assets (*ITTOIA 2005, ss 33A, 307B*).

However intangible expenditure is treated as "non-qualifying" if the trader or property business grants a sub-licence in respect of the asset to another person.

B34.1.5 Deduction of income tax at source

A basic rate deduction of income tax is required for royalties paid that arise from UK patent rights. Where a UK patent is sold outright and the vendor is not resident in the UK, income tax is deductible at source from the consideration paid. This may be reduced or eliminated under the terms of any relevant double tax treaty between the UK and the jurisdiction of the recipient.

Where both the payer and recipient are resident in EU member states, payments may be made "gross" between parties that are "25 per cent associates".

A general requirement to deduct income tax from non-UK source intellectual property was extended to payments of patent royalties, trademarks and certain other classes of intangible property rights when paid on or after 28 June 2016.

B34.2 REFERENCES

Statutory references

CAA 2001, Part 8

ITTOIA 2005, ss 33A, 89, 90, 307B, 587, 595, 600, 601, Sch 2, para 26

ITA 2007, ss 448, 903, 906, 907

Leading cases

None

HMRC manuals

BIM45965, BIM45951

CA75100, CA75130, CA75300, CA75310

See also

B20, **B46**, **B48**

B35

Pensions

B35.1 COMMENT

Tax relief for pensions for the self-employed or partner of a business is only available through the personal reliefs section of the self-assessment tax return. It will either be a personal pension scheme or a retirement annuity scheme. Thus the payment into a pension policy for the business owner cannot be termed a business deduction.

In contrast, paying into a scheme for an employee has long been a common business cost. It has become even more so with auto-enrolment now in place, compulsorily providing pension funding for employees who have not opted out.

B35.1.1 Annuities paid to retired partners

It is common practice for a partnership to pay an annuity (an annual payment) to a retired partner, particularly within professional partnerships. The terms of the annuity will normally form part of the partnership agreement. The tax treatment depends on the level of annuity agreed. If it exceeds particular limits, the capitalised value of the annuity payable is also treated as consideration for the disposal of the retiring partner's fractional interest in the partnership assets. Thus it would be subject to capital gains tax rules in accordance with the disposal and acquisition of fractional shares in partnerships.

The legislation treats the capitalised value of the annuity as consideration for disposal only if it is regarded as more than a reasonable recognition of the retired partner's past contribution of work and effort to the partnership. There is a set scale which determines what is meant by "reasonable" in this context. It considers length of time as a partner and also his average profit share. HMRC's table of calculation is set out in Statement of Practice D12 and at CG28400.

The payment of the annuities may be charged to the partnership's profit and loss account. However, if this is the case, they should be added back in the tax computation. Instead, relief is given in the tax computation by allowing the annuities payable to be allocated to the partners as charges on income.

The allocation is made in accordance with the normal partnership-sharing arrangements.

When an annuity is paid to a retired partner, it must be made net of basic rate tax.

The current partners receive tax relief for the payments through their own individual tax returns. The relief is available because the partner is an individual who makes an annual payment from which tax must be deducted.

B35.1.2 Pension payments for the benefit of employees

Detailed treatment of this significant topic is outside the scope of this publication. Accordingly, brief indicators only of certain areas have been included. Radical changes were made to the pensions legislation from 6 April 2006. None of the earlier regime has been referred to here.

Tax relief on an employer's contribution to a registered pension scheme is given in accordance with the normal tax rules for the deductibility of the expenses of a trade. This is subject to two exceptions:

- contributions are treated as not being capital payments if they otherwise would be; and
- the timing of the deduction for a contribution does not follow its accounting treatment. Relief for a contribution is given for the accounting period in which it is paid and not in the period(s) it is recognised in the accounts (unless it is also subject to spreading rules).

In deciding whether a contribution to a registered pension scheme is allowable, the same rules apply as for any other expense (apart from the two exceptions above). Thus, the contribution must be made wholly and exclusively for the purposes of the trade. HMRC acknowledge that it will be relatively rare, in the context of pension contributions, to have to consider whether there is a non-trade purpose for the employer's decision to make the contribution. Nevertheless, HMRC do consider that it is necessary to view each position on its own facts. It is, of course, only likely to be in doubt where connected parties are involved. It has been raised as an issue where a personal company is involved and pension payments are paid to a controlling director which appear to be out of proportion to his contribution to the company's trade.

Expenditure incurred for the purposes of going out of business, rather than for the purposes of carrying on the business, fails the "wholly and exclusively for the purposes of the trade" test. Therefore, substantial contributions which are outside the normal pattern could be disputed by HMRC as not being made for the benefit of the trade. Nevertheless, HMRC recognise that pension contributions made under contractual obligations in the capacity of employer are deductible, even if they arise on the cessation of the trade.

In *Smith v Incorporated Council of Law Reporting for England and Wales* the Council claimed for the amount of a gratuity, paid to one of their reporters on retirement, to be allowed against its profits. The reporter was not entitled to a retiring gratuity, but it had been the habit of the Council to give a gratuitous pension, or a gratuity, to a reporter who retired after long service. The courts agreed that a deduction was admissible.

In contrast, in *Morgan Crucible Co Ltd v IR Commrs*, the employer company took out an insurance policy to provide it with an equivalent income with which to meet a series of pension payments. The premium paid to the insurers was held not to be deductible. The distinction from other cases, where payment of an annuity had been found to be deductible, was believed to lie in the fact that, in the *Morgan Crucible* case, the taxpayer obtained an asset by reason of the payment; it did not receive direct income.

B35.1.3 Optional remuneration arrangements (salary sacrifice)

The salary sacrifice arrangements were significantly changed from 6 April 2017 by *ITEPA 2003, s 69A*. This change was accompanied by a change of name to 'optional remuneration arrangements' (OpRA). The amendments prevent the benefit from the income tax and NICs advantages previously available under certain salary sacrifice arrangements. Particularly targeted were benefits in kind with a cash allowance option and flexible benefits packages with a cash option.

An OpRA (as with the previous salary sacrifice) happens when an employee gives up the right to part of the cash remuneration due under his contract of employment. An employee may also sacrifice a one-off item, such as a bonus. One of the most common forms has always been for an employee to choose to receive the sacrificed part of his salary as a pension contribution, whether to his own personal pension scheme or an employer scheme.

The new legislation expressly provides that OpRAs will continue to permit a sacrifice of salary in favour of a pension contribution. HMRC at BIM46075 confirm this in their statement:

> "An increased pension contribution by an employer resulting from a salary sacrifice arrangement of the type set out at EIM42750 onwards, is wholly and exclusively for the purposes of the trade and allowable as a deduction in arriving at the employer's taxable trade profits."

There are other exceptions whereby the tax advantages obtainable under salary sacrifice arrangements remain in place under OpRA, such as the provision of cycles and cyclists' safety equipment. They are listed at *ITEPA 2003, s 228A*. Further examination of OpRA is outside the scope of this publication but HMRC helpfully expand on the detail of the new legislation and this can be found in manuals from EIM44000 onwards.

There are strict conditions to be met if an OpRA is to operate properly within the legislation. HMRC make it clear, as indicated above, that those conditions must be in place for the subsequent employer costs, such as pension contributions, to be allowed as a deduction in the employer's profits without also being taxable on the employee.

B35.2 REFERENCES

Statutory references

FA 2004, ss 196–224

ITA 2007, ss 448, 900

ITEPA 2003, s 69A

ITEPA 2003, s 228A

Leading cases

Smith v Incorporated Council of Law Reporting for England and Wales [1914] 3 KB 674, 6 TC 477

Morgan Crucible Co Ltd v IRC [1932] 2 KB 185, 17 TC 311

HMRC manuals

BIM46000 onwards

BIM46075

CG28400

PM31110 onwards

EIM 44000 onwards

See also

SP D12

B36

Political expenditure

B36.1 COMMENT

Payments to political funds, contributions to party funds, and expenses of candidates at elections are all disallowed from being business expenses for tax purposes (see BIM42528). The basis is that there is a purpose other than for the benefit of the trade. On the other hand, HMRC accept that the cost of propaganda undertaken wholly and exclusively to prevent a trader from losing his business and to preserve its assets is admissible (see BIM35570). The latter is supported by case law, an example being when Tate & Lyle mounted a campaign against the proposed nationalisation of the sugar-refining industry.

In the *Breweries* case, it was held that the company's prolonged campaign to relax the licensing laws enabled a revenue deduction, despite HMRC's contention that the cost was capital in nature to enhance the company's asset base. The expenditure was deemed to be akin to advertising which would serve to increase the normal income of the business.

The alternative view was exemplified in the *Boarland* case. There, the costs of producing and circulating a pamphlet were determined not to be "monies wholly and exclusively laid out or expended for the purposes of the trade". The pamphlet was, broadly, an attack on the policy and acts of the then Labour government.

There is a distinction where expenditure is not in the form of a donation to a political party but is instead expended to acquire goods or services which are merely bought with some political purpose in mind. Examples could be conducting a political survey, or researching information on current political policies. If it were thought that a political donation and an allowable business acquisition might both be made to the same recipient, it would be sensible to separate the two payments. An invoice being clearly raised in respect of the allowable item would assist an argument that the tax treatment of the two payments should be differentiated.

B36.1.1 Collective publicity schemes

HMRC acknowledge that contributions by a trader to a collective publicity scheme, organised by a committee or other body representing the general interests of a town or area, are not necessarily prompted by political motivation. In those circumstances the expenditure should be allowed as a deduction. This is subject to the contributions being of a reasonable amount in relation to the benefit likely to accrue to the business.

B36.2 REFERENCES

Statutory references

ITTOIA 2005, ss 33, 34

Leading cases

Boarland v Kramat Pulai Ltd (1953) 35 TC 1

Morgan v Tate & Lyle Ltd (1954) 35 TC 367

Cooper v Rhymney Breweries Ltd (1965) 42 TC 509

HMRC manuals

BIM42528, BIM47435, BIM35570, BIM37035

B37

Post-cessation expenses

B37.1 COMMENT

Relief for post-cessation expenses is available for payments made after the cessation of a trade or business where the expense would have been deductible had the business continued. Post-cessation expenses are relieved on a paid basis rather than an accruals basis.

Individuals may offset some types of post-cessation expenses against other sources of income.

B37.1.1 Method of relief

For individuals, personal representatives, trustees and non-resident companies subject to UK income tax, a deduction for post-cessation expenses relating to a former trade or property business must be claimed first against post-cessation receipts arising in the same tax year. The excess can be carried forward for offset against future post-cessation receipts.

Where a trader has elected to use the cash basis, these rules continue to operate to allow relief for post-cessation expenditure. Where the fixed rate deduction scheme was previously used for motor expenses, post-cessation mileage can be relieved against post-cessation receipts. Similarly where a property business falls within the cash basis post-cessation expenses paid may be offset against post-cessation receipts.

Additional relief for post-cessation expenses may be available where an expense is a "qualifying payment" or "qualifying event" in relation to the former trade, profession or vocation (but not a property business) and this expense arises within seven years of cessation. The amount can be relieved in the following order:

1. The excess over post-cessation receipts can be offset against other sources of income in the same tax year (subject to the same general restriction for the offset of trade losses; i.e. the higher of £50,000 and 25% of adjusted net income for tax years from 2013/14).

2. Any excess may then be offset against chargeable gains arising in the same tax year (before deducting capital losses, the annual exempt amount or other trading losses).

A qualifying payment is restricted to the following categories of expenses:

- Expenses in rectifying defective goods or services provided in the previous trade.
- Damages paid for defective goods or services.
- Legal costs in dealing with a claim for damages.
- Insurance premiums against defective work and insurance covering legal costs for potential claims.
- Costs of collecting trade debts.

When the above expenses are recovered through an insurance claim and that receipt falls in a later tax year, the previous expenses are matched to the year of receipt thus reducing the amount of the qualifying payment available for sideways loss relief.

A "qualifying event" arises when a trade debt is written off post-cessation, under a statutory solvency arrangement. The qualifying event occurs in the tax year of the release and can be claimed as an expense if the debt is still held by the original trader.

Post-cessation expenses that do not fall within the definition of a qualifying payment or qualifying event may only be offset against post-cessation receipts.

B37.1.2 Date of cessation – timing of expenditure

The date of cessation is a question of fact. The discontinuance of a property letting business will usually occur when the last of the properties in a portfolio is sold (or there is a change of use so that the property is no longer let).

Expenditure accrued under generally accepted accounting principles in an accounting period up to the date of cessation will be deductible in arriving at taxable profits or losses in the usual way – subject to satisfying certain conditions where provisions are made (see **B39**).

Certain types of expenses will not be allowable for the purposes of the trade, if the purpose of incurring the cost was for the closure of the business.

The following types of expenditure will be deductible in the final period of trade (either when accrued in the accounts or paid as a post-cessation expense):

- Statutory redundancy payments, contractual liabilities of an employer on the termination of employment, and other employment expenses for which no other relief would have been available for the employer prior to a permanent cessation of trade (e.g. because the payments could not be accrued under general accountancy principles as a provision in the final period of trade).
- Non-contractual redundancy payments up to three times the statutory redundancy payment.
- Employer pension contributions that would otherwise be deductible in future accounting periods under spreading rules.
- Employer contributions to cover deficiencies in a pension scheme.

Post-cessation expenses are not deductible if:

- an amount has already been included as a deduction on an accruals basis in a pre-cessation period; or
- expenses accrued at the date of cessation have not been settled. If accrued expenses are paid in a subsequent tax year, the post-cessation expenses may be claimed in that later tax year.

From 12 January 2012, anti-avoidance applies to restrict relief for post-cessation expenses where the main purpose is to obtain a reduction of income tax.

B37.1.3 Carry back of post-cessation receipts

An election can be made to carry back a post-cessation receipt to the final period of trade when it is received in a tax year beginning no later than six years after the discontinuance of trade.

The election will be advantageous where there were unutilised trade losses at the date of cessation or if a lower marginal income tax rate applied in the tax year of cessation compared to the tax year of receipt. Post-cessation expenses take priority and must first be offset to reduce the amount of the receipt available for carry-back.

The effect of the carry-back is given in the tax year of the receipt, but the additional income tax liability (if any) is based on the difference between the original tax liability in the tax year of cessation and the tax on income by including the post-cessation receipt in the tax year of discontinuance (using tax rates and allowances applicable to the earlier period).

B37.2 REFERENCES

Statutory references

TCGA 1992, ss 261D, 261E

FA 2004, ss 198,199

ITTOIA 2005, ss 76–79, 250, 254, 255, 272, 351

ITA 2007, ss 23, 96–101, 98A, 125

CTA 2009, ss 76–79, 196–199

Leading cases

None

HMRC manuals

BIM90000, BIM90075, BIM90080, BIM90110, BIM90115, BIM90120, BIM38320, BIM40265, BIM46040

PIM2510, PIM3005

See also

B3, **B35**, **B39**, **B42**, **B45**, **B55**

B38

Pre-trading expenditure

B38.1 COMMENT

Expenses incurred before the commencement of a trade are not deductible under general principles, but pre-trading expenditure is treated as incurred on the day on which the trade commences – subject to the expenses being incurred within seven years before that date and satisfying the statutory tests for deductibility. The date of commencement is a question of fact, but is usually taken as the time at which the business is in a position to provide customers with goods or services.

A deduction is only available if the expense would have been allowable had the trade already commenced. Capital expenditure, such as partnership formation expenses, costs associated with acquiring another business or expenditure on fixed assets to be used in the trade, does not qualify.

For traders and property businesses using the cash basis expenses are deductible when paid and relief is deferred until commencement of the trade or business, subject to the specific cash basis rules (see **Chapters 2** and **5**).

B38.2 REFERENCES

Statutory references

ITTOIA 2005, ss 31A, 57, 272, 272ZA

CTA 2009, ss 61, 208, 330, 462, 1045, 1149

Leading cases

None

HMRC manuals

BIM46351, BIM45355, BIM70030

See also

Chapters 3, 4

B39

Provisions

B39.1 COMMENT

The recognition of a provision in the accounts reflects a liability of the business for which the amount of the final settlement may be uncertain. Prior to 1998, the tax deductibility of provisions was based on the overriding principle that losses should not be anticipated. The introduction of the accounting standard FRS 12 "Provisions, Contingent Liabilities and Contingent Assets" codified the conditions under which a provision could be recognised for accounting purposes and this coincided with the introduction of the statutory rule that the profits of a trade should be calculated in accordance with generally accepted accounting practice.

The tax treatment provisions have no application to businesses that elect to use the cash basis.

The application of previous case law on the timing of the deductibility of provisions is now modified by application of accounting principles and this is governed by:

- compliance with Section 21 of FRS 102;
- the nature of the expense (i.e. capital or revenue); or
- whether the provision relates to expenditure that is disallowable under specific statute or case law principles.

The tax treatment outlined below does not apply to:

- general creditors and specific accruals for expenses;
- deferred income;
- valuation adjustments to stock or work in progress (see **B55**);
- accounting for operating or finance leases;
- provisions for bad or doubtful debts (see **B3**);

- depreciation or impairment provisions to write down the value of investments; or
- financial instruments.

The tax treatment for provisions has no general application to traders or property businesses using the cash basis. Where a deduction for a provision has been claimed using GAAP and the taxpayer begins to use the cash basis in a later tax year, no further deduction will be available when the expenses are settled under transitional rules in order to prevent double counting.

B39.1.1 Accounting requirements

From 1 January 2015, the accounting treatment for provisions is found at Section 21 of FRS 102 and is broadly similar to the previous accounting standard, FRS 12.

Generally, a contingent liability is an uncertain obligation and is recognised in the accounts.

The conditions for making a provision in the accounts arise where all of the following conditions apply:

- There is a present obligation (legal or constructive) as a result of a past event as at the balance sheet date.
- It is probable (more than a 50% chance) that a transfer of economic benefits will be required to settle that obligation.
- A reliable estimate can be made of the amount. This will include:
  - using projections and probabilities when a large number of items are under review;
  - an average of a range of values where a number of factors will determine the final settlement;
  - if appropriate, the amount should be discounted to net present value; and
  - the reimbursement of a liability is treated as a separate asset and only recognised if it is nearly certain that the asset is recoverable.

A constructive obligation may be established from a previous pattern of events; for example, if customers buy goods under warranty, this provides a legal obligation for rectifying faults. The experience and history of warranty claims may be sufficient to make an accurate estimate.

Provisions that reflect future anticipated losses, where a legal or constructive obligation has not been entered into at the balance sheet date, are not permissible under FRS 102. Examples of this include:

- A reorganisation of a business where a decision had been made but no announcements on redundancy or other expenditure had been notified or contracted for before the end of the accounting period (*Meat Traders Ltd v Cushing [1997] SpC 131*).

- Provisions for future repair costs for assets if there was no present obligation to incur the expenditure (e.g. lease assets subject to an ongoing legal obligation for service and maintenance: *Johnston v Britannia Airways Ltd (1994) 67 TC 99*).

B39.1.2 Timing of expenditure governed by specific rules

Specific statutory rules apply to the following provisions:

- *Benefits provided to employees:* A deduction is deferred until the year of payment if the provision or accrual for salaries or employee benefits is settled more than nine months after the end of the accounting period.

- *Expenditure on cessation of trade:* Statutory redundancy payments, contractual payments liable by an employer and non-contractual redundancy payments up to three times the redundancy are treated as paid in the final period of trade.

Example – Provision for onerous lease

XYZ LLP has a short leasehold with a remaining term of 10 years, which coincides with a rent review. Rent is set at £50,000 p.a. with a five-year break clause. The LLP has vacated the premises and a sub-lease has been granted at £25,000 p.a. for five years. A provision is made in the accounts for costs associated with the onerous lease:

• Net rental expenses £25,000 p.a. × 10 years	£250,000
• Maintenance costs	£5,000
• Structural alterations on vacating the premises	£10,000

Section 21 of FRS 102 allows a provision to be recognised for obligations under onerous leases when a net loss is identified. The rentals arise from a present obligation for a past event and a reliable estimate of the rental costs, net of expected rent receivable, has been made. The amounts provided should be adjusted to reflect the net present value of the expected obligations.

The provision for the deficiency in net rent covers 10 years but, as XYZ LLP has an option to terminate the lease after five years, only half of

£250,000 should be provided for because it is unlikely that there will be a "transfer of economic benefits" for settlement of further rent costs after that time. The conditions for a provision under Section 21 of FRS 102 are not satisfied, as this limits the amount of the provision for an onerous contract to the "least net cost of exiting from the contract, which is the lower of the cost of fulfilling it and any compensation or penalties arising from failure to fulfil it".

HMRC accept that, where the amount has not been properly calculated but a more accurate estimate can be made (and the other conditions of Section 21 of FRS 102 are satisfied), a deduction can be claimed for part of the provision. Therefore, £125,000 of the £250,000 will be deductible covering the five-year period.

If the provision for maintenance relates to a requirement under the lease, the costs for accounting periods up to the period in which the provision is made will be deductible. Usually, a provision for future maintenance is not allowable, as this arises from part of an executory contract; i.e. where the obligation for ongoing repairs is not a present obligation (*Johnston v Britannia Airways Ltd*). However, as the lease is now onerous, a provision for all expected losses can be made. Subject to identifying any capital expenditure, this part of the provision will be deductible (FRS 102, para 21.1B). If maintenance is recoverable under the sub-lease, the expected future income stream should be taxable (and separately recognised as an asset in the accounts).

There is a legal obligation to make structural alterations to the premises, but no revenue deduction will be available as the cost is capital in nature (this provision should have been made in the accounts when the premises were originally altered and capitalised as a fixed asset at that time).

B39.2 REFERENCES

Statutory references

ITTOIA 2005, ss 36, 38, 76–79

CTA 2009, ss 76–79

Leading cases

Owen v Southern Railway of Peru Ltd (1956) 36 TC 602

Johnston v Britannia Airways Ltd (1994) 67 TC 99

Meat Traders Ltd v Cushing [1997] SpC 131

Herbert Smith v Honour [1999] STC 173

Jenners (Edinburgh) Ltd v CIR (SpC166/98)

HMRC manuals

BIM31100, BIM35210, BIM38395, BIM46500–BIM46565

See also

Chapters 1, B1, B3, B30, B55

FRS 102 Section 21

B40

Quotas

B40.1 COMMENT

These are typically farming issues. In an attempt to control the global and particularly the EU agricultural outputs, production quotas were introduced as one of the weapons.

The main farming products to which production quotas have applied over the years are milk, sugar beet, potatoes, ewe and suckler cow premium, fish. They were gradually withdrawn by the EU, with milk quotas being the last to survive. They were abolished on 31 March 2015.

The right to ownership of milk quotas was originally conferred on all dairy farmers who met the qualifying conditions when they were introduced in 1984. Accordingly, quotas became capital assets. Case law substantiated the view that quota was a separate asset from the land to which it was attached, see *Cottle v Coldicott (HMIT) (1995) Sp C 40*.

Quotas were transferable between farmers by outright sale and purchase. Where the quotas were a fixed capital asset of a farmer's trade, which was the usual position, such transactions had no effect on trading profits for the farmers concerned. The capital treatment was verified in *Terry and Anor v R & C Commrs (2005) Sp C 482*. Instead, proceeds and costs were subject to capital gains tax and the disposal gave rise to a capital receipt. Quotas are included in the list of assets subject to roll-over relief. Accordingly, theoretically this could still be of relevance to farmers who disposed of quota toward the end of their existence. However, at that stage they had very little value.

There had also been a market in the leasing of milk quotas. The essential difference between leasing and sale was the temporary nature of the leasing arrangement. The quota reverted to the original owner at the end of the agreement. This led to a difference in the tax treatment. Payments for quota leasing were allowable deductions in the farmer's accounts. Similarly, receipts from the leasing of quotas were regarded as part of the trading income. Consequently, it was always important historically to determine whether it had been a leased or a purchased milk quota that was in point.

There is an alternative treatment for the income from leasing if the activity to which the quota relates has ceased or substantially reduced. In that instance, the receipt would be dealt with as miscellaneous income. Accordingly, there would only be direct costs, such as leasing agent's commission, available for offset against the taxable income. This could only be of relevance to a taxpayer's position for earlier years, given the present withdrawal of quotas from the agricultural scene.

B40.2 REFERENCES

Statutory references

TCGA 1992, s 155

Leading cases

Cottle v Coldicott (HMIT) (1995) Sp C 40

Terry and Anor v R & C Commrs (2005) Sp C 482

HMRC manuals

BIM55300, BIM55320

B41

Removal expenses

B41.1 COMMENT

A deduction for removal expenses is allowable where the purpose of the relocation:

- does not part of a general scheme for expansion (*Granite Supply Association Ltd v Kitton (1905) 5 TC 168*);
- is to improve the efficiency of the business; or
- is unavoidable, e.g. because an existing lease cannot be extended or the premises are subject to a compulsory purchase order.

If one of the above situations applies, removal costs for relocating trading stock, tools, equipment and employees will be allowable. The amount deductible may be reduced by any compensation or a disturbance allowance received to cover the removal costs.

HMRC also accept that the cost of dismantling and re-siting plant and machinery are deductible in these circumstances (BIM42530). When "old" fixtures or plant are not relocated, the cost of new fixtures will be subject to capital allowances claims in the usual way (*Eastmans Limited v Shaw (1928) 14 TC 218*).

If the relocation of a business forms part of a general scheme of expansion, removal expenses are treated as capital in nature and will be disallowed.

B41.1.1 Relocation of employees

Costs incurred by an employer in the relocation of employees are also allowable (the employee may claim relief against earnings for certain categories of removal costs met by the employer, up to a total of £8,000).

If the employer purchases an employee's residence and the property is sold without being used by the employer, the transaction will not be treated as a capital disposal. Incidental costs, such as legal fees, stamp duty and estate agent costs, are treated as revenue deductions, and the profit or loss on sale is included in the trading result of the business (BIM42531).

B41.1.2 Relocation of partners or sole traders

Payments made by a partnership to relocate a partner are not wholly and exclusively for the purposes of the trade. The expenses are tainted by a duality of purpose for the individual in their capacity as a proprietor, notwithstanding the underlying business purpose (*MacKinlay v Arthur Young McClelland Moores & Co [1989] STC 898*).

B41.2 REFERENCES

Statutory references

ITEPA 2003, ss 271–287

ITTOIA 2005, ss 33, 34

CTA 2009, ss 53, 54

Leading cases

Granite Supply Association Ltd v Kitton (1905) 5 TC 168

Eastmans Limited v Shaw (1928) 14 TC 218

MacKinlay (Inspector of Taxes) v Arthur Young McClelland Moores & Co [1989] STC 898

HMRC manuals

BIM42530, BIM42531, BIM38120

See also

Chapter 3, **B42**, **B44**

B42

Remuneration

B42.1 COMMENT

At first sight, it might seem that "remuneration" is bound to be deductible, being a normal cost of a business, whether unincorporated or otherwise. However, closer examination shows up different areas which could harbour uncertainty. These will be examined as:

- ongoing employment (general earnings);
- redundancy; and
- employing family members.

B42.1.1 General earnings

Employment income is defined as comprising "general earnings" and "specific employment income".

The main importance of specific employment income is in relation to the special rules for taxing the employment of non-UK residents and non-UK domiciles. Broadly, these special rules apply to general earnings but not to specific earnings. The latter are categorised as:

- payments and benefits on termination of employment;
- payments and benefits in respect of non-approved pension schemes; and
- share-related income (including share options).

The remainder of this section focuses on general earnings; specific earnings are outside the remit of this publication.

B42.1.2 Ongoing employment – when has remuneration been paid?

No deduction is allowed for remuneration for an accounting period unless it is paid before the end of the nine months immediately following the end of that period. Whilst this would not generally be an issue, it could be where family members are employed, or for director/shareholders of companies.

Defining the date of payment for tax purposes to employees could be critical in all circumstances, whether families are involved or not, particularly at the end of an accounts or PAYE year and when a bonus might be in point.

Remuneration is paid when it is treated as received by an employee for the purposes of the charge to income tax on employment income.

Cash earnings are treated as received for assessment purposes, and paid for PAYE purposes, on the earlier of:

- the time when either a payment or a payment on account of earnings is actually made, and
- the time when a person becomes entitled to either a payment or a payment on account of earnings.

Actual payment happens when the income comes into the control of the employee such that he can deal with it as he wishes. This means, in respect of different methods of payment:

- for payment by cheque, when the employer posts it or hands it over to the employee. The date the cheque is cleared or put into the bank is irrelevant;
- for payment by credit transfer, when it is passed into a bank or building society account;
- (rarely) when it is credited to an account in the employer's books, but only if the employee can freely draw upon it himself at that point. This is more relevant to directors, where the rule differs (see below); and
- when the income is paid to a third party or it is used in a way directed by the employee. This could apply to a payment agreed by the employee to be taken direct from his earnings.

As indicated above, a payment on account of earnings can determine the payment date in the same way as a precise payment of earnings. A payment on account is not the same as a loan (this is of critical importance when operating RTI); it is a payment in respect of which the employer has no right of recovery, thus contrasting with a loan.

Where a loan has been made to an employee, there can be no recourse to reduce the loan for any purposes on the basis that the employee makes a loan to his employer by being paid salary monthly in arrears. This assumes that he is only entitled to salary at the end of the month. This was determined in *Williams v Todd*.

B42.1.3 Directors and payment of remuneration

Directors are treated differently from other employees when defining the remuneration payment date.

In addition to the earliest of the first two criteria (see above) for all employees, directors add three further criteria for deciding which is the earliest:

- the date when earnings are credited to an account in the employer's books on which the director is not free to draw. Thus any restriction on the director's right to draw the earnings is disregarded for any tax assessment (including deductibility) and PAYE purposes;
- the end of any accounting period for which the earnings have been determined (e.g. by a board meeting or the director's contract of employment); and
- if the earnings are determined after the end of the accounting period, it is when they are determined.

HMRC also recognise the above when arguing the level of the director's loan account at the end of the company's financial year.

B42.1.4 Non-cash earnings

This category of earnings – i.e. "benefits in kind" – has substantial reference material devoted to what is comprised within the charge and the way it is taxed on the employee. In this section, we focus on the deductibility to the employer's business and the relevant cost of providing the benefits.

There is a natural symmetry between benefits taxed on the employee and an allowance in the employer's accounts. Wherever there is a tax liability on the employee, there will be a deduction permitted in the employer's accounts based on the cost to the employer of having provided it. Note that the value on which the employee is taxed is a separate matter and might not be the same as the employer's cost.

The statutes determine the value of the non-cash earnings on which the employee will be taxed. There are two main methods involved, unless specific scale charges or other calculation rules apply. One of those methods is the cost to the provider (usually the employer) and the other is money's worth. The latter is the older method. Effectively, it is the second-hand value, as it looks at the value in the employee's hands. Although it does still apply in limited circumstances, it has largely been superseded by the cost to the employer.

The majority of benefits in kind are reported on form P11D after the end of the tax year, although from 6 April 2016 employers have been able to tax expenses and benefits through their payroll. This is achieved by adding the value of the expense and/or benefit to their taxable income (payrolling) rather than providing them separately. Whichever reporting method is used, the benefits are subsequently taxed on the employee, either through a tax code or the self-assessment tax return. This timing is not relevant to the employer's expense deduction. The latter will have been allowed in his accounts in accordance with GAAP.

The respective timing of submitting P11Ds and charging a cost in the employer's accounts does offer a slight flexibility in the case of the director/shareholder company. There might be an opportunity to review the cost borne by the company before submitting form P11D and decide whether the intention was to charge it to the director's loan account rather than treat it as a company cost.

Note that, when considering benefits in kind provided to employees, it is not correct simply to disallow the costs in the tax computations of company accounts or charge the cost to drawings of a sole trader or partnership business. Unless the employee has agreed to repay the value of the benefit to his employer, once a benefit has been provided it is too late for the employer to ease the tax burden on the employee by forgoing his own tax deduction.

B42.1.5 Redundancy – overview

One of the many matters of concern to an employee being made redundant will be his tax position. The employer should be able to guide him and he must also check his own position in respect of its deductibility against his profits.

There is an exemption from income tax on an employee on a statutory redundancy payment received to the extent that it exceeds the statutory amount. It is dependent on it being a contractual redundancy payment that is made. The legislation (*ITEPA 2003, s 309*) defines the terminology.

The legislation continues to the effect that statutory redundancy payments, additional contractual redundancy payments and other qualifying payments in connection with the termination of employment will be aggregated and only treated as taxable earnings on the excess over £30,000.

Deciding whether a termination payment other than a statutory or contractual redundancy payment qualifies for the £30,000 exemption from income tax is outside the scope of this publication. However, a reminder to employers – changes were made in *Finance (No 2) Act 2017* to tighten the scope of the £30,000 exemption. This brought in 'Post-employment notice pay' (PENP) which is a new concept. It excludes from the £30,000 exemption amounts which, had the individual's employment not been terminated, would have been subject to PAYE and NICs in full. A separate new rule ensures that where an individual receives a payment in lieu of notice (PILON) this will be subject to tax irrespective of whether the payment is contractual or non-contractual. The legislation amendments are at *ITEPA 2003, ss 402A–402E*. All payments to the redundant employee should continue to be allowable deductions from the employer's profits, but if penalties are charged because the PAYE records are incorrect, they will not be allowable (see **B26**).

There is considerable HMRC guidance on termination payments at EIM12805 onwards.

B42.1.6 Redundancy payments – deductible?

For the employer, both statutory and contractual redundancy payments would normally be deductible as revenue expenses in the accounting period when they are made. However, there are two aspects which might deny them:

- for the benefit of the ongoing trade; and
- duality of purpose.

Where payments to employees have been made on the cessation of the business, HMRC have in the past, in limited circumstances, successfully contended that they could not have been made for the benefit of the trade because it was ceasing. This was finally laid to rest in the *Hong Kong* case, on the basis that the payments were deductible because they discharged obligations of the employment contracts entered into during the trading activities. Nevertheless, conditions apply. HMRC will now allow relief for redundancy or severance payments made on cessation of trade, provided the payment is:

- to an employee taken on for the purposes of the trade, and
- under a pre-existing contractual or statutory obligation which was a consequence of the person being employed for the purposes of the trade.

The position is enforced by a statutory provision (*ITTOIA 2005, s 79*) that permits a revenue deduction to be made on the cessation of a business (but not where there is simply a corporate reorganisation) up to a limit of three times the amount of the statutory redundancy pay. If it is made after the business has ceased, it is treated as arising on the last day of trading.

Duality of purpose might prevent a revenue deduction of redundancy payments where:

- they were made for a personal as opposed to a business reason. Payments to a member of the employer's family are the obvious target here. However, the statutory deductions permitting redundancy payments, including the additional "three times" limit, should apply irrespective of a personal relationship; or

- they were of a capital nature. A leading case (*George Peters and Co*) held that certain of the arrangements entered into by the company to secure the proposed sale of its shares were properly of a capital and not of a trading nature. Under current legislation, that would not override payments meeting the criteria for the statutory deduction of redundancy payments, but the principle should be considered for payments that exceeded the relevant amounts.

B42.1.7 Redundancy payments – timing

Redundancy payments are normally deductible when paid. However, they can be allowed in the prior accounting period where conditions are met. For this to apply, it is necessary for a provision to have been made in accordance with GAAP. References to 'Old GAAP' FRS 12, now FRS102, Section 21 are in point. HMRC support this view at BIM46615. This is more likely to occur with companies, where restructuring is planned. In summary:

- the obligation must have arisen under a plan to cease or dispose of the business from which the company cannot reasonably withdraw;
- the redundancy programme had been determined;
- the redundancy calculations have been accurately made and related to employees identified individually; and
- the payments were actually made within nine months of the end of the accounting period.

B42.1.8 Family members

The key to remuneration expenditure being deductible when paid to the employer's family is that it should be commercially genuine. HMRC's arguments against it, in whatever context, fall away where the level of payment properly reflects the individual's contribution to the business and where objective employment conditions prevail.

HMRC guidance (at ESM4155) instructs that a spouse's employment in any capacity other than that of the [paid] employment is to be disregarded.

The strictures of RTI have (hopefully) lessened the occurrence of the classic error of failing to record a spouse's salary in the payroll records. However, the requirement actually to make the payment to the spouse (or any other employee) at least within nine months after the accounting period is strictly upheld. Neither is it adequate to identify other payments (such as household expenses, holidays or gifts) and assert that they constituted salary.

Ideally, there should be a contract of employment. If not, it is worth spending time considering and listing the tasks that really are carried out by the employed individual.

The above principles should be applied equally to remuneration paid to the employer's children. The added constraints of employment law in respect of children must also be observed.

The effect of a failed family remuneration claim by the employer will be different for a company. In that situation, unless the payment is charged instead to the director's loan account, the payment will constitute a taxable benefit in kind on the employed director. For a sole trader or partnership business, it will be treated as the proprietor's drawings.

B42.1.9 Family – scholarships

This is a matter frequently raised by clients. Can they pay for their children's university education through the business and set it against their taxable income? In virtually all circumstances, the answer will be "no". It is referenced in legislation and in HMRC manuals.

The appeal of the idea is significant. Scholarship payments of up to, currently, £15,480 per academic year can, if the conditions are properly met, be exempt from tax in the hands of the recipient at the same time as constituting a business deduction.

The situation is most often met in personal companies where a parent is shareholder/director, although the legislation applies equally to all employees. Where a scholarship is awarded to an individual whose parent is employed by the company providing the scholarship, or where arrangements have been made to secure it, the scholarship income will be treated as taxable earnings of the parent. Even where efforts are made to employ the student in his own capacity, it has been rejected by the courts. HMRC contended that the individuals were not bona fide employees during the periods of time they were at university, despite the fact that they were employed afterwards. As one of the conditions for the scholarship exemption is that the course must be full-time, HMRC's argument is difficult to counter.

It might be feasible, in specific circumstances, for a more remote member of the family to provide the scholarship from a different employer entity from the one where the parent is employed, but that would have to be investigated with care. Any reciprocal arrangements would, of course, prevent any chance of success.

The case of *Kutcha v Revenue & Customs* sets out the difficulty of claiming a deduction for scholarship payments to family members, together with the associated benefit in kind on the employed parent that will ensue.

For an unincorporated business, any such scholarship payment would simply be denied as a deduction.

B42.2 REFERENCES

Statutory references

ITEPA 2003, ss 7, 16, 18, 63 onwards, 212, 309, 401, 403

ITEPA 2003, ss 402A–402E

ITTOIA 2005, ss 79, 776

Leading cases

George Peters & Co Ltd v Smith (1963) 41 TC 264

Williams v Todd (1988) 60 TC 727

Commissioner of Inland Revenue (Hong Kong) v Cosmotron Manufacturing Co Ltd [1997] BTC 465

Kutcha and another v Revenue & Customs [2013] UKFTT 369 (TC)

HMRC manuals

BIM46615, BIM47130

EIM42270, EIM42300, EIM00512, EIM12805

ESM4155

B43

Rent and rates

B43.1 COMMENT

Rental costs and associated expenses, such as business rates, are generally deductible if the expense relates to premises used by the trade.

No deduction is available for rent paid by a sole trader in their capacity as owner of the property; individuals cannot let property to themselves so any "rent" paid is treated as drawings. The situation where a sole trader operates more than one business, and makes charges for rent to reflect an accurate accounting position of each activity, is not entirely free from doubt.

The position of a sole trader differs from that where rent is paid by a partnership to one or more of the partners who hold a property "outside" the partnership. In this case, a deduction is available to the business (BIM38110; *Heastie v Veitch & Co (1933) 18 TC 305*).

When a trading property is vacated, the ongoing rentals or maintenance associated with leasehold or freehold property will continue to be deductible. The "wholly and exclusively" test is satisfied, as the continuing obligation for the expenditure is linked to the original purpose and this is not altered by the decision to move the trade elsewhere. If the property is sublet to offset the rental expenses and other costs, the net losses are treated as a trading deduction (*IRC v Falkirk Iron Co Ltd (1933) 17 TC 625*, *Hyett v Lennard (1940) 23 TC 346*).

The business may make a provision for future losses on an onerous contract in accordance with the accounting standards and obtain relief in the accounting period in which the provision is made – subject to meeting the accounting requirements and ensuring that the underlying costs are not disallowed as capital (see **B39**).

Net income from property that is let temporarily, as surplus to the requirements of the trade, is treated as a trading profit so that the associated letting costs can be deductible as a trade expense (BIM41015).

B43.1.1 Lump sum payments

For the treatment of notional rent for a premium paid on the grant of a short lease, see **B28**. Rent paid under a licence to occupy is deductible on an accruals basis as charged to the accounts.

The underlying legal form of a lease transaction will establish the nature of payments. A facility to pay a fixed premium by instalments does not necessarily entitle the payer to a revenue deduction (*Commissioners of Inland Revenue v Adam (1928) 14 TC 34*). The formulation of a rental charge by reference to the underlying value of a property is not conclusive evidence that the rental payments are capital (*Racecourse Betting Control Board v Wild (HM Inspector of Taxes) (1938) 22 TC 182*).

A lump sum paid by a tenant in lieu of rent is treated as a premium (see **B28**). A payment by a tenant for variation or early surrender of a lease is a capital cost of acquiring additional rights to an asset or making a disposal (*Tucker v Granada Motorway Services Ltd (1978) 53 TC 92*).

B43.1.2 Cash basis and fixed rate deductions

The use of the cash basis allows the taxpayer to obtain relief for rent when paid (see **Chapter 2**).

Sole traders and partnerships (but not companies, LLPs or partnerships which include a corporate member) may use fixed rate deductions for use of home as an office. The monthly rates range from £10 to £26, depending on the hours worked, and cover household utility costs, telephone and broadband (see **B16**).

Property businesses within the cash basis may claim rentals paid on a property that is sublet (see **Chapter 5**). The specific statutory rules for deductions of premiums do not apply to traders and landlords and no deduction is available for lump sum premiums.

B43.1.3 Rent for businesses operating at home

Prior to the rewrite of the Taxes Acts (*ITTOIA 2005* and *CTA 2009*), a rent deduction for businesses occupying residential dwellings was restricted to the relevant proportion of rent paid and was generally capped at two-thirds of the total rental cost (*ICTA 1988, s 74(1)(c), repealed*).

This rule no longer applies, but rent charged by a director for use of their home as a place of business must not be above a market rent. Charging rent offers an alternative method of extracting profits from a company. Rental income less expenses will be taxed as a property trade for the individual and reported as a separate source of income in the self-assessment return.

For the deduction of expenses where the home is used as an office or place of business by an unincorporated trader, see **B59**.

B43.1.4 Tied premises

Expenses of letting tied premises, such as a public house let by a brewery, will be treated as a trading expense; similarly, rent is taxable as a trade receipt (BIM46270, PIM4300).

B43.1.5 Interest treated as rent

Interest expenses incurred by partners or shareholders, on loans to acquire property used by the partnership or a close company, may be treated as deductible in computing the profits of the business instead of charging rent (see **B31**; BIM82075, BIM45755, formerly SP 4/85). The concessionary treatment of interest as notional rent does not extend to interest paid by a partnership on a loan from a third party which is then lent-on to one of the individual partners to purchase property used by the business (*R v Inspector of Taxes ex parte Brumfield [1989] STC 151*).

B43.1.6 Non-resident landlords

Tenants who pay rent to non-UK resident landlords are required to deduct, and account quarterly for deductions of, basic rate income tax on rent paid. There is no requirement to deduct if the property is let via a UK letting agent (who takes on this obligation).

Tenants have a right to withhold income tax from payments made to a non-resident landlord. Where deductions have previously been overlooked, the tenant may offset income tax against future rents payable to the landlord (INTM370030).

B43.2 REFERENCES

Statutory references

ICTA 1988, s 74(1)(c) repealed

ITTOIA 2005, ss 19, 21, 33, 34, 47, 61, 267A

CTA 2009, ss 42, 44, 53, 54

Leading cases

Commissioners of Inland Revenue v Adam (1928) 14 TC 34

IRC v Falkirk Iron Co Ltd (1933) 17 TC 625

Heastie v Veitch & Co (1933) 18 TC 305

Racecourse Betting Control Board v Wild (HM Inspector of Taxes) (1938) 22 TC 182

Hyett v Lennard (1940) 23 TC 346

Tucker (HM Inspector of Taxes) v Granada Motorway Services Ltd (1978) 53 TC 92

HMRC manuals

BIM35305, BIM38110, BIM41015, BIM45744, BIM46270, BIM46810, BIM47800–BIM47825

INTM370030

PIM4300, PIM1214

See also

B16, **B28**, **B31**, **B39**, **B59**

B44

Repairs and renewals

B44.1 COMMENT

Whether or not expenditure on repairs qualifies as a deduction in calculating business profits is determined in accordance with ordinary principles. Therefore, it will be necessary to consider the "wholly and exclusively" and the "capital expenditure" rules.

A repair involves restoring an asset to its original condition. Where the expenditure represents an improvement, alteration or an addition to an asset, that is capital, and is consequently disallowed for tax purposes in trading accounts.

B44.1.1 Repairs – buildings and structures

The phrase "original condition" must be interpreted in context and does not necessarily mean the condition when first constructed. Thus, if repair work is carried out following the purchase of an existing building, the costs would only be allowed if the building had immediately been fit for the purpose for which it was acquired. If not, the assumption is that there was a discount in the purchase price to allow for the capital expenditure needed before the building could be used. This is frequently encountered in residential properties acquired for letting. If it is to be contended that it was merely the new owner's choice to redecorate and repair, or the convenience of doing so while the property was empty, a detailed record and photographs on acquisition might assist.

An analysis of the condition of an asset on purchase has been built up through the courts. In *Law Shipping*, repairs to a ship acquired in a defective condition and necessary before it could become seaworthy were held to be capital. The ship was not capable of being used to earn profits until the repairs had been carried out.

In contrast, in *Odeon Theatres* the repairs to the theatre after acquisition were prevented by wartime scarcity of materials. When, several years later, the repairs could be carried out, the court judged them to qualify as deductible costs. Part of the reasoning was that the purchase price had not apparently been reduced because of the state of its repair. In addition, the building was deemed fit for profitable use immediately when bought. Importance was also placed on the accounting treatment. This is a principle still relied on to a considerable extent, with *ITTOIA 2005, s 25* adding legislative strength.

HMRC state that a change to the external size of a building will invariably be regarded as an improvement. Despite this, an increase just to the number of windows, or the use of slightly different materials because technological improvements have led to the demise of the originals, will not deem the repairs to be capital. HMRC highlight that in their "Capital v Revenue Expenditure Toolkit". As an example, the replacement of single-glazed windows by double-glazed equivalents would be deductible as a repair cost.

It is accepted that there is a distinction between replacement of the entirety of an asset (capital) and renewal of a subsidiary part of an asset (repair). Unfortunately, not every set of circumstances neatly fits the definitions. Case law only assists to a limited extent. The two classic cases here are those involving the replacement of a factory chimney. In one of them, it was held that the entirety was the chimney and thus the expenditure was capital (*O'Grady v Bullcroft Main Collieries*). For the other, it was determined that the entirety was the factory and so the expenditure on the chimney, which was a mere part of the factory, was revenue (*Samuel Jones & Co (Devonvale)*). Thus the facts of each situation must be considered in conjunction with legislation and guidance before drawing a conclusion.

Expenditure on "repairs" is either capital or revenue, following the "wholly and exclusively" rule. It cannot be both. Neither can a notional repair cost be deemed from the capital cost of an improvement. Thus, if an extension to a building is constructed, an estimated cost of re-plastering or re-roofing the original, had it not been demolished, cannot be claimed as a deductible repair. This is supported by case law (see *William P Lawrie* and *Lowestoft Water Co*).

Consequently, where the expenditure is found to result in the creation of a new asset, no apportionment may be made. The case of *Curtin v 'M' & Co Ltd [1960] IR 59* is used by HMRC to emphasise this. The conclusion is also referred to in the "Capital v Revenue Expenditure Toolkit". However, it is sometimes possible to apportion the total expenditure on a renewal as being specific parts as capital and other specific parts as revenue. In the *Conn v Robins* case the cost of capital expenditure on fixtures, underfloor heating and toilets was separately identified and the remainder of the cost was justified as repairs to the original structure.

Another case where the tribunal reviewed a split between capital and revenue expenditure was that of *Wills*, where the accounts showed around £63,000 as capital expenditure and nearly £44,000 as repairs. The latter related to work on an outbuilding attached to a rental property. HMRC sought to classify the whole as an improvement, together with a change of the character of the asset. The Tribunal found that the reality was repairing and restoring the original, with its end use not having been changed.

Despite their own insistence on an entirety of works done being either capital or repair, HMRC do concede (at PIM2020) that work commissioned on a property may include expenditure on capital works and also separate expenditure on repairs at the same time. HMRC accept in those circumstances that the expenditure on repairs remains allowable. They state that expenditure may be apportioned on a fair and reasonable basis to estimate the amount attributable to the repair element, perhaps using an apportionment based on the contractor's bill.

HMRC include a review of the nature of repairs in their "Capital v Revenue Expenditure Toolkit", referred to above. HMRC also focus on analysis points for properties for letting in their Property Income Manual. They usefully introduce the capital allowance regime and the way in which it adds to the "revenue or capital" debate. HMRC have also drafted "Revenue and Customs Brief 5 Guidance on repairs and renewals of assets", which they say is relevant both to those carrying on a trade or a property business. It applies equally to individuals and companies incurring expenditure on repairing business assets.

B44.1.2 Timing of a deduction

Reliance on accounting standards here is significant but not overriding. Thus, substantial expenditure on the refurbishing of a property might lead to it being capitalised in the accounts and released to the profit and loss account over its expected useful life. The tax treatment does not have to follow this. Instead, the detail of the whole expenditure should be analysed carefully into its component tax elements:

- repairs;
- capital (structure);
- capital (plant and machinery); and
- capital (integral features).

Based on that analysis, the components can then be taxed appropriately in the year in which the cost of repairs has been charged to the accounts.

Where a provision for future repairs has been correctly made in accordance with GAAP, it is an allowable expense in that year rather than the year invoiced, unless there are specific tax rules to the contrary.

B44.1.3 Repairs – plant and machinery

Exactly the same principles apply to distinguish repairs from capital for plant and machinery (which includes fixtures and fittings, where appropriate) as for buildings and structures. It is the result that differs. It is also far easier, at least for plant and machinery, to determine whether a new asset has been acquired or an old one has been repaired.

Fixtures and fittings can be more difficult to identify separately from the structure of the building. A fixture is an asset which is installed or otherwise fixed in or to a building or land so as to become part of that building or land in law. An asset can still be a free-standing asset even if it is connected to another structure. Courts have developed two key factors for determining whether a particular asset is a fixture or free-standing:

- the method and degree of annexation; and
- the object and purpose of annexation.

The distinction between a free-standing asset and a fixture is important in many aspects of tax legislation. In the context of business deductions, if it has been determined that particular expenditure is capital not a repair, then for a free-standing asset, capital allowances within the regime of plant and machinery are available. If it is a fixture, it will have become part of the structure. In that case, only if the type of asset falls within the category of integral features will there be any revenue deduction. This will be within the capital allowances regime. If not an integral feature, a fixture will be part of the land or building to which it is fixed and subject to tax legislation as such.

The detail of the capital allowances regime is outside the scope of this publication. However, certain aspects of integral features have relevance here. There are five categories of integral features. They are:

- an electrical system (including a lighting system);
- a cold water system;
- a space or water heating system, a powered system of ventilation, air cooling or air purification, and any floor or ceiling comprised in such a system;
- a lift, an escalator or a moving walkway; and
- external solar shading.

Integral features qualify for the annual investment allowance (AIA) in the same way as other plant and machinery. To the extent that expenditure exceeds the AIA, it is transferred into a special pool and not the main pool. Thereafter, a writing down allowance of 8% is applied to the pool.

The particular issue with integral features and repairs is the special definition of "replacement asset" that applies. If the repair expenditure represents the whole or more than 50% of the cost of replacing an integral feature, either all at once or within any period of 12 months, that cost is to be treated as capital expenditure on the replacement of that integral feature for capital allowances purposes. As a result, instead of the repair being a revenue deduction, the cost will be capital. HMRC provide clarification on this aspect at CA22340. With the current fairly high rates of AIA, this will only make a significant difference to taxable profits in rare cases. However, at such time as the AIA limits reduce substantially again, the lower writing down allowances would bite and the special definition of "replacement asset" for integral features could make an unwelcome impact.

B44.2 REFERENCES

Statutory references

CAA 2001, ss 33A, 33B

ITTOIA 2005, ss 25, 33, 34(1)(a)

Leading cases

Law Shipping Co Ltd v IR Commrs (1930) 12 TC 621

O'Grady v Bullcroft Main Collieries Ltd (1932) 17 TC 93

Margrett v The Lowestoft Water & Gas Co (1935) 19 TC 481

Samuel Jones & Co (Devonvale) Ltd v IR Commrs (1951) 32 TC 513

William P Lawrie v CIR (1952) 34 TC 20

Curtin v 'M' & Co Ltd [1960] IR 59

Conn v Robins Bros Ltd (1966) 43 TC 266

Odeon Associated Theatres Ltd v Jones (1971) 48 TC 257

Wills v Revenue & Customs [2010] UKFTT 174 (TC)

HMRC manuals

BIM46900 onwards, BIM46930

CA22340

PIM2020

Capital v Revenue Expenditure Toolkit

B45

Restrictive undertakings

B45.1 COMMENT

Payments made for restrictive undertakings by an employer are eligible for deduction under specific statutory provisions (*ITTOIA 2005, s 69*) if the amount is taxable as income for the employee (*ITEPA 2003, ss 225, 226*).

The purpose of a restrictive undertaking is to prohibit an employee from competing with the employer and typically covers confidentiality, solicitation of specific customers or working within a defined area. The payment may cover existing restrictions in the employment contracts or new restrictions, and will generally form part of an overall settlement agreement to prevent either party from making further claims in respect of the employment.

If the amount is not taxable as earnings in the hands of the employee, the employer may still be able to claim a deduction for the payment under general principles. Compensation payments by a company that are linked to a disposal of an interest in share capital may be disallowed if this is linked to a disposal of shares rather than for the purpose of the trade (*James Snook and Co Ltd v Blasdale*).

Damages or compensation paid by the former employee in breach of restrictive covenants is not an allowable deduction in computing profits of the trade, as duality of purpose will be evident where the payment relates to the previous employment (*Knight v Parry; Philip McMahon v HMRC*; see **B30**).

Where a payment is made to establish a commercial advantage, for example to restrict a competitor to limit business within a geographical area and this secures a permanent advantage, the payment is likely to be capital in nature and if so the amount will not be allowable on first principles.

B45.2 REFERENCES

Statutory references

ITEPA 2003, ss 225, 226

ITTOIA 2005, s 69

CTA 2009, s 69

Leading cases

James Snook and Co Ltd v Blasdale (1952) 33 TC 244

Knight v Parry (1972) 48 TC 580

Walker v The Joint Credit Card Co Ltd [1982] 55TC617

Philip McMahon v HMRC [2013] UKFTT 403 (TC)

HMRC manuals

BIM35595, BIM37717, BIM47005, BIM47200

EIM03605

See also

Chapter 3, **B14**, **B30**, **B42**

B46

Royalties

B46.1 COMMENT

Article 12 of the OECD Model Tax Convention describes royalties as follows:

> "... payments of any kind received as a consideration for the use of, or the right to use, any copyright of literary, artistic or scientific work including cinematograph films, any patent, trademark, design or model, plan, secret formula or process, or for information concerning industrial, commercial or scientific experience."

Royalties payable under copyright licences for the performance or use of creative artistic works, a registered design or public lending rights are deductible on an accruals basis if the expense is incurred for the purpose of an unincorporated trade, profession or vocation. A deduction is disallowed if the royalty is set above a commercial rate. Transfer pricing rules require an adjustment to royalties to reflect an arm's length price if the payer receives a potential tax advantage (see **B32**).

Where there is no trade activity, relief may be obtained for royalties paid as "qualifying annual payments" and can be offset against miscellaneous income derived from intellectual property rights. Therefore, if a copyright is part of a sub-licensing arrangement, royalties payable (and other costs such as agents' commissions) may be deductible.

Anti-avoidance applies from 5 December 2012 to restrict a deduction of royalties as an annual payment against income generally. Royalty payments made in connection with a trade, profession or vocation, or income from a particular source, are not affected.

Mineral royalties are deductible as rental payments for the use or exploitation of land.

Know-how is not a separate intellectual property right and exists alongside registered rights such as copyrights, trademarks and patents. The tax treatment is covered at **B20**.

For companies, the tax treatment of royalties is dealt with under the corporate intangibles regime (*CTA 2009, Part 8*), and these provisions do not apply to unincorporated businesses.

Traders and property businesses using the cash basis can claim a deduction for recurring royalties and licence fees when paid.

The treatment of payments for intellectual property rights that are capital in nature are covered at **B34**.

B46.1.1 Deduction of income tax

The payment of royalties is subject to deduction of basic rate income tax at source.

Deduction of income tax for copyright royalties is required, whether these are periodic payments or a lump sum (*IRC v Longmans Green & Co Ltd (1932) 17 TC 272*).

Royalties paid to a non-resident owner of certain types of intellectual property are also subject to deduction of UK income tax. With effect from 28 June 2016, the type of royalties for which a deduction is required is aligned to terminology used in the OECD model treaty and includes royalties in respect of patents, trademarks, copyrights (excluding film related copyrights), registered design rights or public lending rights (see also **B34**).

Income tax may be reduced or eliminated under the terms of a double tax treaty between the UK and the jurisdiction of the recipient. Payments may be made without deduction of income tax when the payer and recipient are "25 per cent associates" and both parties are resident in an EU member state.

B46.2 REFERENCES

Statutory references

CAA 2001, ss 452–462

ITTOIA 2005, s 12, Chapter 2, Part 5

ITA 2007, ss 900–914

CTA 2009, s 39, Part 12

TIOPA 2010, Part 4

Leading cases

IRC v Longmans Green & Co Ltd (1932) 17 TC 272

HMRC manuals

BIM45965, BIM50725

DT2140

INTM400010

See also

Council Directive 2003/49/EC

OECD Model Treaty – 18 December 2017

B20, **B32**, **B34**, **B48**

B47

Security

B47.1 COMMENT

The term "security" has two separate contexts for tax allowable deductions from profits:

- security of persons and property; and
- security of an asset placed to underpin borrowings.

B47.1.1 Persons and property

There are special, and strict, rules which provide that certain expenditure on personal security measures can result in a business deduction through qualifying under the capital allowances regime. If conditions relating to these special rules are not met, the expenditure must be considered on general principles. The criteria must all be met and are set out at *CAA 2001, s 33*, a summary of which follows:

- a "relevant qualifying activity" is being carried on by an individual or partnership (but not a company);
- the individual or partnership incurs the expenditure in connection with the provision of a security asset;
- if the special rules did not apply, no tax relief would otherwise be due either in calculating the income from the qualifying activity or under the capital allowances legislation;
- the asset is provided or used to meet a special threat to the individual's personal physical security;
- that threat arises wholly or mainly because of the relevant activity; and
- the sole object of incurring the expenditure is to meet that threat.

Although *CAA 2001, s 33* excludes a company, an equivalent provision is available to a corporate employer and employee at *ITEPA 2003, s 100*. This removes, from the charge to tax on the employee, the cost of a benefit provided by the employer company where the personal security threat conditions have all been met. The *Hanson* case referred to below is a classic example.

Whilst much of the expenditure might be allowable under normal capital allowances rules for the business, there are key additions in this legislation.

First, the type of asset on which capital allowances can be claimed extends to a structure (such as a wall) and an asset which becomes fixed to land. Specific exclusions are:

- a car, ship or aircraft; or
- a dwelling or grounds appurtenant to a dwelling.

Secondly, on disposal of the relevant asset, its proceeds are deemed to be nil. This prevents there being any addition to a capital allowance pool (for example, whether the asset has ultimately outlived its useful life or whether it has remained fixed to a building that has been sold or taken into personal ownership out of the trade). The legislation itself determines that ownership at the outset lies with the individual or partnership making the expenditure.

The legislation is interpreted strictly by HMRC. There must be a real threat to an individual's personal security. The threat must have come about as a result of the business and not personal issues. The asset must either be entirely used for security purposes, or be a clearly defined part of an asset that is so used. HMRC manuals expound on their views, citing alarm systems, bullet-resistant windows, reinforced doors and windows, perimeter walls and fences as included assets. HMRC also provide situation examples.

Where a security asset has been properly identified and allowed, revenue expenditure associated with it, which would not otherwise be allowed, is permitted. The type of expenditure envisaged is that which would ordinarily be disallowed through not being wholly and exclusively incurred for the purpose of the business. This might be, for example, personal body guards.

The *Hanson* case, although it related to employment expenses and a benefit in kind charge, gives a good example of the type of situation envisaged. Lord Hanson, through his business position as executive chairman of Hanson Plc, had become a target for the IRA. It was also found that the sole object of the company in providing the security services was to meet that threat. The court decision determined that Lord Hanson was not liable for a tax charge on the security measures provided by the company.

Separately from the above special legislation, allowable under the normal capital allowances regime is the cost of guard dogs. Provided it is clear that they are genuinely used to enhance security, their acquisition falls within plant and machinery and the allowable deductions follow accordingly.

Note that the special legislation does not extend to threat to property. There is no particular deduction available for defence of property, but normal rules (such as those on capital allowances, staff costs and contractors) are all available, where appropriate. This was exemplified in *Brockhouse and Ors (t/a A5 Aquatics) [2011] TC 01235.* Mr Brockhouse was a member of a partnership whose business was that of selling fish, aquariums, ponds and associated products. The partnership had installed fencing around the property, which included Mr Brockhouse's own residence as well as the partnership's retail premises. The purpose of the new fencing was to improve security because they had suffered from poachers. The FTT found that there was far too little evidence to conclude that Mr Brockhouse faced a special threat to his personal physical security. As a consequence, the conditions of *CAA 2001, s 33* were not met and Mr Brockhouse's appeal against HMRC's disallowance of the expenditure failed.

B47.1.2 Underpinning borrowings

This use of the term "security" is merely touched upon here for completeness. Loan and overdraft interest is dealt with in **B31**. The security envisaged here is not in itself expenditure which qualifies as a deduction, but it enables interest charged on a loan secured on a particular asset to qualify, when all conditions are met.

The key point to be drawn is that it is not the nature of the asset itself on which security has been charged which determines the deductibility of loan interest; it is the use of the loan itself which is the determining factor. Thus a sole trader or partner might use his home as security for a loan for working capital for his business, or to buy an asset for the business. This might be by way of a new mortgage or an extension of an existing home mortgage. Provided the loan itself is used by the business, the fact that the home is the structure to provide the security is irrelevant. Interest would still be deductible. The converse also applies. Using a business asset as security does not automatically enable the interest on a loan raised thereon to qualify as a business deduction. However, a different position might be available where the finance raised by a loan is used by the business to repay monies effectively loaned to the business by the sole trader or partner.

B47.2 REFERENCES

Statutory references

CAA 2001, ss 27(1), 33, 63(5)

ITEPA 2003, s 100

ITTOIA 2005, s 81

Leading cases

Lord Hanson v Mansworth (HMIT) [2004] SpC 410

Brockhouse and Ors (t/a A5 Aquatics) [2011] TC 01235

HMRC manuals

BIM47301, BIM47305, BIM47310

CA22270, CA 21200

B48

Software

B48.1 COMMENT

There is no statutory definition of "software" within the *Taxes Acts*. HMRC describe software as "computer programs of any type and data of any kind" and "a set of instructions in digital form".

A revenue deduction is available for recurring licence fees for use of non-exclusive software rights for the purpose of a trade. HMRC's view is that software is essentially a tool of the trade, and general case law distinguishing payments between capital and revenue has limited application. By concession, where payments for software are for rights covering a period of less than two years, the cost will be deductible in full in the year of payment (where the amount is written off in the accounts).

If periodic payments for software are instalments for an outright purchase of software rights, so that the purchaser has exclusivity to use or sub-license the intellectual property (e.g. for use in a trade of developing and licensing software), this type of expenditure is capital in nature.

The purchase of software as a capital asset may include the acquisition of a bundle of other intellectual property rights, such as trademarks, copyrights, or "show-how" and the tax treatment is then dependent on the underlying rights (see **B34**, **B46**).

Traders or property businesses using the cash basis may claim relief for software expenses. From 6 April 2017, where the expense is of a capital nature then a deduction is allowed if the rights fall within the definition used in the accounting standard for Micro-entities, FRS 105, Section 13 "Intangible Assets other than goodwill".

Intellectual property is defined as:

- patents, trademarks and registered designs, plant breeder rights (UK registered or similar rights registered overseas);
- unregistered information or techniques with industrial, commercial or other economic value; and

- licences in connection with the above rights.

Capital expenditure on software that comprises the above types of intellectual property will qualify for relief if the rights to use the software expire within 20 years of the date of purchase.

For companies, the tax treatment of software is generally dealt with under the corporate intangibles regime (*CTA 2009, Part 8*) and these provisions do not apply to unincorporated businesses.

B48.1.1 Capital allowances

If a business acquires "a right to use or otherwise deal with computer software" by making a lump sum payment this is deemed to be expenditure on plant, and relief is then obtained through claiming capital allowances. This treatment applies whether or not the licence fee is incurred in conjunction with a purchase of computer hardware. If an Annual Investment Allowance is not available, a short-life asset election may be appropriate to ensure that the deduction for software is obtained over its useful life.

Proceeds taken to the capital allowances pool on disposal of software rights are limited, in the usual way, to the original cost. A disposal includes an outright sale or grant of a user licence (or series of licences). Unlike other types of qualifying plant, no disposal arises if the business permanently ceases or the rights are no longer used for a qualifying activity.

Capital allowances cannot be claimed by taxpayers using the cash basis.

B48.1.2 In-house software development

The economic function of software used in the trade will determine the tax treatment, and this applies to in-house expenses of an IT department. The dividing line between costs to bring into existence an asset or advantage as fixed capital for the business and recurring revenue expenditure is a question of fact (*McVeigh v Arthur Sanderson & Sons Ltd (1968) 45 TC 273*).

If the accounting treatment requires that costs are capitalised or treated as deferred then tax deductions will follow generally accepted accounting principles; e.g. capitalised staff costs that are revenue in nature are deductible when amortised to the profit and loss account.

Expenses that are capital in nature will be disallowed, even if the prescribed accounting treatment is to write off the expenditure, but may qualify for capital allowances.

Income tax is not deductible at source on royalties paid for a non-exclusive software licence (typically where this comprises widely available rights to generic software). A payment for the exploitation of bespoke software rights may be subject to deduction at the basic rate. This depends on the location of the supplier and the nature of the underlying bundle of intellectual property which is comprised in the software. For example if software includes copyrights or know-how then a deduction may be required when payment is made to a non-UK resident supplier (see **B46**).

B48.2 REFERENCES

Statutory references

CAA 2001, ss 71, 72

ITA 2007, ss 906, 907

CTA 2009, s 815

Leading cases

McVeigh v Arthur Sanderson & Sons Ltd (1968) 45 TC 273

ECC Quarries Ltd v Watkis (1975) 51 TC 153

HMRC manuals

BIM35801, BIM35805, BIM35810, BIM35822

CA23410, CA23430

INTM342630

See also

Chapter 3, **B34**, **B46**, **B63**

HMRC Capital v Revenue Expenditure Toolkit: 2016–17 Self-Assessment and Company Tax Returns (published August 2017)

B49

Staff welfare costs

B49.1 COMMENT

As with certain other payments where employees are involved (see **B42**), a key issue is not just the deductibility of expenditure on staff welfare to the employer business, but also the knock-on effect on taxable benefits of the employees.

Consideration should therefore be given to those that are:

- general staff costs, such as providing tea and coffee;
- general staff costs that cross the line to become benefits in kind; and
- welfare costs that are tax exempt in specific circumstances.

All of the above costs should remain deductible business costs to the employer, unless provided in the course of his ordinary domestic and personal relationships. It is the way in which the costs are handled for the employee that differentiates between them. Whilst a detailed analysis of staff benefits is outside the scope of this publication, indicators are included where they could assist an employer in selecting which welfare costs to undertake.

B49.1.1 Capital or revenue?

In addition to the above cost categories, HMRC are watchful in case expenditure has been outlaid on capital items. Examples of capital items are:

- the cost, whether incurred voluntarily or under compulsion, of additions or structural alterations to business premises, made to meet the welfare requirements of employees; and
- the cost of sports pavilions, clubhouses, and providing specialised sports grounds.

HMRC contrast the above with examples of costs which would be deductible against profits:

- the rent and cost of maintenance of recreation grounds, canteens, ambulance rooms, rest rooms, lavatories, or day nurseries for use by employees;

- salaries of welfare superintendents; and
- provision of protective clothing and cost of their repair and laundering.

B49.1.2 General staff costs – not taxable benefits

All the costs discussed here should be deductible to the employer in his trading accounts. They are only examples of expenditure that an employer can provide which staff could enjoy as perks without being taxed on them.

The position relating to "trivial benefits" changed from 6 April 2016. Prior to that, HMRC's internal guidance stated (at EIM21861) that "trivial benefits" should be ignored for all practical purposes. However, there was no set monetary limit to distinguish those costs from "minor" benefits. The latter were primarily taxable albeit of not significant value, unless other specific legislation exempted them (such as welfare counselling). The principle prior to 6 April 2016 was to look at the circumstances with a common sense approach. It was the cost to each employee, and not the overall cost to the employer, that was being judged. The salary level of the employee was irrelevant. HMRC explained that a benefit that rewarded an employee was less likely to be classed as trivial than expenditure on staff welfare.

From 6 April 2016 there is a statutory exemption in place for trivial benefits. Items under £50 are classed as trivial. There is no limit to the number of trivial benefits that an individual employee can receive, except where directors of a close company are involved. In that case an annual cap of £300 per person per tax year applies. The detail is set out at *ITEPA 2003, ss 323A, 323B,* which should be checked for the conditions which apply. Particularly, cash and cash vouchers are excluded from being trivial benefits in this context. HMRC provide a useful commentary at EIM21864 to EIM21868.

Providing tea, coffee and water from a cooling dispenser is specifically exempted from being a taxable benefit if the facilities are available to all staff. If not, the provision would be classed as a trivial benefit. This facility is extended to providing free or subsidised meals to staff without being a taxable benefit if particular conditions are met. The meals must be:

- provided in a canteen or on the employer's premises;
- of a reasonable cost;
- available to all staff at the same location, although some may be subsidised to a greater extent and the choices available need not be the same for all staff;
- not part of a salary sacrifice (optional remuneration arrangements) or flexible working arrangement; and

- hotel and catering staff have separate arrangements permitting them to dine in a designated section of the public dining area.

B49.1.3 General staff costs viewed as taxable

As above, the facilities mentioned here will be deductible for the employer, although see **B13** on entertaining for the full picture of that specialised area. The range is very wide, and only a very few are highlighted here, showing the line where the non-taxable ones selected above cross to becoming taxable.

The employer providing staff benefits of cash, "money's worth" or non-cash vouchers will always be taxable. Even if they are of low value, they will not be classed as "trivial benefits".

The general exemption from a taxable benefit charge where meals are provided in a canteen does not extend to meals provided in premises available to the general public, such as restaurants, cafes or public houses. Unless another exemption applies, such as subsistence (see **B50**), even those of modest scale will be taxable benefits.

Private medical and dental insurance provided to staff by an employer will always be a taxable benefit, unless it is work-related (e.g. travel insurance for an employee working overseas). The exact way that the tax and NIC charge is levied will depend on the particular type of arrangement involved. Each method will result in a deductible expense for the employer.

B49.1.4 Welfare costs tax exempt on the employee

For comment where welfare counselling provided by an employer is not taxable as a benefit on the employee, see **B7**.

Statutory powers are set out in *ITEPA 2003, s 210* so that the Treasury may make selected benefits free from tax on employees. Already included are: annual health screenings, provided they are available to all employees; and medical check-ups, again to be available to all employees, or all of those identified as having a condition that requires them.

More loosely categorised as "welfare" benefits are sports and recreational facilities provided free to employees and their families. Again, these will not be taxable benefits on the employees if certain conditions are met. These include the facilities being available to all employees, and that they should not be open to the general public.

Eye tests can be provided free of tax to any employees who use a computer screen in their work. If it can be certified by an optician that part of the need for spectacles results from using computers at work, the spectacles can also be funded, either fully or in part, by the employer without a taxable benefit arising.

B49.1.5 Finally

By way of clarification, all of the costs incurred by an employer, whether sole trader, partnership or company, in providing welfare benefits to staff will be deductible expenses unless they are of a capital nature. The choice as to which benefits (if any) are to be provided is likely to be influenced by the value perceived by the employee. That is bound to be affected by any attendant tax charge.

B49.2 REFERENCES

Statutory references

ITEPA 2003, ss 210, 317, 320A. 323A, 323B

Leading cases

None

HMRC manuals

BIM47070

EIM21860, EIM21861, EIM21863, EIM21864 to EIM21868

B50

Subsistence

B50.1 COMMENT

The context here is the deductibility of subsistence costs for the unincorporated business, whether sole trader or partnership. The tax treatment for employees and directors in receipt of subsistence provided by their employer is outside the scope of this publication.

Obtaining a tax deduction, even where common sense implies that one should be available, is not easy for the self-employed. The problem is the "wholly and exclusively" rule in *ITTOIA 2005, s 34*. Historically, HMRC have achieved significant success in the courts in denying a deduction for subsistence, based on duality of purpose. Undeniably, human beings require food to live, not just to work. Any claim to apportionment failed because, by so claiming, partial private use was thereby admitted and "wholly and exclusively" was ruled out.

The *Caillebotte v Quinn* case demonstrated this perfectly. Mr Quinn was a carpenter who was working some 40 miles from home. Buying his lunch cost him 40 pence (this was in 1975!) compared with his home-made sandwiches of 10 pence. Accordingly, he claimed 30 pence per day as a business deduction and the judge ruled against him.

The *Watkis v Ashford* case was an important one, changing to a limited extent HMRC's view. The nature of the costs in dispute varied. The firm of solicitors claimed to deduct:

- the cost of food and drink at lunchtime partnership meetings;
- the cost of food and drink at evening partnership meetings;
- accommodation, food and drink at the firm's annual conference; and
- the provision of a room, food and drink at a conference with other firms.

At the initial appeal hearing before the Special Commissioner, the firm Ashford, Sparkes and Harward were successful in claiming all of the above as deductible costs. HMRC appealed. In response, Nourse J determined that:

- The cost of food and drink was disallowable on general principles of "wholly and exclusively". Accordingly, the costs of food and drink for partnership lunchtime and evening meetings were not deductible.
- Costs of the accommodation for the annual conference were incurred solely for the purposes of the business. No distinction was to be made between the cost of overnight accommodation on the one hand and food and drink on the other. Therefore the costs of the weekend annual conference were allowed in full.
- The cost of the provision of the room for the conference with other firms was outlaid entirely for business reasons. It was separately identified from the cost of the food and drink. This led to the cost of room hire succeeding as a deduction, but the cost of food and drink failing on duality of purpose.

As a result of the *Watkis v Ashford* case, HMRC now allow reasonable expenditure on meals that are taken in conjunction with overnight accommodation, whether or not paid on the same bill.

In practice, HMRC have for some years relaxed the strict principle in certain circumstances. They have permitted a deduction for "reasonable expenses" incurred where the following applies:

- the business is by its nature itinerant; and
- the costs relate to occasional business journeys outside the normal pattern.

Subsequently (and currently the position, effective from 2009/10), a statutory footing was imposed to replace the informal practice that had developed. *ITTOIA 2005, s 57A* clearly creates a link between travel costs which are allowable as a business deduction and associated costs of food and drink. In this way, it is akin to employee subsistence costs. These, in general, follow the treatment of the employee's travel costs when determining whether a deduction against employment income is available. This is normally, but not necessarily, associated with the employer having borne the cost of the travel and subsistence.

There are specific conditions to be met in *section 57A* for the cost of food and drink to be allowable to the self-employed. The section states:

> "(1) In calculating the profits of a trade, a deduction is allowed for any reasonable expenses incurred on food or drink for consumption by the trader at a place to which the trader travels in the course of carrying on the trade, or while travelling to a place in the course of carrying on the trade, if conditions A and B are met.
>
> (2) Condition A is met if–

(a) a deduction is allowed for the expenses incurred by the trader in travelling to the place, or

(b) where the expenses of travelling to the place are not incurred by the trader, a deduction would be allowed for them if they were.

(3) Condition B is met if–

(a) at the time the expenses are incurred on the food or drink, the trade is by its nature itinerant, or

(b) the trader does not travel to the place more than occasionally in the course of carrying on the trade and either–

(i) the travel in connection with which the expenses are incurred on the food or drink is undertaken otherwise than as part of the trader's normal pattern of travel in the course of carrying on the trade, or

(ii) the trader does not have such a normal pattern of travel."

The link with travel for a deduction for subsistence to be allowed was shown in *Jain [2015] TC 04788*. Dr Jain was a consultant orthopaedic surgeon, employed by a local NHS Trust. He was also in private practice, undertaking consultations and operations in another local hospital. In addition, he carried out work providing medical reports for litigation purposes under contract for various agencies. Dr Jain visited each hospital once a month and stayed overnight at local hotels. He then prepared the reports and dealt with administration in relation to the work at his home. Dr Jain claimed deductions for travel and subsistence expenses in relation to his travel between the hospitals and his home. These HMRC disallowed on the basis that the expenses had a duality of purpose and so were not incurred wholly and exclusively for the purposes of the trade or profession.

The FTT found that there was sufficient similarity to the *Samadian* case (see **B33**) in the regularity and predictability of Dr Jain's visits to the hospitals to make them places of business. It therefore followed that the costs of travel between the hospitals and Dr Jain's home were not incurred wholly and exclusively for the purposes of the business and were not deductible. Whether Dr Jain's subsistence expenditure could be deducted was dependent on the treatment of the related travel expenses, under *ITTOIA 2005, s 57A*. Consequently the FTT found that following *Caillebotte v Quinn (1975)* expenditure on food had a duality of purpose which disallowed it, and, as a result of the decision on travel expenses, neither was it deductible under *section 57A*.

B50.1.1 Subsistence when working overseas

HMRC have always had a more lenient attitude to both accommodation and subsistence costs when the individual's business has caused him to travel abroad and to stay there for a time. BIM47710 still refers to their views expressed in Statement of Practice A16 but the opinion remains current. It states that:

> "Where an individual who is resident in the UK and chargeable to tax on the profits of a trade, profession or vocation carried on wholly or partly in the UK (either alone or in partnership) spends time abroad on business, the cost of living abroad personal to him will not be disallowed under *s34 Income Tax (Trading and Other Income) Act 2005* if the absence abroad is for the purposes of the trade, profession or vocation. Private expenditure, for example, on holidays taken in the course of a business trip, should, however, not be allowed. Living expenses are regarded as including the cost of accommodation, food and drink attributable to the individual trader or partner. If he is accompanied by his family or other dependants, the costs attributable to them will not be allowed."

The above HMRC statement does not mean that they abandon that cornerstone of legislation, "duality of purpose", in connection with overseas business costs. Where a business trip is combined with, for example, a holiday, the entire costs are likely to be disallowed. The *Bowden v Russell* case tested this. A solicitor travelled with his wife to the USA and Canada to attend the annual meeting of the American Bar Association and the Empire Law Conference. However, he and his wife combined this with a holiday. Initially, an appeal by the solicitor to the General Commissioners against HMRC disallowing his share (he had excluded those of his wife) of the costs incurred was mainly successful. HMRC appealed the case to the High Court. One of the key points on which the solicitor failed was that it was clear – indeed, he had stated – that his intention had always been to combine the conference trip with a holiday. That in itself enforced the "duality of purpose" principle. A point also raised by HMRC, but on which the judges decided that they did not need to reach a conclusion because the case had already been proven on duality, was that the subject matter of the conference was remote from the type of work and clients that the firm dealt with.

B50.1.2 Self-employed lorry drivers

The approach to subsistence and accommodation set out above applies equally to self-employed lorry drivers. However, there is a practical difference for lorry drivers, in that many of them use specially adapted cabs and sleep there overnight. HMRC confirm (at BIM37670, and originally in their Tax Bulletin of 8 August 1993) that the reasonable cost of meals is deductible when associated with drivers sleeping in their cabs in the same way as if they had taken other overnight accommodation.

B50.1.3 Hotel proprietors

The issue in this context usually turns from one of deductible expenses to deemed income. Hotel proprietors and, frequently, the owners of restaurants and public houses might benefit from food purchased for their business. In that position, the owners should be assessing a fair and reasonable value of these notional sales and accounting for them in their trading accounts.

B50.1.4 Reminder

None of the considerations here override the fundamental principles relating to the deductibility of costs of entertaining (see **B13**).

B50.2 REFERENCES

Statutory references

ITTOIA 2005, ss 34, 57A

Leading cases

Bowden v Russell & Russell (1965) 42 TC 301

Caillebotte v Quinn (1975) 50 TC 222

Watkis v Ashford, Sparkes and Harward [1985] BTC 391

Jain [2015] TC 04788

Samadian v Revenue and Customs Commissioners [2014] BTC 504

HMRC manuals

BIM37660, BIM37670, BIM47710

B51

Tax (foreign)

B51.1 COMMENT

Many UK businesses have some overseas income which forms a part of their trade. Where it comes about by trading with another business overseas, as opposed to a private customer, it will often be the case that the tax jurisdiction in which the customer is based will require tax to be withheld from the payment. Double tax treaties usually ensure that relief for the amount withheld has the potential to be reclaimed in the country where the supplier business resides.

The fundamental rules relating to claiming relief against UK tax, for foreign tax that has been deducted against the same income, are similar whether the income in question relates to the trade of an unincorporated business, that of a company or an individual's personal income.

There are two methods by which the tax charged by a foreign country is relieved against that levied in the UK. The one that potentially provides the maximum tax reduction is tax credit relief.

The legislation decrees that the foreign tax can only be offset against the UK tax charged on the person's identical income (or gains). It cannot be offset against any other income, nor can it be carried forward or back against income from the same (or any other) country in a different accounting period.

Accordingly, the UK tax on that income for that person in the relevant year is calculated first, ignoring the foreign tax. Next, the UK tax thus calculated is compared with the amount of the foreign tax. Under the tax credit relief system, the foreign tax simply reduces the UK tax. If the foreign tax is lower, it can be utilised entirely by the offset. If it is higher, the reduction is limited to the UK tax itself, and the surplus foreign tax is wasted.

The case of *Ward [2016] TC 04902* demonstrates the restrictions on the relievable foreign tax credit. This was one of five issues heard by the FTT. Mr Ward was an Australian citizen seconded to the UK and he became UK resident during that period. His secondment was subsequently extended and for a while he transferred back to the Australian payroll. In his UK tax return he claimed a substantial credit for Australian tax against his UK tax liability. However, it transpired that Mr Ward had claimed loss relief which reduced his Australian tax liability considerably. The FTT upheld HMRC's contention that the foreign tax credit set against his UK tax could not exceed the amount of foreign tax actually paid.

The second method of relief is always available to the person making the claim, but usually comes into play when there are losses in respect of the income on which the foreign tax was charged. It offers relief by deduction against the income as an expense. Thus, if there are losses, the foreign tax increases them because it is treated as an expense of the trade and, in that way, will be included in whatever loss relief mechanism is chosen.

Whilst the deduction option would not provide as much tax reduction as the tax credit option where the latter is fully available, where there are losses it would be better than no relief at all.

Where the deduction method is required, the tax credit relief under *TIOPA 2010, s 18* is disclaimed under *s 27*. *Section 112* then permits the tax to be treated as a deduction.

The deduction of foreign tax from trading income reviewed above relates to foreign taxes levied on income. However, a deduction may also be allowed from UK trading profits for other annual taxes charged on a person resident in the UK in respect of his overseas trading. Examples are taxes on trade purchases or turnover and social security taxes in respect of employees. The tax in question would need to be examined in each individual case to determine whether it would be allowable as a deduction or not (see BIM45901 and BIM45905 for further guidance).

The *Legal & General Assurance* case was important in establishing that the amount of foreign tax can only be offset against UK tax on that foreign income, and not against the whole of the company's profits. This point has now been legislated so is beyond doubt and not reliant upon case law. That case related to the particular instance of insurance companies, but the principle has been extended so that the position is clear for all businesses.

The significance of relating the income on which the foreign tax has been deducted to the income which is subject to UK tax should not be overlooked. In *R & C Commrs v Anson*, a UK resident individual suffered US tax on his share of the profits distributed by a Delaware LLC. For US tax purposes, a Delaware company is treated as transparent. However, HMRC treated the LLC as opaque, which resulted in the UK taxpayer's income becoming a distribution by way of dividend by the LLC. However, in the US it was not a dividend, so there was no tax credit to be set against the UK tax liability. The case was heard initially by the Upper Tribunal, but subsequently the Court of Appeal upheld the decision.

B51.2 REFERENCES

Statutory references

TIOPA 2010, ss 18, 27, 112

Leading cases

Legal & General Assurance Society Ltd v Thomas [2005] SpC 461

R & C Commrs v Anson [2012] BTC 1,552

Ward [2016] TC 04902

HMRC manuals

BIM45901, BIM45905

INTM161050, INTM161080

B52

Trade subscriptions

B52.1 COMMENT

Under general principles, a subscription made for the purpose of the trade is deductible. No relief is available where the motive for the expenditure has a dual purpose; e.g. fees paid by an unincorporated business for a proprietor's membership of the local golf club are likely to have more than an incidental private purpose.

Initial entrance fees to join a professional body or other organisation are generally not allowable, as the amount is capital in nature being a one off expense to secure an enduring benefit.

HMRC maintain a list of approved professional organisations for employees as guidance for subscriptions that qualify for a deduction against earnings (*ITEPA 2003, s 333*). A subscription paid by a self-employed trader to an organisation included on the list may be deductible where this is relevant to the trade. Subscriptions to other professional and trade associations that are not listed (including foreign trade associations) may also be allowable.

Fees paid to a trade association are deductible if the amount is applied for a business purpose; i.e. costs incurred on behalf of the member would have been deductible had these been incurred directly (*Lochgelly Iron & Coal Company Ltd v Crawford (1913) 6 TC 267*). Trade organisations can obtain guidance from HMRC to clarify the nature of entrance fees and subscriptions paid by their members (BIM47425).

The payment of a subscription that entitles the trader to purchase discounted goods and services for the purposes of the trade will be allowable (*Elwood v Utitz CA (NI) (1965) 42 TC 482*).

Charitable donations in cash made by a sole trader are disallowable, as the personal motive for making the payment, except for the following:

- If a trader has a direct connection to a charity and there are clearly defined promotional benefits for the business in linking itself to that organisation, in which case HMRC accept that modest subscriptions may be claimed.

- Subscriptions to a charity aimed at providing benefits to employees of the business may be allowed, e.g. to a local hospital (*Bourne and Hollingsworth Ltd v Ogden (1929) 14 TC 349*).
- Contributions or subscriptions to certain benevolent societies; for example, HMRC accept that annual contributions to the Chartered Accountants' Benevolent Association qualify for a deduction where the amount does not exceed the annual voting subscription rate to a member of the ICAEW.

B52.2 REFERENCES

Statutory references

ITTOIA 2005, s 34

CTA 2009, s 54

Leading cases

Lochgelly Iron & Coal Company Ltd v Crawford (1913) 6 TC 267

Thomas v Richard Evans & Co Ltd (1927) 11 TC 790

Bourne & Hollingsworth Ltd v Ogden (1929) 14 TC 349

Elwood v Utitz CA (NI) (1965) 42 TC 482

HMRC manuals

BIM37500, BIM47410, BIM47415

See also

B5, B36

Approved list of organisations for deductions by employees for subscriptions: www.hmrc.gov.uk/list3/list3.htm

B53

Trade tools

B53.1 COMMENT

The rules on deductions for the replacement and alteration of trade tools are repealed for expenditure incurred on or after 6 April 2016. The definition of "tools" was wide ranging and allowed claims for items that were not intended to qualify for relief. For example the deduction could be claimed by landlords letting part-furnished accommodation who were unable to access relief through the "wear and tear" allowance (now superseded by Replacement of Domestic items relief – see **B62**).

Abolition of the relief will not unduly restrict relief for traders if an Annual Investment Allowance under the capital allowances regime is available. Landlords of residential properties (except for furnished holiday letting) cannot claim capital allowances so certain items may no longer qualify for relief under the narrower definition used for domestic items.

Traders and property businesses using the cash basis may obtain a revenue deduction for certain categories of capital items that are depreciating assets.

B53.1.1 Replacement and alteration of tools – Pre-6 April 2016

A statutory deduction is available for the replacement or alternation of trade tools on expenditure incurred before 6 April 2016 where otherwise the item would be treated as capital under general principles. A tool for this purpose is defined as "any implement, utensil or article".

Under the tools relief the initial cost of purchase is treated as a capital expense and is not eligible for a deduction but may instead qualify for relief under the capital allowances rules.

Replacement tools are treated as revenue expenditure if a deduction would not otherwise be available under general principles, e.g. as a repair. Where the accounting treatment is to write off the cost of tools in full when the items are replaced, no adjustment is necessary in the computation of taxable profits.

Alternatively, if the accounting treatment capitalises or defers the cost of renewing tools (e.g. as part of stock or work in progress), a revenue deduction can be claimed in the accounting period when the costs were incurred.

The dividing line for an implement or utensil for residential property letting may have included moveable items such as soft furnishings and kitchen utensils but not carpets, curtains, fridges or cookers (see **B62**).

A previous claim for capital allowances on tooling does not restrict a revenue deduction for replacement items (BIM46965).

HMRC interpreted the meaning of "tool" narrowly and gave the following as examples:

- glasses in a public house;
- spanners used by a car mechanic; and
- cutlery in a cafe.

Examples of items that did not qualify as tools include:

- bakers' ovens;
- hairdressers' chairs;
- haulage lorries; and
- free-standing "white goods".

The renewals basis for tools did not apply for traders that elected to use the cash basis (see **Chapter 2**).

B53.2 REFERENCES

Statutory references

ITTOIA 2005, ss 33A, 311A, 56A, 68 (repealed)

FA 2016, s 72

Leading cases

None

HMRC manuals

BIM46960, BIM46965

See also

Chapter 2, **B44**, **B55**, **B62**

B54

Trading and property allowance

B54.1 COMMENT

A fixed expense allowance was introduced from 6 April 2017 with the intention of excluding individuals from self-assessment if they have trading or property income of £1,000 or less. Where the allowance covers the income in full no entry is required in a self-assessment return.

B54.1.1 Trading allowance

The trading allowance is available to individuals who would otherwise be taxed as a sole trader. The following cannot claim the allowance:

- individuals operating in partnerships;
- an activity that qualifies under the "rent a room" scheme as a trade, as the exemption takes priority.

The allowance is given by reference to "relevant income" and comprises:

- trading receipts from an individual's relevant trades*; plus*
- miscellaneous income, ignoring the trading allowance and before deduction of any expenses (*ITTOIA 2005, ss 687–689A*).

Trade receipts may be calculated by reference to the cash basis (if an individual is eligible) or under generally accepted accounting practice. Miscellaneous receipts are on an arising basis.

The following types of income or profits are *not* included as part of relevant income:

- post-cessation receipts (see **B37**), which do not fall within the definition of relevant income;
- adjustment income on a change of accounting policy (see **B1**).

If relevant income is less than £1,000 the trader allowance applies automatically to reduce taxable profits to nil. Where a taxpayer uses the allowance no further relief is available for actual expenses incurred. An election can be made to disapply the allowance on or before the first anniversary of the self-assessment filing deadline. This may be beneficial if actual expenses generate a loss which may then be relieved against other income, or if overlap relief is available on the cessation of a trade.

An election for partial relief can be made when relevant income exceeds £1,000. The allowance may be allocated between more than one trade or source of miscellaneous income.

The trading allowance is not available against:

- income that is within rent-a-room relief (e.g. a bed and breakfast business) where:
  - receipts are within the limit of £7,500, (divided where income is received jointly) and the taxpayer elects out of rent-a-room rules; or
  - receipts are above the limit but the taxpayer does not elect to use rent-a-room for receipts under the "alternative calculation" method but chooses instead to deduct actual expenses;
- relevant income that is from an employer, spouse or civil partner;
- payments that are received from a partnership in which the individual is a partner, or company in which they are a participator;
- trading income that includes a receipt from a close company where the trader is also a participator or associate of a participator in the company.

B54.1.2 Property allowance

A separate allowance, in addition to the trading allowance, may also be available to taxpayers for property income up to £1,000 p.a. from 6 April 2017. Joint property owners are entitled to an allowance of £1,000 each.

The allowance covers income from UK or overseas property that would otherwise be taxable.

Property income from the following is not within the definition of relevant business property:

- rent-a-room;
- an Authorised Investment Trust; or
- a distribution from a Real Estate Investment Trust.

The allowance cannot be used to provide relief in the following circumstances:

- to reduce restricted interest costs for a non-deductible proportion relating to a dwelling related loan (see **B31**).
- for rental income which could be within rent-a-room, but where the taxpayer does not elect to use the relief (see **54.1.1**);
- income is from an employer, spouse or civil partner;
- payments are received from a partnership in which the individual is a partner or company where the individual is a participator;
- rental income includes a receipt from a close company where the landlord is also a participator or associate of a participator in the company.

B54.2 REFERENCES

Statutory references

ITTOIA 2005, s 22A, Part 6A (ss 783A–783BQ), ss 687–689A, Part 7

Leading cases

None

HMRC guidance

www.gov.uk/guidance/tax-free-allowances-on-property-and-trading-income

See also

Chapter 3, B37

B55

Trading stock and work in progress

B55.1 COMMENT

For businesses using generally accepted accounting practice the cost of inventory is recognised as an expense in the accounting period in which sales revenue is recognised. Therefore an adjustment is required, at the end of each accounting period for stock and work in progress held at the balance sheet date, to calculate accounting profits or losses in compliance with generally accepted accounting principles.

Trading stock and work in progress is part of circulating or working capital of a business and includes goods and services at various stages of production held for the purposes of sale. An asset will be classed as stock where it is used in the ordinary course of trade, rather than a fixed asset that is used permanently in the business. In cases where the classification is uncertain, the balance sheet disclosure, description of the activities in the financial statements and other documentation, such as a partnership agreement, may be persuasive in determining what type of assets are held as stock.

The intention of the trader may alter over time (see *Vodafone Cellular Ltd v Shaw (1997) 69 TC 376*, *Simmons v IR Commrs [1980] STC 350* and *Kirkham v Williams [1991] STC 342*). If stock is temporarily used for hire, this will not necessarily change its classification to fixed capital (*Gloucester Railway Carriage and Wagon Company Ltd v CIR*).

The valuation of stock and progress is not relevant to traders who use the cash basis for computing taxable profits, where a deduction is allowed when the stock is purchased (see **Chapter 2**).

B55.1.1 Accounting framework

The deductibility of stock and progress follows generally accepted accounting practice. From 1 January 2015 the accounting requirements are dealt with under "Inventories" at Section 13 of FRS 102, including raw materials, work in progress and finished goods. The new standard is similar to its predecessor, SSAP 9 "Stocks and Long-Term Contracts".

Accounting for long-term contracts including construction projects (previously dealt with under SSAP 9) and contracts for uncompleted services not represented by a physical asset is covered by Section 23 "Revenue Recognition" (previously FRS 5 Application Note G and UITF 40). Specialist activities, including agriculture and mineral extraction, are dealt with at Section 34 of FRS 102.

Cost of sales generally comprises:

- opening stock and work in progress brought forward, plus
- purchases during the period, less
- the closing value of stock and work in progress.

The effect of the above is that, for each accounting period, the profit and loss is debited or credited the movement on opening and closing stock values. The accounting mechanism for this adjustment is achieved by charging opening stock to the accounts at the beginning of the accounting period and crediting the closing amount at the end of the period.

When goods are purchased on sale or return, the legal ownership will generally be transferred to the trader when the item is sold. The tax treatment will follow the correct accounting treatment.

B55.1.2 Valuation methods

The basic rule for the valuation of physical stock and work in progress at the end of the accounting period is based on the lower of cost and "estimated selling price less costs to complete sell", i.e. net realisable value.

Manufactured stock includes all or some of the following:

- raw materials;
- direct production expenses; and
- relevant proportion of overhead costs.

The accounting treatment used for valuing physical stock depends on the nature of the goods and services produced. The following methods are acceptable:

- "first in first out" ("FIFO");
- replacement cost (this method is commonly used by car dealers – BIM52001);
- discounted selling price (selling price less average gross margin); or
- base stock (commonly used when there are a large number of smaller stock items and the holding does not fall below a defined level).

Mark to market valuations may be used for certain types of financial instruments.

FRS 102 no longer permits stock to be valued on a "last in first out" ("LIFO") basis. LIFO assumes that recently purchased stocks are sold first and the closing stock valuation is based on the cost of older items.

B55.1.3 Impairments

Stock values may be adjusted for events after the balance sheet date; so, if sale prices realised after the end of the accounting period are less than cost, the value of closing stock may be reduced (FRS 102, Section 32). This write down is an allowable expense when recognised in the profit and loss account.

A business with a large number of inventories may use a formulae approach to calculate provisions against closing stock values, and the deduction will be allowable if an appropriate methodology is used to calculate the impairment. A provision against slow-moving stock will not necessarily be allowable unless there is other evidence that the realisable value of the underlying items is less than cost.

Partially complete contracts for services or physical work in progress on long-term construction contracts are valued on a percentage completion method and, if appropriate, a proportion of profits will be recognised under accounting rules for revenue recognition (FRS 102, Section 23). This accounting treatment also requires costs to be written off immediately when it is probable that total contract costs will exceed total contract revenue (FRS 102, para 23.26).

B55.1.4 Disallowed expenses included in stock

Production costs in valuing stock may include the absorption of fixed or variable overheads. When non-deductible expenditure, such as depreciation, is deferred as part of the valuation of closing stock and work in progress, the disallowance will be deferred and adjusted for in computing taxable profits in a later accounting period in which the stock is written off as part of cost of sales (*HMRC v William Grant & Sons Distillers Ltd; Small v Mars UK Ltd [2007] UKHL 15*).

Example – Depreciation and finance costs allocated to work in progress

In the year ended 31 March 2015, XYZ Partnership charges £50,000 depreciation for production plant to the profit and loss account (allocating the cost of the asset over its useful economic life, in accordance with FRS 102, Section 17). The closing valuation of work in progress and finished goods includes £10,000 as a proportion of depreciation overhead (as prescribed by FRS 102, Section 13). The net disallowable depreciation for that accounting period is £40,000 (i.e. £50,000 debited as depreciation, less £10,000 credited and included in the valuation of closing stock).

Certain finance costs, such as interest or hire purchase finance charges, may be absorbed as part of trading stock. The timing of the deductions for interest expenses will also follow the accounting treatment.

Replacement tooling costs incurred before 6 April 2016 are deductible in the accounting period in which the cost is incurred, notwithstanding that the expense may have been included in closing stock. The effect of this is that tooling costs were deductible in an earlier accounting period than recognised for accounting purposes. This treatment does not apply for tooling expenditure incurred after 5 April 2016 (see **B53**).

B55.1.5 Discontinuance of trade

A discontinuance of trade brings about a disposal of stock and work in progress (including long-term contracts) based on a sale at open market at the date of cessation.

The market value disposal rule also applies to traders that have adopted the cash basis.

If stock is sold to another person carrying out a trade in the UK and the parties are not connected, the acquisition price is the agreed price (which corresponds to the vendor's sale proceeds), plus associated acquisition costs.

Where the seller and purchaser of stock are connected persons (*ITA 2007, s 993*) an arm's length price must be adopted by both parties to account for the value of stock. A joint election can be made to use a lower value if the consideration paid does not exceed the arm's length price, so that the value used by the connected seller and purchaser will be the higher of:

- book value for the vendor; and
- the sales value agreed between the parties.

A trader using the cash basis is deemed to bring a receipt into charge for a tax year where there is a permanent cessation of trade, being the value of any trading stock at that time.

Example – Discontinuance: stock purchased by a connected party

A Ltd disincorporates its trade and the company distributes its assets, including trading stock, to the shareholders who then commence trading in partnership. The stock is shown at £30,000 in the final balance sheet of A Ltd, and the market value on the cessation of trade is £45,000. No consideration is given by the shareholders who receive the company's assets as a distribution on the winding up. The parties are connected and a joint election may be made to transfer stock at book value (*ITTOIA 2005, s 178; CTA 2009, s 167*). No taxable profit is realised by A Ltd on the transfer of closing stock, and the cost of opening stock for the partnership is £30,000.

Stock transferred to a person who is not carrying out a trade in the UK is treated as a deemed disposal based on the open market value at the date of cessation.

The discontinuance rules do not apply on a change in partners' interests unless this coincides with a cessation of the partnership.

The value of work in progress for an unincorporated profession or vocation on discontinuance will be the amount agreed between the parties if the purchaser continues to trade in the UK. A joint election can be made to transfer work in progress at cost, and the election is available whether or not the parties are connected. Any amount received in excess of cost is taxed on the seller as a post-cessation receipt.

In all other cases, work in progress is deemed to be sold at an arm's length price at the date of cessation.

On the death of a sole trader, the closing stock and work in progress are deemed to be sold at the lower of cost and net realisable value. If the trade is continued by the executors, stock is taken at market value and any uplift in value is not taxable in the estate of the deceased. HMRC accept that where the business passes directly to a beneficiary, trading stock is also treated as acquired at market value (BIM33520).

B55.1.6 Barter transactions

If a trader purchases stock for non-cash consideration, the cost of stock will be based on value of the consideration given where the parties are not connected.

Where business assets are acquired on incorporation in consideration for the issue of share capital ("incorporation relief" under *TCGA 1992, s 162)* the company (purchaser) will acquire stock at market value. A joint election to transfer stock at a lower value (e.g. book value) does not apply in these circumstances.

B55.1.7 Transactions not at arm's length

Stock purchased at below market value will be treated as purchased for the amount paid, unless the transaction involves fraud.

The cost of stock or work in progress may be adjusted to an arm's length price if the parties to the transaction are under common control, a tax advantage is obtained and the purchaser is within UK transfer pricing rules (see **B32**). Previously where transfer pricing rules applied, these took priority over the valuation of stock on transfers to or from fixed assets. This is amended for transactions from 8 July 2015 where the open market value of stock now trumps the transfer pricing value (if different).

Stock acquired as part of the purchase of a business may be revalued under fair value accounting rules with adjustments being made against the value of purchased goodwill (see FRS 102, Section 19). When computing taxable profits it is the amount paid for stock and work in progress that is used to compute taxable profits.

B55.1.8 Appropriation from stock

Sharkey v Wernher (1954) 36 TC 275 established the principle that, where a trader takes goods for own use, the disposal is treated as a sale at market value, so the difference between market value and the cost of the stock will be taxable as income. The rule does not apply to services.

The application of *Sharkey* was thrown into doubt following changes introduced by *FA 1998, s 42* (now *ITTOIA 2005, s 25*), which confirmed that the starting point for computing taxable profits must be based on accounting profits prepared in accordance with generally accepted accounting principles – which does not necessarily recognise accounting profit on an appropriation of stock.

The *Sharkey* principle has now been legislated so that in calculating the profits a receipt is brought into account, less any consideration received for the appropriation. The following transfers of stock will be treated as a disposal at market value:

- an appropriation of stock for use outside the business; and
- a transfer of stock to fixed assets for use as fixed capital.

Stock is narrowly defined for this purpose as items "… sold in the ordinary course of trade, or which would be sold if it were mature or its manufacture, preparation or construction were complete …" (*ITTOIA 2005, s 172A*). Raw materials, services performed in the ordinary course of trade, and materials used for services are specifically excluded. Therefore, only finished goods or partially completed physical work in progress are subject to the market value rule.

The boundary between an appropriation on which profit should be brought into charge, rather than a disallowance of expenses due to private use by the proprietor is not always free from doubt. Where a proprietor uses raw materials rather than a completed stock item from the business a deemed profit does not arise.

Furthermore, the parameters to establish market value are not always clear. For example, at the end of each day a restaurateur may take home perishable food that can no longer be used in the business. Arguably, these items are worthless; if so, no deemed profit will arise. Alternatively, if goods are taken for personal use by a retailer which attract a higher selling price than identical products sold by a competitor, the value for applying the own use principle is not entirely free from doubt.

When computing the profit attributed to the trader on an appropriation, the deduction for the cost of the stock should include any non-recoverable input VAT (see **B60**).

For a property development trader, an appropriation of stock to fixed assets may result in an unexpected taxable profit. The accounting classification should, if possible, be established at the commencement of construction and shown as fixed assets in the course of construction, rather than stock and work in progress.

The market value rule for appropriation of stock does not apply to traders using the cash basis; an apportionment would be necessary to disallow the cost of stock that was used for non-trading purposes.

A deemed receipt and corresponding profit is not brought into account where stock is donated to a charity (see **B5**).

B55.1.9 Transfer of fixed assets to stock

The appropriation of assets from fixed assets to stock in trade is treated as a disposal at market value for capital gains tax, if the asset is a chargeable asset (*TCGA 1992, s 161*). An election may be made to effectively "hold over" the gain (*TCGA 1992, s 161(3)*), which will be deferred and subsequently realised on the sale of the stock as part of trading profits.

The appropriation of stock legislation, which was brought in to deal with the *Sharkey* principle *(FA 2008)*, requires that when stock is introduced to the business this is acquired at market value on the date of transfer (*ITTOIA 2005, s 172C*). This conflicts with the capital gains tax hold-over rule that applies when an election is made on the contribution of a chargeable asset. The hierarchy of income tax over capital gains tax suggests that the stock is not reduced by the held-over gain, but the interaction of the respective statutory provisions is not free from doubt.

For appropriations made on or after 8 March 2017 the election under *s 161* can only be made to defer a gain. Prior to that date, where an asset had fallen in value, it was possible to elect to hold-over a capital loss and later realise a trading loss on the sale of the stock.

An election cannot be made to hold-over gains or losses (from 8 March 2017) that are "ATED related", i.e. arise wholly or partly for gains on the appropriation of a high value residential property.

Note that an election is not available to "hold-over" profit realised on a transfer *from* stock to fixed assets.

Chargeable assets transferred between spouses or civil partners, where the transferee receives the asset as stock in trade, is a disposal at market value under capital gains tax rules (*TCGA 1992, ss 17, 18*). The "no gain/no loss" rule for transfers of chargeable assets does not apply in these circumstances (*TCGA 1992, s 58*).

B55.2 REFERENCES

Statutory references

TCGA 1992, ss 17, 18, 58,161, 162, 165

ITTOIA 2005, ss 33A, 97A, 127, 172A–172F, 173–186

ITA 2007, s 993

CTA 2009, ss 156–161, 162–171

TIOPA 2010, Part 4

Leading cases

Gloucester Railway Carriage and Wagon Company Ltd v CIR (1925) 12 TC 720

A–Z of Business Tax Deductions

Spiers & Son Ltd v Ogden (1932) 17 TC 117

Sharkey (HM Inspector of Taxes) v Wernher (1954) 36 TC 275

Threlfall v Jones; Gallagher v Jones (1973) 66 TC 77

Simmons (as liquidator of Lionel Simmons Properties Ltd) v Inland Revenue Commissioners [1980] STC 350

Kirkham v Williams (Inspector of Taxes) [1991] STC 342

Vodafone Cellular Ltd and ors v Shaw (1997) 69 TC 376

HMRC v William Grant & Sons Distillers Ltd; Small v Mars UK Ltd HL [2007] STC 680

HMRC manuals

BIM33015, BIM33100, BIM33300, BIM33450, BIM33600, BIM33715, BIM51625, BIM52001, BIM60030, BIM60060, BIM70025

CG69200

See also

Chapters 1, 2, B1, B32, B53, B60

Sections 13, 23 and 34, FRS 102

HS232 Farm stock valuation (2018)

B56

Training courses and examination fees

B56.1 COMMENT

This section should be read in conjunction with **B7**. However, **B7.1.3** "Re-training relaxation?" is reproduced in full, as follows:

> "Changes to the limitation of a revenue deduction to training costs incurred for a trade existing when the course is undertaken are in the air. At the time of publication of this chapter a consultation is in progress on an extension to include supporting individuals needing to upskill or retrain. It is particularly aimed at those wanting to change career or improve their earnings. It focuses on both employees and the self-employed, hoping to align their respective positions more closely than at present. HMRC intend that the design of the extended relief should protect against its misuse on recreational activities and personal purposes. They also want it to be as simple as possible. The consultation period ran from 13 March to 8 June 2018. HMRC publication of the outcome is to follow, but is not available at the time of publication of this chapter."

The remainder of this chapter focuses entirely on the rules in place prior to the consultation outcome. The key task when considering whether the cost of training courses is deductible for the self-employed or a partnership is to differentiate between training for new skills and training to update current skills.

HMRC acknowledge that the costs of training undertaken to update their existing expertise constitutes an allowable deduction for the purposes of the owner's trade.

The *Dass* case (referred to in **B7**) exemplifies a re-training position as opposed to training costs for expertise used in the current business. Mr Dass's claim for the cost of an examination fee of a solicitor's qualification was dismissed by the Special Commissioner because its purpose was to open up a new skill and not just to maintain the level of skill used in his established business. Accordingly, it was capital and not revenue in nature.

The *Azam* case (also referred to in **B7**) highlighted a failed deduction based on duality of purpose. Here, the personal benefits gained by the therapy sessions on which the costs had been incurred were found to be more than incidental, and so the deduction was disallowed completely through duality of purpose.

The distinction between capital and revenue is the most frequent problem with the cost of training courses and, particularly, examination fees. The very nature of the latter indicates that a new skill is being acquired. That it was incurred wholly and exclusively for the purpose of the business would not be disputed. HMRC would probably find grounds to contend that the qualification would put the individual in the position to earn a living (a capital cost) as opposed to maintaining the skills which supported the existing business.

An argument might be sustainable where an examination was being undertaken to provide marketing credibility to clients where the skills involved were already in use in the taxpayer's business, but he simply had not achieved a paper qualification to support it.

HMRC in their "Capital v Revenue Expenditure Toolkit" propose that training costs (which presumably would include examination fees, where appropriate) for new skills could fail to be deductible in a trading account on the grounds of both *sections 33* and *34* of *ITTOIA 2005*. The costs could fail the *section 33* test by being the cost of an enduring benefit to the trade (capital) and also *section 34* by not being expended wholly and exclusively for the trade. It was a future trade that was envisaged, and not the existing one.

B56.2 REFERENCES

Statutory references

ITTOIA 2005, ss 33, 34

Leading cases

Dass v R & C Commrs [2006] SpC 570

Azam v Revenue & Customs [2011] UKFTT 18 (TC)

HMRC manuals

BIM42526, BIM35660

B57

Travel expenses

B57.1 COMMENT

In comparison with the topic of employee travel, there is little in the legislation and in HMRC guidance relating to travel costs of the self-employed. We need to understand the indicators that are available and apply those deduced principles to each individual taxpayer's circumstances.

This section has links with **B50**. As commented therein, current legislation on the deductibility of subsistence costs means that the availability of the latter largely follows that of travel expenses. It is therefore all the more important to assess the position accurately in respect of travel costs so that the treatment of subsistence expenditure will also be correct.

B33 on mileage allowances also has relevance; in particular, **B33.1.1** and **B33.1.2** are vital starting points to this section and should be read before proceeding further here.

B57.1.1 Travel by vehicle

When reviewing the travel expenses incurred by the owner of an unincorporated business, in determining the validity of a claim to deduct the costs of travel it matters not the type of vehicle that the individual uses. There is no different treatment accorded to the use of a van, goods vehicle or motor cycle compared with the smartest of cars. The business owner is free to choose his mode of travel and spend however much he wishes on the vehicle of his choice. It will only make a difference to the amount of the claim if he opts to use the fixed rate deductions for assessing the cost of each mile of travel.

Once business travel by vehicle has been established, each eligible person, whether sole trader or in a partnership, has the choice of using actual costs or fixed rate deductions in arriving at the cost to be claimed in the accounts (see **B16** for the detail of the latter method of costing). Note that, once a fixed allowance for business mileage has been used for a particular vehicle, this method of calculation must continue to be used for as long as the vehicle remains in the business.

Further detail on fixed rate deductions for mileage is given at BIM75005 (still referred to as "simplified expenses"). **B33.1.3** (under its "Actual costs" heading) illustrates this method of claim for vehicles, as opposed to fixed rate deductions.

B57.1.2 Travel – business proportion

Continuing from the "Mileage allowances" sections, we know that *ITTOIA 2005, s 34(2)* permits a claim for business travel to be apportioned out of a journey that combined it with a private purpose – provided there is an identifiable portion that was solely for business purposes. That underlines the vital role that good quality records play if an individual wishes to maximise his costs on which he can obtain tax relief.

There is no specific guidance provided by HMRC as to the way in which records should be maintained to verify vehicle travel claims. Experience shows that a sensible and consistent effort will gain rewards. Ideally, of course, the individual should keep a pad in the car and record the mileage of each and every trip, or at least the ones that he wishes to claim as being for business travel. Certainly, he should have a record taken from his car of its mileage reading at the start and end of his financial year. If he cannot form the habit of recording the mileage of each business trip, he should at least do so for sample periods. Even a week of accurate records every three months would assist, particularly if consistency is established.

Maintaining a diary of his business trips is another key record that HMRC would expect to see in support of his travel claims. If actual car mileage readings have not been taken, there are plenty of systems available which can provide distance between locations if they are identified in a supporting diary. This can be a fall-back position if contemporaneous mileage records have not been maintained.

B57.1.3 Travel – centre of operations

From **B33.1.2**, we understand the challenge of claiming home as office for the start point of every business journey: *Samadian*, *Jain* and *Sargent v Barnes* demonstrated the failed arguments, while *Horton v Young* showed the principles of a valid claim.

Jones [2015] TC 04643 provided yet another judgment in favour of HMRC relating to medical consultants working within both the NHS and private hospitals. Yet in this case, Dr Jones was a self-employed anaesthetist. This resulted in the FTT finding that hypothetically, given the taxpayer's position as a subcontractor to surgeons, his attendance at the hospitals may not have been 'regular and predictable'. However, in reality such a pattern was clear and the hospitals were therefore places of business. Consequently the travel costs between them and his home were not deductible as they were not incurred wholly and exclusively for the purposes of the business.

The case of *Jackman v Powell* resulted in another judgment against using home as the start point for business travel. Being aware of the logic could be useful when assessing the claims by other businesses. Mr Powell had a milk round. He was an independent contractor who travelled from home to a milk depot to collect his float and milk for onward delivery to his customers. When HMRC disallowed the costs of travel between home and the depot, Mr Powell appealed to the Special Commissioners. There he won his case, on the basis that the expenditure on travel to the depot was exclusively incurred for the purpose of enabling him to earn profits in his trade. The expenditure had no other purpose. The taxpayer was in fact travelling from his base of operation to his customers. Stopping at the depot was an intermediate point on the way to carry out an activity exclusively referable to his trade, enabling him to pick up his milk float, milk and other goods.

The findings on behalf of Mr Powell were reversed when HMRC appealed to the Chancery Division of the High Court. The judge's determination was that the Special Commissioner had erred in law. She had taken the view that the round, which was a collection of some 35 fixed streets, could not be a base of operation because it was an area as opposed to a single place. The judge disagreed; consequently, Mr Powell's journey from home to the start of his round (which commenced at the depot) was for private purposes, as it was the round itself which constituted the base of operations.

In the case of *White v Revenue & Customs* the taxpayer, a self-employed senior flying instructor and examiner, gave flying lessons and examined pilots at two airports. He had no other permanent work centre and otherwise operated his business from home. He had claimed travel costs from his home to the airports as a business deduction. The First-tier Tribunal determined that the real basis of his operations was to be found at the two airports. The visits to the airports were regular and predictable to carry out Mr White's professional activities. The fact that Mr White was only contacted at his home to arrange flying lessons or examinations did not mean that the airports where Mr White invariably carried out those activities were not also places of business. Accordingly, it was concluded that the travel expenses claimed by Mr White in respect of the journeys between his home and the airports were not incurred wholly and exclusively for the purposes of his profession as a flying instructor and examiner; they were also as a result of his decision to live away from the two airports where he carried on his business. It followed that Mr White was not entitled to deduct the expenses of travelling between his home and the airports.

We can deduce from the above cases (and others) that having no other location which is a permanent base forming the focal point of the business's functions is the key for travel from home claims. The taxpayer's home must be his true base of operations in respect of the fundamental premise of the work that he carries out to earn his business income.

B57.1.4 Nature of the journey

Expenses incurred on business travel, whether in the UK or abroad, will be deductible provided the business purpose is the sole purpose of the journey. This is exemplified by the contrasting cases of *Edwards v Warmsley* and *Bowden v Russell*. In the *Russell* case (examined in **B50**), the deduction claim for all the expenses (save a £20 registration fee for the overseas conference itself) failed because the intention at the outset was to combine holiday with business.

The *Walmesley* case demonstrates the opposite. An international conference held in the USA was again at the centre of the claim. This time, the representative partner of a firm of chartered accountants which had overseas clients attended the conference. The extension of his stay by seven days more than the actual (seven-day) conference was taken up with visits to accountancy firms and business contacts. There was no indication that the partner was considering a visit to the USA for social purposes. Consequently, the firm won its appeal against HMRC's disallowance of the cost in their partnership accounts, first before the Commissioners and next in the High Court.

In *Sargent v Eayrs* the expenditure at issue represented the cost of a visit to Western Australia by the taxpayer, who farmed in Gloucestershire, to investigate farming conditions with a view to emigration and buying a farm there. The expenditure was held not to have been incurred wholly and exclusively for the purposes of the farmer's existing trade. Instead, it was of a capital nature because Group Captain Eayrs had a view to setting up a new or extended business in Australia. Although, if undertaken, it would have similarities to his current UK business, it was not a part of his existing trade. This judgment was delivered in the High Court, after the Commissioners had decided that the travel costs to Australia were allowable against his business income.

B57.1.5 Summarising

To establish a valid claim for travel costs from home, it must be clearly the base of the operations on which the business is founded. It is not sufficient merely that the taxpayer does not have any other formal office.

The nature of any journey on which business travel (and, therefore, associated costs such as subsistence and accommodation) claims are made should be evaluated against the risk of "duality of purpose". The purpose itself of the journey cannot be split by apportioning some costs. It will either fail or succeed entirely, depending on whether or not there was a single, business reason for the journey.

B57.2 REFERENCES

Statutory references

ITTIOA 2005, ss 33, 34(1) and (2)

Leading cases

Bowden v Russell & Russell (1965) 42 TC 301

Edwards v Warmsley, Henshall & Co (1967) 44 TC 431

Sargent (HM Inspector of Taxes) v Eayrs (1) (1969–1973) 48 TC 573

Horton v Young (1971) 47 TC 60

Sargent v Barnes (1978) 52 TC 335

Jackman (HMIT) v Powell [2004] BTC 336

Samadian v Revenue & Customs [2013] UKFTT 115 (TC)

Samadian v Revenue & Customs Commissioners [2014] BTC 504

Jain [2015] TC 04788

Jones [2015] TC 04643

White v Revenue & Customs [2014] UKFTT 214 (TC)

HMRC manuals

BIM75005, BIM37600 to BIM37635, BIM37675, BIM42115, BIM42525, BIM37935

B58

Unremittable amounts

B58.1 COMMENT

Bad debt relief as a deduction against profits is only allowable where it is specific and in accordance with *ITTOIA 2005, s 35*. That section does not take into account the position where the customer resides outside the UK, the debt itself is agreed and payable as far as it can be by the customer, but other constraints prevent receipt of the funds by the supplier.

The position envisaged is where the jurisdiction of the customer prohibits the transfer of funds out of its territory. The prohibition might take various forms, but the UK legislation which deals with it should cover each particular issue. Originally, the relief was available through ESC B38 in the context of overseas trade debts, but that was enacted into its present *ITTOIA 2005* format.

The relief applies where all of the following apply:

- an amount received by, or owed to, a trader is brought into account as a receipt in computing his profits;
- it is paid or owed in a territory outside the UK; and
- some or all of it is unremittable.

For the purposes of the relief, an amount is "unremittable" if:

- it is received but cannot be transferred to the UK because, and only because, of foreign exchange restrictions;
- it is owed but temporarily cannot be paid in the overseas territory, due only to such restrictions; or
- it is owed and can be paid in the overseas territory, but the amount paid there would not be transferable to the UK, due only to such restrictions.

Foreign exchange restrictions are defined as restrictions imposed by the law of the overseas territory by any executive action of its government, or by the impossibility of obtaining currency there which is transferable to the UK.

B58.1.1 Form of the relief

Relief is given for the amount in question by deducting it from profits, but it cannot create a trading loss. Instead, any excess of unremittable amounts over profits in that year is carried forward to the next period of account. In that next period, the excess would be aggregated with any newly determined unremittable amounts, and the cumulative total would be used to offset that year's profits. Again, no loss can be created. Excess amounts continue to be carried forward until such time as there are profits against which they can be relieved.

B58.1.2 Restrictions on the relief

If the UK business decides, and is able, to use the amount in question to finance expenditure or investment outside the UK, or it is otherwise applied outside the UK, the relief is not available.

If circumstances change, such that the terms of bad debt relief become available on the amount and it is deductible as an expense, the relief accorded to unremittable amounts is denied.

If an insurance recovery is received in respect of the unremittable amount, no statutory relief is available.

Where any of these occurrences take place in an accounting period after the relief has been obtained, it is withdrawn and steps must be taken to adjust for it. This includes the position where expenditure outside the UK has taken place in a subsequent accounting period. Similarly, it includes any part of the amount which is exchanged for, or discharged by, an amount that is not unremittable.

The method of adjustment is to treat the amount as a trading receipt for the period of account in which the withdrawal event occurs.

B58.1.3 Cash basis

For the avoidance of doubt, *ITTOIA 2005, s 188A* sets out that the deduction from taxable profits on account of unremittable amounts does not extend to users of the cash basis. Of course, this is hardly surprising, as implementation of the cash basis rules would result in the receipt not having been recorded in the trading account.

B58.2 REFERENCES

Statutory references

ITTOIA 2005, ss 35, 187–191

CTA 2009, ss 172–175

Leading cases

None

HMRC manuals

BIM42750 (refers throughout this section)

B59

Use of home as office

B59.1 COMMENT

Before thinking about the costs which can be applied in a claim for using a part of the home as an office, the fundamental basis of the claim should be evaluated. To assist, see **B57.1.3**. The explanations and the case references given (see below) show that the centre from which the business earns its income might not be in the home – it could be at a location such as (in those cases) an airport, hospital or milk depot. However, those findings did not preclude the home from being used at all as a place of business; it was simply not the main centre of operations.

Keeping those opening remarks in mind, then assess the use of the particular home in question. If there is a remote centre, the extra costs of using the home as office could be lower than if there is none other. Nevertheless, the principle to apply remains constant: what is the extra cost of using the home that would not otherwise have been incurred?

HMRC have set out their own review plan based on core business activities. These are:

- providing goods and/or services;
- maintaining business records; and
- marketing and obtaining new business.

HMRC accept that, in principle, costs of the home that could be incurred for business purposes include:

- running costs (such as heat, light, power, cleaning, metered water); these are included in HMRC's fixed rate deductions; and
- fixed costs (such as council tax, insurance and mortgage interest, where an identifiable proportion can be attributed to business use); where appropriate, these can be claimed in addition to the fixed rate deductions;
- telephone and broadband/internet are not included in either of the above two categories, as they are deemed not to relate to the home itself. See

below 'Calculating the cost' for further guidance on assessing allowable business proportion.

It is paramount that the "wholly and exclusively" rule set out in *ITTOIA 2005, s 34* must not be breached if a cost is to be claimed successfully as a business deduction. As explained elsewhere in this publication, it is *section 34(2)* that permits a claim where an expense covers both private and business elements. It does so by accepting a claim where the business share is separately identifiable. In interpretation in the context of home as office use, this does not mean that every bill must show the two parts separately; it means that, where such separation is not available, there must be a reasoned basis for any apportionment used.

Neither, in interpretation, is it required that a particular part of the home should be used entirely for business, with no private use at all. Indeed, that would be damaging from a capital gains tax point of view (see below).

Summarising, use of the home "wholly and exclusively" in respect of a business deduction means that, when part of the home is being used for the trade, that is the sole use for that part at that time. Thus, if the part of the home used for trade purposes is also, at the same time, used for some other non-trade purpose, no deduction is due. Accordingly, writing up the business records during an evening in the room where one's partner is watching television would fail the test. Move into the room next door and the "separate use" test is met.

B59.1.1 Calculating the cost

There are two methods available for quantifying the claim for use of home as office

- actual costs, apportioned appropriately where necessary; and
- fixed rate deductions, also known as simplified expenses.

The latter option has been dealt with in **B16**; the detail is not repeated here. However, to aid comparisons, the rates are set out below.

At the date of this publication, the rates per month are:

–	Working 25 to 50 hrs/month in the home	£10
–	51 to 100 hrs/month in the home	£18
–	More than 100 hrs/month in the home	£26

There is no prescribed way to assess actual costs where there is no separate billing. Where there is documentary evidence, that should be used. Thus, telephone bills which detail the calls and their duration, even if the individual cost is within a fixed package, should be apportioned on that basis. If that seems impractical for every bill, at the very least it should be done adequately to establish a consistent percentage. Where private use of telephone and broadband service is not significant, HMRC can accept that the full cost could be claimed as a business expense.

For other domestic costs, the factors to be taken into account when apportioning an expense include:

- *Area*: what proportion in terms of area of the home is used for business purposes? An alternative basis, depending on the layout of the home and the type of use, might be the number of rooms.
- *Usage*: how much is consumed? This is appropriate where there is a metered or measurable supply, such as electricity, gas or water. However, if applying a percentage arrived at (such as by methods explained below), that too is adequate.
- *Time*: how long is it used for business purposes, compared with any other use?

Unless the use of home as office is minor, it is likely that an overall percentage can be produced, based on a combination of the above factors – say, proportion of area or number of rooms, combined with the proportion of time. That percentage might well be appropriate for both running costs and fixed costs.

HMRC set out guidance on how to work out the business proportion of these costs at BIM47820 and examples of their ideas at BIM47825.

B59.1.2 Capital costs

The distinction between revenue and capital expenses applies equally to use of home as office as it does elsewhere in the legislation on deduction of costs against business income. If a room is extended to accommodate the additional working at home facilities required by the business, that remains an improvement and will be disallowed entirely on the basis of being capital expenditure.

If items of equipment are purchased, their cost is capital and not revenue, but will be subject to claims for capital allowances, including annual investment allowance, in accordance with the legislation. If there is mixed use, such as a computer used personally as well as in the business, provided an identifiable separate business use apportionment can be made, that element can be claimed.

The way in which the business use element is determined does not have to be the same for every item. Thus, the percentage basis considered above might be applied to the running costs and fixed costs, but the cost of a new carpet in one specific room that is used more (or less) than the average could be apportioned differently, for capital allowance purposes, in accordance with its own facts.

B59.1.3 Capital gains tax

This was mentioned above, in the context of assessing the amount of use that a particular room or part of the home has for business purposes. In the focus on income tax deductions, other taxes should not be overlooked. If there is absolutely no private use at all of an area of the home, then at such point as it is sold that portion will not benefit from the main residence exemption. This is set out at *TCGA 1992, s 224(1)*.

It is valid to argue that the way in which the running costs of particular areas of the home have been assessed, as between private and business use, from time to time should not determine the way in which the home has been used throughout its ownership. However, cases of consistent claims in tax returns that a particular room, or perhaps a converted outbuilding, has incurred 100% business use are likely to result in part of the capital gains tax exemption being lost.

HMRC's own view is that the apportionment required, where there is use of a room exclusively for the purposes of a trade, business, profession or vocation, should be made by reference to the facts relating to the dwelling house. This implies that it is the long-term use of the house as a whole that is the determining factor. Indeed, HMRC state that "any private use fraction agreed for the purposes of computing profits chargeable as income provides a poor guide to the apportionment required by TCGA92/S224(1) and should only be used if no other evidence is available".

HMRC explain also that the "exclusive use" test is a stringent one. It is clear that HMRC would not seek any restriction to relief for a room which has some measure of regular residential use. Nevertheless, occasional and very minor residential use would be disregarded. HMRC use an example of a doctor keeping some private possessions in a room used as his or her surgery. HMRC believe that it should still be regarded as exclusively in the business use of the surgery.

Furthermore, the *section 224* exemption requires (at *s 224(2)*) that, where there has been a change of use during the ownership period, the relief accorded by the exemption should be reduced. Therefore the circumstance of, say, former stables being converted to an office, which is subsequently used entirely for business purposes, would require a time-apportioned reduction in the exemption from capital gains tax on that part of the dwelling.

B59.2 REFERENCES

Statutory references

TCGA 1992, s 224

ITTOIA 2005, ss 33, 34, 94H

Leading cases

Caillebotte v Quinn (1975) 50 TC 222

Jackman (HMIT) v Powell [2004] BTC 336

Samadian v Revenue & Customs [2013] UKFTT 115 (TC)

White v Revenue & Customs [2014] UKFTT 214 (TC)

See generally those listed at **B56**

HMRC manuals

BIM75010, BIM47825, BIM47800–BIM47825

CG64650, CG64760, CG64663

B60

VAT

B60.1 COMMENT

A trader that is VAT registered will account for output tax on taxable supplies and reclaim input VAT on goods and services.

VAT payable to or recoverable from HMRC comprises balance sheet entries in the accounts, and generally no VAT is credited or charged to the profit and loss account, so that the pre-tax profit or loss used as starting point for computing taxable profits excludes VAT.

If a trader is not registered for VAT (e.g. because the turnover threshold is not exceeded), the business is taxed on a "VAT inclusive" basis and:

- turnover will be invoiced without charging VAT and therefore credited to the accounts "net"; and
- non-recoverable input VAT incurred on the purchase of goods and services will be expensed to the profit and loss account "gross".

Input VAT will be allowable unless it relates to non-deductible expenses.

For traders entering the cash basis for income tax purposes, from 2017/18 the limit is the higher of £150,000 and the VAT threshold (or £300,000 where the individual receives universal credits). Therefore the VAT and income tax turnover are no longer directly linked. The cash basis is now available to more traders who are likely to be VAT registered (whether using the main scheme or the flat rate scheme).

Property businesses using GAAP or the cash basis may be required to register for VAT (e.g. where a commercial property has an option to tax and rents are treated as taxable supplies).

All registered business on the cash basis should account for VAT in the usual way. Payments and receipts excluding VAT will be treated as deductible and taxable.

B60.1.1 Flat rate scheme

Traders who use the flat rate scheme account for output VAT at a fixed percentage of turnover. This scheme applies to businesses with an annual turnover up to £150,000 (excluding VAT). A special flat rate scheme also operates for farmers.

Supplies of goods and services to customers are subject to VAT at the appropriate rate in the usual way, but input VAT is not recoverable on supplies to the business. Instead, output tax is accounted for at a reduced rate, so that effectively a fixed percentage of input tax is recovered based on turnover. The percentage used to account for output tax is based on the type of trade; for example, accountancy and book-keeping businesses account for tax at a rate of 14.5%, and butchers, off licences or greengrocers at 4% of turnover. A fixed rate of 16.5% applies to "limited cost traders" being businesses that have minimal purchases of goods.

The effect of the flat rate scheme for income tax is that:

- expenses charged to the profit and loss account are inclusive of input VAT; and
- turnover in the accounts will be VAT inclusive, less the reduced rate of output tax paid to HMRC under the fixed rate scheme.

B60.1.2 Partially exempt businesses

Non-recoverable input tax arising from an exempt or partially exempt activity will be deductible. The allocation of input tax between recoverable and irrecoverable amounts may result in VAT expenses relating to the purchase of capital items. HMRC will accept a deduction if the amounts are relatively small (BIM31450).

B60.1.3 Disallowable VAT

Input VAT is not recoverable on business entertainment expenditure, and the VAT charged to the accounts will be disallowed together with the cost of the entertainment.

Fuel supplied by a business to a partner, sole trader or employee that is used for private purposes is treated as a deemed supply. For accounting periods commencing on or after 1 February 2014, VAT is calculated on scale charges based on CO_2 emissions. Output VAT on private fuel will be written off in the accounts as motor expenses.

HMRC guidance on deductibility for the VAT in relation to employees' private fuel is not entirely free from doubt (BIM31550). Where an employee is provided with private fuel as part of a remuneration package, arguably the VAT cost to the employer is deductible, as the additional cost is incurred arguably for the purpose of the trade.

If private fuel is provided to the proprietor of the business, the associated output VAT will also be disallowed as a private expense.

When a proprietor takes goods for non-business use, VAT is accounted for on the cost of the goods at that time (which may be different from the original cost). If the VAT is written off as an expense to the profit and loss account (rather than debited to drawings), the amount is disallowable. See **B55**.

B60.1.4 Bad debts

A VAT-registered business will account for output VAT at the time of supply (unless the trader uses the VAT cash basis). If a debt is bad or doubtful, VAT can be recovered. The VAT element should not be included as part of the charge for bad debts written off in the accounts, and it is not a deductible expense.

B60.1.5 Capital goods scheme

Adjustments to input tax under the capital goods scheme arise when an asset is no longer used in the business or the proportion of partially exempt activities alters. The rules apply to certain classes of assets, such as computers costing more than £50,000 and land and buildings costing more than £250,000.

If, at the time additional VAT is paid:

- capital allowances were available;
- the asset has not been disposed of; and
- the qualifying activity is continued,

the VAT is treated as further qualifying expenditure for capital allowances. Corresponding provisions apply to treat a VAT refund as disposal proceeds.

B60.1.6 Penalties and repayment supplements

VAT penalties, interest paid and repayment supplements are not deductible or taxable.

B60.2 REFERENCES

Statutory references

CAA 2001, ss 61, 234–246

ITTOIA 2005, ss 31A, 33, 34, 54, 777

CTA 2009, ss 53, 54, 1286, 1303

Leading cases

None

HMRC manuals

BIM31525, BIM31530, BIM31535, BIM31540, BIM31560, BIM31610

CA29230

See also

VAT Notice 733

B1, **B13**, **B26**, **B55**

B61

Wayleaves

B61.1 COMMENT

B61.1.1 Wayleaves as income

Wayleaves are typically receivable in return for permitting electricity or telephone poles to be situated on land owned by a person.

The nature of a wayleave is such that it is taxable as a receipt in full, apart from any direct costs incurred. The particular heading under which it is taxed is variable according to the status of the recipient. It is treated as a miscellaneous receipt under *ITTOIA 2005, s 614* if no other charging statute overrides it. This gives little leeway for any excess of direct costs to be relieved.

Where the same person who is in receipt of the wayleave is already carrying on a property business, the sum receivable can be amalgamated within the property business. In that way, profits and losses relating to the property business can be offset against the wayleave net income (or loss).

Similarly, where a person is carrying on a trade, the receipts may be brought into account as part of the receipts of that trade instead of as other income. Again, that permits the income and associated expenditure (e.g. maintenance of the areas surrounding, and access to, the poles) to be accumulated with the income and expenses of a trade. Typically, the trade concerned would be that of farming.

The above considerations might indirectly permit certain expenses that would not otherwise be relievable to be deducted against the income of a property business or a trade. The position of the business making the payment also has special considerations granted by legislation.

B61.1.2 The business granting the wayleave

ITTOIA 2005, s 147 enables the cost of acquiring rights to use telecommunications cable systems and similar products to be treated as deductible revenue expenditure for income tax purposes rather than as capital expenditure. Without this specific provision, such costs would rank as capital expenditure, but they do not qualify to benefit from capital allowances. The basic position is that, where amounts relating to the acquisition or disposal of telecommunication rights (as defined) fall to be treated as revenue items under GAAP, they are so treated for income tax purposes. That ensures that only accounts determined in accordance with accountancy principles will be able to treat the cost of acquisition of telecommunication rights as a revenue deduction.

Interestingly, *ITTOIA 2005, ss 147 and 148* still refer to "in particular FRS 10" rather than FRS 102 as the relevant "accounting standard in relation to ascertaining generally accepted accounting practice". Hopefully the tax issues involved are sufficiently uncontroversial that this would not cause any problems through the courts.

The need for separately defined treatment for unincorporated businesses arose after 1 April 2002 when, for corporation tax purposes, such income and associated expenditure came within the intangible assets regime.

This legislative concession does not apply to businesses using the cash basis. However, in practice it is unlikely that those businesses to which the legislation is targeted would be qualified to use the cash basis.

B61.2 REFERENCES

Statutory references

ITTOIA 2005, ss 22, 144A–148, 344–348, 614

Leading cases

None

HMRC manuals

PIM1115, PIM1118

B62

Wear and tear

B62.1 COMMENT

The statutory deduction for wear and tear for residential property letting is repealed for expenditure incurred on or after 6 April 2016 and superseded by relief for "replacement of domestic items".

A domestic item is defined as furniture, furnishings, household appliances and kitchenware. It specifically excludes anything installed or fixed to a dwelling house so does not permit claims for expenditure on items such as boilers and water filled heating systems, bathroom fittings and fitted cupboards. However, repairs to fixtures that are revenue in nature may qualify for a deduction under general principles (see **Chapter 3**, **B44**).

Property landlords using the cash basis or GAAP may obtain relief for replacement of domestic items subject to satisfying the following conditions:

- the property business consists of a dwelling house;
- the domestic item is provided solely for use by the tenant;
- the old item being replaced must no longer be used;
- the expenditure would otherwise be non-deductible as it is capital expenditure and no capital allowances are available.
- the letting activity is not furnished holiday accommodation or within rent-a-room relief.

The cost of the replacement item is deductible as an expense without a specific claim being required by the taxpayer but only if the new item is not a significant improvement on the old (by comparison to its condition at the time it was originally purchased).

Where the old item is sold or part exchanged the proceeds or value must be taken into account to reduce the expenditure on the new item.

B62.1.1 Wear and tear allowance – Pre-6 April 2016

A statutory allowance is available by election, to cover "wear and tear" for items provided in furnished accommodation. This is intended to provide relief for capital expenditure incurred before 6 April 2016 made in connection with a UK or overseas letting of a residential dwelling.

No wear and tear allowance was available for unfurnished lettings or commercial property lets. Furnished holiday lettings are treated as a deemed trade, and capital allowances can be claimed for this type of letting.

For tax years 2011/12–2015/16 inclusive, a taxpayer could elect to use the wear and tear allowance, which is calculated at 10% of net rents being rents receivable less utilities and council tax and other expenses "normally borne by the tenant" (*ITTOIA 2005, s 308C, repealed*).

The following were examples of expenditure that the wear and tear allowance was intended to cover:

- movable furniture or furnishings, such as beds or suites;
- televisions/DVD players;
- fridges and freezers;
- carpets and floor coverings;
- curtains and blinds;
- linen; and
- crockery and cutlery.

If no wear and tear election was made, expenditure on replacement furnishings prior to 6 April 2016 may have been claimed on a renewals basis as "tools" (see **B53**) but this did not cover large or durable items (e.g. white goods).

B62.2 REFERENCES

Statutory references

CAA 2001, ss 15, 35

ITTOIA 2005, ss 311A, ss 308A–308C (repealed)

Leading cases

None

HMRC manuals

PIM3200, PIM3210

See also

Chapter 3, **B44**, **B53**

B63

Websites

B63.1 COMMENT

For unincorporated businesses that use GAAP, rather than the cash basis, a deduction for website expenses is determined by the nature of the underlying expenditure and the functionality of the website in the context of the business. Expenditure on updating or maintaining an existing website may be a deductible revenue expense when costs are charged to the profit and loss account.

HMRC regard a new website as analogous to a shop window and the creation of an asset or advantage of enduring benefit for the trade, so that initial expenditure in setting up a new website or making enhancements to an existing website will be capital in nature (BIM35815).

The following types of costs are capital in nature:

- initial design and content, including the creation of logos or trademarks;
- registration of new domain names;
- hardware and software expenditure (see **B48**); and
- consultancy and staff costs.

Capitalised staff or external consultancy costs that are revenue in nature will be deductible when charged to the profit and loss account, e.g. yearly or bi-annual website maintenance expenditure that is deferred to match revenue recognition.

Alternatively, if consultancy expenditure or in-house staff costs relate to the creation of intellectual property or other assets with an enduring benefit for the business, these amounts will be permanently disallowed, regardless of the accounting treatment. Capital allowances may be claimed if this expenditure results in the creation of software rights and is used for a qualifying activity.

Traders and property business using the cash basis, can claim deductions for revenue website expenses but also for capital expenses, including:

- purchase of computer hardware; and
- software and intangibles in setting up a website (paid on or after 6 April 2017).

Capital expenditure on intangibles may be deductible if it includes rights within the definition used in the accounting standard for Micro-entities, FRS 105, Section 13 ("Intangible assets other than goodwill").

Relief is available for internally generated intangibles or intellectual property, and includes:

- patents, trademarks and registered designs;
- unregistered information or techniques with industrial, commercial or other economic value; and
- licences in connection with the above rights.

However the expenditure on an intangible will only qualify where the asset, or right to an asset, will cease to exist within 20 years of acquisition.

For companies, expenditure on website development may be deductible under the corporate intangibles regime (*CTA 2009, Part 8*). This legislation does not apply to unincorporated businesses.

B63.2 REFERENCES

Statutory references

CAA 2001, ss 33A, 71, 72, 307B

Leading cases

Anglo-Persian Oil v Dale (1931) 16 TC 253

McVeigh v Arthur Sanderson & Sons Ltd (1968) 45 TC 273

ECC Quarries Ltd v Watkis (1975) 51 TC 153

HMRC manuals

BIM35505, BIM35815

CA23410

See also

Chapter 3, B2, B48

FRS 105 – The Financial Standard applicable to the Micro-entities Regime (revised March 2018)

HMRC Capital v Revenue Expenditure Toolkit: 2016–17 Self-Assessment and Company Tax Returns (published August 2017)

Appendix

Case summaries

Note: This is not an exhaustive list of all the cases listed within the publication, but provides further detail for those cases where this has not already been given within the main commentary.

Acornwood LLP and others v Revenue and Customs Commissioners [2014] SFTD 694 ("Icebreaker Partnerships")

Payments made by five limited liability partnerships to companies for a guaranteed income stream, and for exploitation services relating to intellectual property, were part of a structured investment scheme. The amounts paid were matched by borrowings by the individual members. It was held that the payments were capital in nature and not allowable as they were lump sums to acquire rights to future income streams.

Alliance & Leicester plc v Hamer

See **Halifax plc v Davidson**

Anglo-Persian Oil Company Ltd v Dale (1931) 16 TC 253

A lump sum payment to an overseas sales agent to release a company from an onerous agreement was revenue in nature as this was connected to the circulating capital of the trade rather than fixed capital.

Arizona Copper Company v Smiles (CES) (1891) 3 TC 149

A bonus paid on the redemption of a loan in addition to annual interest payments was held to be made in settlement of the loan and not related to the profits earned by the company and therefore disallowed.

Associated Newspapers Group Ltd v Fleming (1972) 48 TC 382

A publisher providing hospitality to journalists to obtain news stories was held to be disallowable as the costs were not incurred in the ordinary course of its trade, which was to provide news to the general public and not entertainment or hospitality.

Atherton v British Insulated and Helsby Cables Ltd (1925) 10 TC 155

A lump sum paid by a company to set up the nucleus of a pension fund established for its employees was held to be capital (3:2 majority decision in HL). The annual contributions thereafter were agreed as a revenue deduction.

Auckland Gas Co Ltd v CIR (2000) 73 TC 266 and Transco Plc v R A Dyall [2002] SpC 310

These cases considered the deductibility of the costs in replacing gas pipe networks and show the contrast between maintenance costs that include an element of enhancement (*Auckland Gas Co*) and are therefore capital in nature, compared to a "like for like" replacement that did not alter the overall functionality of the network (*Transco*).

Ayeni [2016] TC 05329

The First Tier Tribunal decision of *Ayeni* considered the deductibility of a range of expenses in connection with an appellant's accountancy business. The Tribunal allowed a deduction for a proportion of the cost of premiums of life assurance policies where these were attributed to incidental costs of obtaining finance under *ITTOIA 2005, s 58*. This contrasts to the general rule that payments for life cover are not deductible as generally these are for a dual purpose.

Ball UK Holdings Ltd v CIR [2017] FTT 0457

In the First Tier Tribunal decision *Ball UK Holdings Ltd [2017 FTT 0457]* a UK holding company's functional reporting currency was changed to US dollars and the effect was to recognise a large foreign exchange loss in the company's accounts which potentially resulted in a tax deduction. Following conflicting expert accounting evidence, the Tribunal concluded that the functional currency of the company was sterling and that the accounting standard (then FRS 23) had been misinterpreted by the company and its auditors (PwC). Note: this case is listed for appeal before the Upper Tribunal, in November 2018.

BMW (GB) Ltd v Customs and Excise [1997] STC 824

BMW arranged race track days to entertain customers free of charge. Independent dealerships contributed to part of the cost, but most of the cost was borne by the taxpayer. It was held that input VAT was restricted to the entertainment cost net of contributions from the dealers.

BSC Footwear Ltd v Ridgway (1971) 47 TC 495

This case considered the basis of valuing closing stock. The taxpayer used replacement cost discounted by the gross profit margin, which was agreed as an accepted accounting policy. The Inland Revenue argued that this methodology led to anticipation of losses, and this view was upheld by the House of Lords.

Beauchamp v F W Woolworth plc (1989) 61 TC 542

A foreign currency loan with a five-year term was applied for trading purposes. However, this did not classify the realised exchange loss on repayment of the debt as trading in nature, as the underlying borrowing was not working capital of the business but represented long-term funding.

Bentleys, Stokes and Lowless v Beeson (1952) 33 TC 491

This case considered the nature of hospitality and established the principle that this type of expenditure was gratuitous so that the relationship between the parties was that of host and guest.

Bolam (HM Inspector of Taxes) v Regent Oil Co Ltd (1956) 37 TC 56

Contributions made by a petrol supplier to independent filling stations to cover the costs of decoration, re-siting petrol pumps and maintenance in return for exclusive supply arrangement covered periods of between one and five years and were based on sales or future sales revenues. It was found that the contributions were in the nature of rebates. The payments of a lump sum in advance did not alter the nature of the payments.

Bombay Commissioner of Income Tax v Ahmedabad New Cotton Mills Co Ltd [1929] 8 ATC 575

The basis of a stock valuation did not comply with an accepted commercial accounting method and it was held that adjustments to annual profits were required for both opening and closing stock values in order to compute taxable profits.

Bourne & Hollingsworth Ltd v Ogden (1929) 14 TC 349

Modest annual subscriptions paid by a business to a local hospital were allowable, as the recipient was able to provide medical care for minor illnesses to the taxpayer's employees. However, no relief was available for large payments, as the purpose of the taxpayer was unclear.

Britax International GmbH v CIR (2002) 74 TC 662

When computing the disallowance for car hire charges, it was held that, when computing the restriction, the hire charge includes interest and irrecoverable VAT.

Bullcroft Main Collieries Ltd v O'Grady (1932) 17 TC 93 and Samuel Jones & Co (Devondale) Ltd v IRC (1952) 32 TC 513

In *Bullcroft* the company traded as a colliery and replaced a chimney which had become unsafe. The new chimney was built on an adjacent site and the taxpayer conceded that it was an improvement on the original. This was held to be a replacement of an entirety and, as such, was capital expenditure. This contrasted to the decision in *Samuel Jones* where the company's trade was processing paper. A chimney was replaced because it was unsafe but the replacement did not include any appreciable improvement and was located within the factory building. The costs were held to be revenue as the entirety, being the factory, had not been affected.

Bullrun Inc v Inspector of Taxes [2000] SpC 248

A lump sum surrender payment to dispose of an onerous lease was held to be capital in nature. The taxpayer's argument that a lease at a rack rent without a premium was not an asset was rejected. This contrasts with the decision of *Herbert Smith (a firm) v Honour (1999) 72 TC 130*, where a provision made for future rents under an onerous lease was deductible, as this did not include a legal assignment or surrender.

C Connelly & Co v Wilbey (1992) 65 TC 208

A dispute between two partners of an accountancy practice led to dissolution of the partnership, and the individuals continued to operate as sole traders. On the facts, it was held that the costs related to the dissolution and therefore were not for the purposes of the partnership trade.

Cattermole v Borax & Chemicals Ltd (1949) 31 TC 202

An out-of-court settlement was reached for a claim against a US parent company under US anti-trust laws, the costs of which were disallowed. The cost of advice sought by the directors of the UK subsidiary was allowable, as the purpose was to consider what action should be taken to protect the trade of the UK company.

Celtic Football & Athletic Club Ltd v Customs and Excise [1983] STC 470

This case considered the recovery of input VAT for hospitality provided under a contractual arrangement. Celtic Football Club paid for hotels and meals on behalf of visiting European teams and this was required under UEFA tournament rules. When Celtic played away, reciprocal arrangements were made by the overseas team to accommodate the players. Celtic were contractually obliged to incur the costs and the visiting team effectively did not receive free accommodation and meals as they were required to provide the same facilities on the return leg of the tournament. The costs were not business entertainment and input VAT was recoverable.

Charles Bay Marsden & Sons Ltd v CIR (1919) 12 TC 217

An advance made to a third party supplier to facilitate fulfilment of an order by the taxpayer was not a trade debt and no deduction was available when the debt proved to be irrecoverable.

Commissioners of Inland Revenue v Alexander von Glehn & Co Ltd

See **Commissioners of Inland Revenue v EC Warnes & Co Ltd**

Commissioners of Inland Revenue v Adam (1928) 14 TC 34

A contract to enable a trader to dispose of waste over an eight-year period for a fixed amount was held to be non-deductible as a capital sum. The taxpayer argued that payments made as half-yearly instalments characterised the amounts as revenue deduction. It was held that the method of payment did not influence the nature of the transaction, which was the purchase of a right.

Commissioners of Inland Revenue v Carron Company (1968) 45 TC 18

The taxpayer company claimed a deduction for legal costs in obtaining a new charter, defending an action by two dissenting shareholders and making payments to buy their shares. The previous charter was antiquated and this created problems for the trade. The expenditure repaired the corporate structure but did not alter or enhance the business. The costs were held as allowable revenue expenses on the grounds that this removed obstacles to profitable trading. The decision was made on the principle that "... in some sense or other an asset of a capital nature, tangible or intangible, positive or negative, must be shown to be acquired".

Commissioners of Inland Revenue v EC Warnes & Co Ltd (1919) 12 TC 227 and Commissioners of Inland Revenue v Alexander von Glehn & Co Ltd (1920) 12 TC 232

In both of these cases, the taxpayers incurred penalties under the *Customs (War Powers) Act 1915* by contravening export regulations. The penalty and associated legal fees were disallowed.

Conn v Robins Bros Ltd Ch D (1966) 43 TC 266

A 400-year-old property that was unsafe required complete refurbishment. It was held that the use of modern materials did not, of itself, imply an improvement or enhancement to the asset if the items merely took account of updated techniques or technology. The taxpayer had not claimed enhancement costs for underfloor heating and a new WC, and it was established that an apportionment of costs between capital improvements and revenue repairs can be made where the work is clearly defined.

Cooke v Quick Shoe Repair Service (1949) 30 TC 460

The taxpayer settled liabilities on behalf of the former owner of the business because the vendor failed to settle outstanding trade creditors. There was no contractual obligation for the taxpayer to arrange payment which was made in order to maintain suppliers and continue the trade. It was held that the payments were revenue expenses as they preserved but did not enhance the business.

Craig v HMRC [2012] UKFTT 90 (TC)

The taxpayer was a controlling shareholder and director of a company that provided consultancy services to his sole trader business. HMRC challenged the commercial basis of recharges made by the company and the accounting adopted for deductions claimed by the unincorporated business. HMRC conceded that the charges were deductible. The Tribunal did not agree with this view but proceeded to consider how generally accepted accounting principles should be applied to spread the deduction. It was held that the charges should be apportioned on a straight line basis as, on the facts, there was no other evidence to support a different treatment.

Crown and Cushion Hotel (Chipping Norton) Ltd [2016] TC 05492

The deductibility of sponsorship expenditure paid to an aspiring Formula 1 racing driver was held to be deductible on the specific facts: a company operated three hotels close to Silverstone racetrack and entered into a sponsorship agreement with the 15 year old daughter of the controlling shareholder director. In racing circles the driver was considered to have significant potential and her age and sex meant that she commanded attention. Evidence of the financial and other advertising benefits of the sponsorship arrangement was provided by the company and this was corroborated by evidence given by the racing driver's grandfather. The Tribunal concluded that the sole object was to promote the company's business and that this was the main purpose. Any benefit arising from the personal relationship of the parties was regarded as incidental.

Customs and Excise v Kilroy Television Company Ltd [1997] STC 901

A studio audience were reimbursed travel costs and provided with a buffet. It was held that the services provided by the studio audience were not provided free of charge but provided in return for their attendance. It was not necessary to determine whether the refreshments were made available under a contractual obligation or provided voluntarily.

Customs and Excise v Shaklee International [1981] STC 776

The taxpayer company organised residential courses and regular monthly meetings for training a pyramid sales force. The company's director gave evidence that the food and accommodation were provided for the convenience of the participants, and it was concluded that this was not integral to the business activity. Input VAT on food and accommodation was held to be irrecoverable. The question of whether attendance at the course was quid pro quo as part of services provided was not considered (see *Kilroy* case).

Darngavil Coal Co Ltd v Francis (1913) 7 TC 1

Payments under an agreement for an option to purchase were held to be divisible into consideration paid for the use of wagons, being the finance or hire charge, and capital payments for an option at a future date to purchase an asset at a nominal price.

Dixon v Revenue and Customs Commissioners [2006] STC (SCD) 28

A shop and a private residence were purchased as one transaction, and this was funded by the taxpayer from his own resources together with a business mortgage. A deduction for all of the interest expense was claimed on the basis that the mortgage related to the business property, so that the personal funding had been used to purchase non-business assets. The mortgage application did not support the taxpayer's argument that the purpose was solely to fund the purchase of the business. It was held that, as the assets were acquired through a single transaction, the mortgage related to the whole. Therefore a disallowance of interest should be apportioned by reference to the cost of the private residence against the whole purchase price.

Duckmanton v Revenue and Customs Commissioners [2011] UKFTT 664 (TC), [2012] SFTD 293

The taxpayer was charged with gross negligence, manslaughter and attempting to pervert the course of justice following a fatal road traffic accident involving a lorry operated by him. He was convicted on the count of perverting the course of justice but acquitted of manslaughter. Arguments were put forward by the taxpayer that the purpose in incurring the legal fees was to retain the operating licence for the business. It was held that the fees were incurred to protect his liberty and personal reputation and, accordingly, were not deductible.

ECC Quarries Ltd v Watkis (1975) 51 TC 153

The accounting treatment of costs is not conclusive in determining the tax treatment. The costs of an unsuccessful planning application were not deductible as a revenue expense, notwithstanding that the amounts were written off in the accounts.

Earlspring Properties Ltd v Guest (1995) 67 TC 259

Remuneration paid to a director of a property investment company was found to be excessive and, on the facts, a deduction was limited to 5% of taxable profits.

Eastmans Limited v Shaw (1928) 14 TC 218

No deduction was allowed for fixtures on fitting out new butcher's shops. The taxpayer had argued that the cost of new fixtures, net of proceeds received for fixtures sold, was revenue in nature because the relocation of shops was integral to the business. It was held that the shops were part of the permanent structure of the trade and therefore the net expenditure was capital and not deductible as a revenue expense.

Elwood v Utitz CA (NI) (1965) 42 TC 482

This case concerned a deduction against earnings for a director on payment of subscriptions to a London club that enabled the employer company to obtain cheaper accommodation for business trips. It was held that the cost was wholly, exclusively and necessarily in the performance of the director's duties.

Executive Network v O'Connor [1996] STC (SCD) 29

A recruitment consultancy company sponsored an equestrian business operated by the wife of the controlling shareholder. It was held that the benefits of the arrangements for the sponsor could not be commercially justified and that there was more than an incidental personal benefit in making the payments.

Firestone Tyre & Rubber Co Ltd v Evans Ch D 1976

A foreign exchange loss on the settlement of a liability by a UK company to its US parent was held to be long-term funding and therefore disallowed as capital expenditure.

G Pratt and Sons v HMRC [2011] UKFTT 416 (TC)

The taxpayer resurfaced a farm drive with a concrete covering. The costs were held to be allowable as a repair. The use of a different material did not alter the functionality of the asset and, on the facts, no enhancement or alteration was made to the existing track.

Gloucester Railway Carriage and Wagon Company Ltd v CIR (1925) 12 TC 720

The taxpayer company manufactured railway wagons and these were sold directly or hired to customers. This was treated as a single trading activity so that the hired units were not part of the fixed capital of the business. The hire of wagons did not alter the nature of the item, which was stock in trade for resale. The sale of the wagons was a disposal of stock and, accordingly, surpluses on sale were taxable as trade receipts.

Granite Supply Association Ltd v Kitton (1905) 5 TC 168

It was held that the costs of moving granite and taking down and re-erecting two cranes on moving to a new yard was capital, as the new premises facilitated an expansion of the business and the expenditure contributed to the enhancement of the business.

HMRC v Lansdowne Partners Limited Partnership CA [2012] STC 544

The rebate of fees to a limited partnership were allocated to partners but treated as deductions in the taxpayers' returns. This treatment was incorrect, as the amounts were a distribution of profits to the partners and not an expense of the business.

HMRC v William Grant & Sons Distillers Ltd; Small v Mars UK Ltd HL [2007] STC 680

The outcome of these appeals in the House of Lords was to defer the disallowance of depreciation included in the value of closing stock to a later accounting period when it was expensed to the profit and loss account. This overturned the decision of *Secan v CIR (2000) 74 TC 1*, which had previously decided that the statutory disallowance for depreciation (and other capitalised expenses) was in the period when first charged to profit and loss (i.e. the year of manufacture rather than sale).

Halifax plc v Davidson [2000] SpC 239, Woolwich plc v Davidson [2000] SpC 240, Northern plc v Davidson [2000] SpC 241 and Alliance & Leicester plc v Hamer [2000] SpC 242

The nature of expenses incurred on the demutualisation of building societies was considered in this collection of Special Commissioners' decisions. The costs included in-house staff administration expenses, communications and public relations, together with external advisers' fees. It was agreed that the costs were properly expensed to profit and loss account. It was held that the costs did not alter the underlying trades but only affected the regulatory regime in which the businesses operated. Accordingly the expenses were allowed as revenue. Note: the costs of payments for statutory cash bonuses to members were not claimed as a deduction.

Hammond Engineering Co Ltd v IRC (1975) 50 TC 313

Following the death of a controlling shareholder, the company's board of directors took steps to protect the business after the appointment of the receiver. This included indemnifying employees against legal costs in jointly defending against actions that might have resulted in a cessation of trade. It was held that expenses for a dispute relating to the control of the company and its shareholders were disallowable.

Heastie v Veitch & Co (1933) 18 TC 305

It was held that rent paid to a senior partner for the use of premises by the firm was not an allocation of profits. The treatment of rent and salaries were distinguished.

Heather v P-E Consulting Group Ltd (1972) 48 TC 293

Payments made to an employee trust fund to allow staff to purchase shares in their employer company was held to be deductible. The purpose of the expenditure was to incentivise the staff and, as such, amounts were not capital in nature. The company's intention was to ensure that employees would obtain control of the company to avoid interference by outside shareholders who had previously appointed managers who had upset senior professional staff. In this case, Lord Denning also commented on the accounting treatment (at page 32):

> "The courts have always been assisted greatly by the evidence of accountants. Their practice should be given due weight; but the courts have never regarded themselves as being bound by it. It would be wrong to do so. The question of what is capital and what is revenue is a question of law for the courts. They are not to be deflected from their true course by the evidence of accountants, however eminent."

Herbert Smith (a firm) v Honour (1999) 72 TC 130

A provision made for future rents under an onerous lease for a property that was no longer used by the business longer required was held to be deductible. The Special Commissioners found that the accounting concept of prudence could not take precedence over the rule that losses must not be anticipated. The High Court overturned this decision in favour of the taxpayer on the grounds that there was no rule of law that restricted the anticipation of a liability.

IRC v Falkirk Iron Co Ltd (1933) 17 TC 625 and Hyett v Lennard (1940) 23 TC 346

The taxpayers in each of these cases incurred net losses on sub-letting former trading premises, and the ongoing net rental costs were held to be deductible as trade expenses.

IRC v Longmans Green & Co Ltd (1932) 17 TC 272

A lump sum was paid to a non-resident author for the acquisition of rights to a book based on a formula for units sold that subsequently was not achieved. It was held that the lump sum represented a non-refundable royalty payment, as payment on account of royalties.

Ingenious Games LLP and others [2017] TC 05893

The First Tier Tribunal considered whether expenditure on film rights were capital or revenue in nature in order to determine if the write-off in the accounts, made in accordance with GAAP, was deductible for the LLP. The Tribunal affirmed that no single test had been devised to distinguish capital and revenue payments and case law decisions should be applied to consider which indicators of the capital and revenue divide were of most importance. The question of whether or not it was absurd or unfair to deny relief for a deduction was rejected. Furthermore, the appellants' analogy that the film rights were akin to raw materials or stock was not supported by the accounting treatment. There was an enduring benefit to the business as the income stream was expected to arise over five years and the rights may have some residual value for up to 30 years. It was this last point that the Tribunal considered to be the most important factor and they concluded that the rights were capital in nature and the write-off was not deductible.

Interfish Ltd v CRC [2014] EWCA Civ 876

The taxpayer company carried out a trade of fishing and associated activities. It made a number of payments to a local rugby club which were initially for the purpose of supporting the club financially and improving the squad by signing up new players. The controlling shareholder of the sponsor company had significant personal links to the club and it was found that the payments were made primarily for the benefit of the club. The Upper Tribunal commented that the "wholly and exclusively" test did not translate to defining expenditure as private or business related but concluded that, unless the expenditure was solely for a business purpose of the sponsoring party, the test was not satisfied.

James Snook and Co Ltd v Blasdale (1952) 33 TC 244

A deduction was not available for compensation for loss of office to a director and major shareholder, as the taxpayer company was unable to demonstrate that the termination payment and share sale were unconnected and treated compensation as disguised proceeds for the sale of shares.

John Smith & Son v Moore (1921) 12 TC 266

It was held that the sum paid for "unexpired contracts" represented goodwill and was not deductible, as it related to the fixed capital of the business.

Johnston v Britannia Airways Ltd (1994) 67 TC 99

Accruals for the cost of a major overhaul were provided for by reference to the number of hours for which aircraft were used. It was held that, as the provisions were based on the ordinary principles of commercial accounting in force at the time, the expense would be allowable during the accounting period in which it was charged in the accounts. Note: this accounting treatment is no longer valid under FRS 102, as no obligation for the repairs would have arisen when the provisions were made.

Kato Kagaku Co Ltd v HMRC [2007] SpC 598, [2007] SSCD 412

Relief for an indemnity paid by a borrower to compensate a bank on the early repayment of a loan, in accordance with the terms of the loan agreement, was an allowable incidental cost. Inclusion of the indemnity in the loan terms did not preclude the payment from being an incidental cost.

This case also considered compensation paid to the lender for foreign currency movements on the early repayment of a loan. The amount was disallowed as it indemnified the foreign exchange loss due to the early termination of a swap transaction.

Key IP Ltd v Revenue and Customs Comrs [2011] UKFTT 715 (TC), [2012] SFTD 305

Proceedings for defamation were brought by a company and its sole director/shareholder against another company to protect the plaintiff company's reputation. Inclusion of the individual as one of the plaintiffs increased the likelihood of the claim succeeding but did not undermine the main purpose of the expenditure, which was to protect the reputation of the business. Consequently, all of the fees were held to be allowable.

Kirkham v Williams (Inspector of Taxes) [1991] STC 342

The taxpayer acquired land for use as an office and storage by his business. The site was later developed as a dwelling house. It was held that the subsequent development did not undermine the initial intention, which was to hold the asset on capital account. It could not be inferred that development was an adventure in the nature of trade, and therefore the land had not been appropriated to trading stock.

Knight v Parry (1972) 48 TC 580

The costs of a solicitor defending himself against a claim from his former employers for breach of an employment contract were disallowed on the grounds that the expenses were not for the purpose of the taxpayer's new trade. Furthermore, the costs were for protecting the taxpayer's professional reputation and, as such, were not wholly and exclusively for the purpose of the trade.

Law Shipping v IRC (1923) 12 TC 621

Repairs expenditure incurred shortly after the purchase of a ship, to place the vessel in a condition where it was seaworthy, was held to be capital in nature.

Lawson v Johnson Matthey plc (1992) 65 TC 39

As part of a financial rescue plan, a parent company (JM) made a payment to its insolvent subsidiary that carried out a trade in banking, as part of an arrangement under which the Bank of England would buy the subsidiary's share for a nominal amount. The Revenue had argued that the contribution made by the parent company was a capital expense connected to the sale of the shares. The taxpayer presented evidence that, if the payment had not been made, its own financial stability was in doubt and therefore the purpose was to protect its own trade. The House of Lords agreed that the payment was a revenue deduction.

Linslade Post Office and General Store v HMRC [2012] UKFTT 457 (TC)

Legal costs were incurred by two partners who successfully defended a claim by another party who had declared an interest in the partnership. It was held that the expenses were not capital in nature, as the purpose was to preserve the business; the expenses were not a dispute between the individuals in their capacity as partners and, accordingly, the expenses were deductible.

Lochgelly Iron & Coal Company Ltd v Crawford (1913) 6 TC 267

It was held that subscriptions paid to a conciliation board and used to avoid disputes between employers and employees were an allowable expense for the contributing member. However, costs applied by the board to the mining governing organisation for research into the effects of coal dust were disallowed.

Lurcott v Wakely & Wheeler [1911] 1 KB 905

The Revenue argued that the replacement of an entire wall was not a revenue expense. This case was one of the first to consider the concept of "entirety" and found in favour of the taxpayer.

MacKinlay (Inspector of Taxes) v Arthur Young McClelland Moores & Co [1989] STC 898

The reimbursement of a partner's removal expenses was held to be disallowable on the grounds of duality of purpose by providing assistance to the partner to establish a new home. The House of Lords rejected the taxpayer's arguments that the size of the firm, the number of partners and the expectation that they would be required to move in order to advance the interests of the business were sufficient to make any private benefit incidental to the business purpose.

McKnight v Sheppard (1996) 171 TC 419

Legal expenses incurred to remove a suspension imposed by a professional body to enable a stockbroker to continue trading were treated as allowable, notwithstanding the imposition of penalties for misconduct (which were disallowed).

McQueen v Revenue and Customs Commissioners [2007] STC (SCD) 45

A company incurred expenses in funding amateur rallying events in which the controlling shareholder/director competed to publicise the company's coach hire business. On the facts, it was held that the director's personal satisfaction was incidental to the main business purpose and the costs were treated as allowable.

McVeigh v Arthur Sanderson & Sons Ltd (1968) 45 TC 273

Staff salaries relating to the costs of developing fabric designs and printing blocks were held as capital in creating assets with an enduring benefit but did not qualify as plant for the purposes of claiming investment allowances.

Mallett v Staveley Coal and Iron Company Ltd (1928) 13 TC 772

A company made payments to be released from two mining leases and argued that the payments represented the commutation of annual rentals. It was held that the payments were capital in nature, as these related to the fixed capital of the business.

Markets South West (Holdings) Ltd v Revenue and Customs Commissioners [2011] UKUT 257 (TCC), [2011] STC 1469

A trader breached the conditions of a licence to operate a local market and incurred legal fees to defend an enforcement notice from the local authority.

The taxpayer contended that it already had the right to trade without restriction. The enforcement notice was treated as an application for the grant of planning permission, which may be retrospective. The First-tier Tax Tribunal held that the costs were to modify an intangible asset, being the right to secure an increase in the days on which the market could operate. The Upper Tribunal held that the legal costs should be apportioned on the basis that part of the expense related to a breach of the existing licence and part related to applying for permission to extend the licence (analogous to an improvement and repair to a building).

Marshall Hus & Partners Ltd v Bolton Ch D (1980) 55 TC 539

The profit and loss account information for a property development company covered six accounting periods for corporation tax purposes but comprised only a small number of sales. The taxpayer argued that it was necessary to apportion the total profits on a time basis. It was held that, as the profits of each accounting period could be ascertained by reference to the underlying transactions, this should be used as a basis for arriving at the accounting profit before tax.

Meat Traders Ltd v Cushing [1997] SpC 131

A provision for future operating losses was disallowed as an anticipation of future losses. The basis of the provision would no longer be valid under FRS 12/FRS 102.

Morgan v Tate & Lyle Ltd (1954) 35 TC 367

Expenses in running an anti-nationalisation campaign were held as allowable. It was found that the primary purpose was to prevent the loss of the company's business and to preserve all of its assets. As in *Southern v Borax Consolidated Ltd*, there was no evidence of enhancement or improvement.

Netlogic Consulting Ltd v Revenue and Customs Commissioners [2005] STC (SCD) 524

The taxpayer contended that all of the costs of a function that was held to attract prospective new clients were allowable as part of general advertising expenses. It was held by the Special Commissioners that the refreshments were disallowable as entertainment expenses. Other expense, such as room hire, was allowable and was not incidental entertainment expenditure in view of the overall purpose of the event.

Northern plc v Davidson

See **Halifax plc v Davidson**

Odeon Associated Theatres Ltd v Jones (1971) 48 TC 257

The taxpayer acquired cinemas during the late 1940s and the state of repair was found not to have influenced the purchase price. The Revenue argued that part of the expenditure relating to the pre-acquisition period should be disallowed as capital. The costs of repairs were written off to profit and loss accounting and expert evidence was given on behalf of the taxpayer to support that treatment. It was held that the repairs were revenue. The *Law Shipping* case was distinguished (at page 258) on the grounds that "(a) the purchase price was substantially less than if the vessel had been in a fit state of repair; (b) the vessel could not continue as a profit earning asset without being repaired shortly after acquisition; (c) there was no evidence of accountancy practice".

Owen (HM Inspector of Taxes) v Southern Railway of Peru Ltd (1956) 36 TC 602

The taxpayer had a legal obligation to pay staff when they left the company and this was calculated by reference to salary and length of service. The Revenue argued that, as the payment was contingent on the departure of an employee, a loss was anticipated. It was held that the accounting methodology was in accordance with accounting practice but that no effort had been made to accurately calculate the amount and so the taxpayer failed to secure a deduction.

Parnalls Solicitors Ltd v Revenue and Customs Commissioners [2010] SFTD 284

This First-tier Tribunal decision considered the effect of a transfer of a liability on incorporation. The obligation to pay recurring annuities had been agreed between the former partnership and a retiring partner and this liability was transferred on the purchase of the business by the company. It was held that: "The payment of the lump sum in commutation of the annuity was not to extinguish a contractual obligation to make recurring revenue payments and was not itself a revenue payment, but extinguished an obligation to make payments of capital expenditure and was a capital payment. The lump sum was not an allowable deduction in computing the taxpayer company's profits".

Pattison v Marine Midland HL (1983) 57 TC 219

It was held that foreign exchange differences on long-term US dollar borrowings, used by a bank to hedge its foreign currency exposure on short-term lending to customers, were not taxable or deductible to the extent that no profit or loss was recognised in the accounts and the foreign currency borrowings were used to hedge assets in the same currency.

Pearce v Woodall Duckham Ltd (1978) 51 TC 271

The company changed the valuation of stock, and the old and new methods were equally valid as a basis of accounting. It was held that profits arising on the revaluation of opening stock, that were taken directly to reserves in the accounting period in which the change of policy took place, were taxable in that accounting period.

Philip McMahon v Revenue & Customs [2013] UKFTT 403 (TC)

The facts of this tribunal hearing were similar to those in *Knight v Parry*. The legal fees arose from a settlement made for breach of an employment contract and did not relate to the business of the taxpayer.

Pyrah v Annis & Co (1957) 37 TC 163

Legal costs to vary a licence to increase the number of vehicles operated by a company were held to be the acquisition of an asset and were disallowed as capital.

Racecourse Betting Control Board v Wild (HM Inspector of Taxes) (1938) 22 TC 182

Rent paid under a licence to occupy by reference to an annual amount was allowable as a revenue expense, notwithstanding that the amount was set by reference to a percentage of the cost of construction of the buildings by the landlord.

Reid's Brewery v Male (1891) 3 TC 279

A trade deduction was allowed for irrecoverable loans made by a brewery to its customers, as these facilities were integral to the trading relationships with the publicans. This contrasts with the decision of *CIR v Hagart & Burn-Murdoch (HL) (1929) 14 TC 433*, where it was held that irrecoverable loans made by a solicitor to a client were not customary and therefore not deductible.

Samuel Jones & Co (Devondale) Ltd v IRC

See **Bullcroft Main Collieries Ltd v O'Grady**

Sharkey (HM Inspector of Taxes) v Wernher (1954) 36 TC 275

The owner of a stud farm transferred horses for use in horse-racing that was a hobby activity. The House of Lords held that the transfers should be treated as disposals at open market values.

Silk v Fletcher [1999] STC (SCD) 220, [2000] SpC 239

A partner in a firm of accountants, on leaving the partnership, took loans to finance an allocation of work in progress, fixtures and other trade assets under the terms of a deed of partition. The accounts of the new sole trader practice showed overdrawn balances reflecting an excess of drawings over net profits that cumulatively were equivalent to the original loans. It was held that:

(i) The sole trader's capital account (comprising cumulative net profits) was insufficient to fund the drawings. Therefore a proportion of the interest on the loans used to fund drawings in excess of net profits was disallowed, as this did not relate to the business.

(ii) As no capital was contributed by Mr Silk, interest on drawings was funded by realising work in progress and book debts (excluding any realised profit element) and was also disallowed.

(iii) The basis of the apportionment of interest was to be adjusted by identifying net realised profits (using a crude cash basis), so that depreciation was ignored and a reduction was made for the excess of debtors over creditors.

Simmons (as liquidator of Lionel Simmons Properties Ltd) v Inland Revenue Commissioners [1980] STC 350

A company had a record of holding properties as investments. Prior to liquidation, the whole property portfolio was sold. The taxpayer contended that, while some properties were held as fixed assets, others were owned either as trade stock or fixed assets – there was a mixed motive. The House of Lords held that the assets could not have a dual or intermediate status and, on the facts, it was determined that all of the properties were held as fixed assets.

Small v Mars UK Ltd

See **HMRC v William Grant & Sons Distillers Ltd**

Smith's Potato Estates Ltd v Bolland (1948) 30 TC 267

The accounting and legal costs of contesting an assessment to tax were not deductible. The payment of a tax liability determines the financial resources of a business; however, it was held that tax was assessed as payment to the Exchequer and was not for the purposes of earning profits of the trade.

Southern v Borax Consolidated Ltd (1940) 23 TC 597

Expenditure made in defending the title to land by a US subsidiary (trading as a UK branch) was regarded as revenue expenditure as no alteration or improvement was made to the asset and the expenditure was akin to maintenance.

Southwest Communications Group Ltd v Revenue and Customs Commissioners [2012] UKFTT 701 (TC)

The First-tier Tribunal considered an application for the appellant's costs following HMRC's withdrawal from an appeal against the deductibility of sponsorship expenses that had been paid in excess of amounts agreed under a sponsorship contract with Exeter Chiefs Rugby Club. The chairman and controlling shareholder/director of the taxpayer was also the chairman of the club. HMRC did not pursue the appeal on the grounds that there was no duality of purpose on the basis of evidence presented by witness statements.

Spiers & Son Ltd v Ogden (1932) 17 TC 117

The taxpayer company was a builder who occasionally let properties before sale. It was argued that the company was not carrying out a trade as a property dealer if properties were rented. Taking into account the objects in the company's memorandum and the method of financing the business, it was held that the properties were stock in trade and there was only one activity based on the initial intention, which was to sell on the properties at a profit.

Stephenson v Payne, Stone Fraser & Co Ch D (1967) 44 TC 507

It was held that a charge made for office services and staff administration provided by a management company to a partnership, under common control, was excessive. Only the costs incurred by the company plus a modest profit were allowed.

Strick v Regent Oil Co Ltd (1965) 43 TC 1

In order to secure exclusive supply contracts, lump payments were made by a petrol wholesaler to independent garages for the grant of leases over petrol stations, and the amount was based on expected future sales. The premises were leased back at a nominal sum, with covenants for the retailer to take supplies from Regent. It was held that the payment was capital in nature, as it related to a lease of land.

Thomas v Richard Evans & Co Ltd (1927) 11 TC 790

Subscriptions to a central fund to cover compensation for accidents were held as allowable.

Thompson v CIR [2005] SpC 458, [2005] STC (SCD) 320

The Special Commissioners rejected error or mistake claims for bad or doubtful debts where hindsight was applied in ascertaining the time at which a debt became irrecoverable; only events affecting the recovery of debts at the balance sheet date may be taken into account.

Threlfall v Jones; Gallagher v Jones (1993) 66 TC 77

These cases with similar facts concerned the timing of the deduction of lease payments. The taxpayers argued that expenditure was deductible when paid in the first accounting period that resulted in large losses. The Inland Revenue argued that the payments should be spread and this was based on expert accounting evidence. It was held that tax deduction should follow proper accounting principles.

Transco Plc v R A Dyall

See **Auckland Gas Co Ltd v CIR**

Triage Services Ltd v Revenue and Customs Commissioners [2006] SpC 519, [2006] STC (SCD) 85

The taxpayer company acquired stock, goodwill, and plant and machinery as a going concern. At the same time the taxpayer company secured service contracts with the vendor. No pre-existing customer contracts were transferred, and the vendor did not assign the trade name. It was agreed that the consideration for the purchase would be £8m for the assets. An amount was recognised in the accounts as goodwill arising on the settlement of liabilities transferred with the business. It was held by the Special Commissioners that the discharge of the assumed liabilities was not a revenue deduction, as the acceptance of liabilities represented a one-off commercial advantage and this was for goodwill. The fact that trade contracts and the business name were not acquired did not alter this conclusion (see also *Cooke v Quick Shoe Repair Service*, where no transfer of liabilities was made to the purchaser).

Tucker (HM Inspector of Taxes) v Granada Motorway Services Ltd (1978) 53 TC 92

A lump sum payment to amend a lease, by commuting payments for additional rent based on sales revenues, was held as capital in nature as an enhancement of the additional asset – notwithstanding that the lease remained unassignable, had no balance sheet value and that the effect was to reduce future rentals that would otherwise have been deductible as revenue expenses.

Vallambrosa Rubber Company Ltd v Farmer (1910) 5 TC 529

It was held that the costs of maintaining a rubber estate were deductible as revenue expenses, regardless of whether these were attributed to productive areas or parts that were under cultivation for later production. A distinction was made between recurring expenditure before and after the commencement of trade. Preparing the land prior to commencement of trade was "once and for all" and capital in nature. Note this principle has been superseded by statute that allows relief for pre-trading expenses (*ITTOIA 2005, s 57*).

Van den Berghs Ltd v Clark (1935) 19 TC 390

This case considered the nature of a receipt on the settlement of a dispute with a competitor. The parties had previously entered into anti-competition and collaboration agreements. The payment made to cancel these arrangements was received by the taxpayer and held to be capital, as the rights under the agreements related to the fixed capital of the business and were fundamental to the structure for earning profits.

Vodafone Cellular Ltd & Others v Shaw (1997) 69 TC 376

A payment made by Vodafone to release the company and its subsidiary from an onerous licence agreement was held to be revenue in nature. The case considered the impact on the structure of the business and referred to the principles established in *Anglo-Persian Oil Company Ltd* and *Van den Berghs Ltd* that considered whether a payment (or receipt) was related to the underlying structure of the business or part of working capital. The nature and effect of the payment on the business was considered at the time the payment was made, at which point the licence had become worthless. The question of whether the payment was wholly and exclusively for the trade was also considered. It was found that there was no conscious motive to make the payment on behalf of a subsidiary, and the effect on the inter-group finances was irrelevant when considering the "wholly and exclusively" test.

Walker v The Joint Credit Card Co Ltd (1982) 55 TC 617

A payment made to a competitor to facilitate the cessation of its trade was held to be capital, as it represented a payment of goodwill for closing down a rival.

Watneys London Ltd v Pike; Watney Combe Reid & Co Ltd v Pike (1982) 57 TC 37

Payments were made to tenants of tied public houses to obtain vacant possession and enable the business to be run by the taxpayer's own management. The payments were held to be capital, notwithstanding the taxpayer's argument that no identifiable new asset had been created by the payments.

William P Lawrie v CIR (1952) 34 TC 20

On repairing a roof, the taxpayer raised the roof height and modified the design. Notional repair costs were calculated by reference to the original area of the old roof. It was held that notional repairs could not be claimed as a revenue expense.

Woolwich plc v Davidson

See **Halifax plc v Davidson**

Index

[All references are to paragraph number]